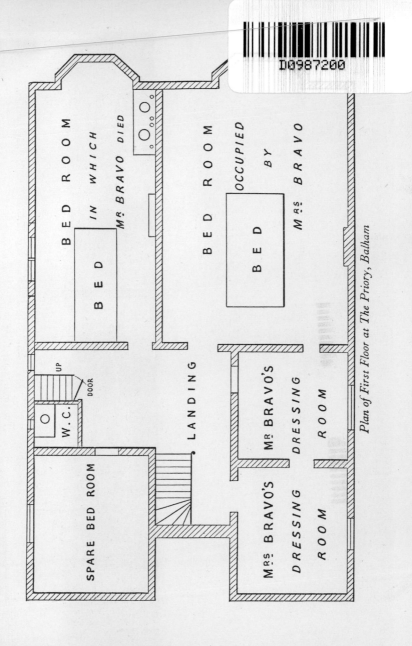

Plan of First Floor at The Priory, Balham

BED ROOM IN WHICH MR. BRAVO DIED

BED

BED ROOM OCCUPIED BY MRS. BRAVO

BED

UP

DOOR

W.C.

LANDING

SPARE BED ROOM

MR BRAVO'S DRESSING ROOM

MRS. BRAVO'S DRESSING ROOM

HOW CHARLES BRAVO DIED

By the same author

SAINT—WITH RED HANDS?
The Chronicle of a Great Crime

HOW
CHARLES BRAVO
DIED

The Chronicle of a Cause Célèbre

YSEULT BRIDGES

THE REPRINT SOCIETY
LONDON

FIRST PUBLISHED 1956
THIS EDITION PUBLISHED BY THE REPRINT SOCIETY LTD.
BY ARRANGEMENT WITH JARROLDS PUBLISHERS (LONDON) LTD.
1957

PRINTED IN ENGLAND BY
HAZELL WATSON AND VINEY LTD
AYLESBURY AND LONDON

To

RODNEY MAINGOT, F.R.C.S.

"I count myself in nothing else so happy
As in a soul remembering my good friends."

KING RICHARD THE SECOND:
Act II, Scene III

CONTENTS

CONTENTS

PART I
ANTECEDENTS AND BACKGROUND

PART II
THE TRAGEDY

PART III
THE SECOND INQUEST

PART IV
THE SOLUTION

LIST OF ILLUSTRATIONS

Between pages 32 and 33

Charles Delaunay Turner Bravo, barrister-at-law. At the age of 25

Florence Ricardo. At the age of 25. "A face of delicate contours, violet-blue eyes and glorious chestnut hair"

James Manby Gully, M.D. From a *Vanity Fair* cartoon, 1876. "The ancient lover"

Between pages 64 and 65

Florence Bravo. From a photograph taken on her honeymoon at Brighton

The Priory, Balham. "A perfect example in miniature of early 19th-century Gothic"

Jane Cannon Cox. At the age of 30. "Her strain of Asiatic blood was clearly apparent"

Page 119

Sketch of Charles Bravo's bedroom

Between pages 160 and 161

The four medical men summoned on the "fatal Tuesday"

Mrs. Robert Campbell. The wife of the County magnate

Mr. Joseph Bravo. The city merchant of Jamaican origin

Between pages 192 and 193

Sir William Gull, Bart., M.D. From a *Vanity Fair* cartoon, 1875. "His sense of the mystery of the universe was deep"

AUTHOR'S NOTE
AND ACKNOWLEDGMENTS

RECOGNITION of the fact that major criminal cases constitute a very valuable part of our social history is long overdue. Not only do they disclose the day-to-day lives of whole families with an intimacy undiscoverable by any other means, not only do they reveal the impact of contemporary ideology upon the individuals involved, but they demonstrate the actual processes of our legal machinery in action at a particular period, and furnish the grounds from which the improvements of our criminal code have sprung. For these reasons—as well as those of justice—as much careful study should be given to the background of such cases, and to the incidents and issues which lead up to the climax, as to the climax itself.

That invaluable series, *Notable British Trials*, has made *verbatim* accounts of the legal proceedings in famous cases—each prefaced with a scholarly and lucid essay—available to the student, to which he can turn with ease and assurance for his information. But for the cases which, though equally dramatic and powerful, never for one reason or another occupied the time of a Judge and jury he must resort to the yellowing files of the contemporary Press for an equally reliable source of information.

The modern tendency to pack half a dozen full-scale tragedies into the compass of a single volume all too often leads to the sacrifice of accuracy to sensation; and since such books are popular—and it is a human foible to find guilt more stimulating than innocence—errors once committed are apt to be repeated until they grow to be accepted as facts. An outstanding instance of this was the case of Constance Kent, chronicled in my previous book, *Saint—With Red Hands?* In the present one I deal in a similar manner with the mystery which surrounds the death of Charles Bravo.

I owe a debt of deep gratitude to Dr. C. A. Malcolm of the

Signet Library, Edinburgh, for lending me, and allowing me to retain for several months, the copy of *The Balham Mystery* without which I should never have been able to write this book. This copy of a rare contemporary volume, profusely illustrated with skilful drawings—some of which are reproduced here—is made rarer still by the addition of the photographs of Florence Bravo and Dr. Gully, and by the *Vanity Fair* cartoons, which I have had permission to include. I am also grateful to Dr. Malcolm for entrusting me with the originals of Sir Arthur Channell's and Mr. Fortescue Kemp's letters. My debt is also great to Mr. W. N. Roughead for putting me in touch with Dr. Malcolm and the Signet Library to which he has presented all his father's— the late Mr. William Roughead's—criminological books.

I have, too, to thank the Wandsworth Borough Librarian and his staff for their generous assistance in my preliminary researches; Dr. W. D. Nicol for advice on certain medical points; the Rev. W. H. Evans, Rector of Buscot, for searching his parish registers on my behalf; Mr. E. Dashper Horley for information concerning various legal personalities; Sir Travers Humphreys for permission to quote from his book, *Criminal Days*; Mr. F. J. P. Veale for permission to quote from his monograph on the Bravo case in the series *Verdict in Doubt*; and the following publishing houses for similar permission in the case of the works given against their names:

Messrs. John Lane the Bodley Head Ltd.:	*The Bravo Mystery and Other Cases* (Sir John Hall, Bart.)
Messrs. William Heinemann Ltd.:	*Cases in Court* (Sir Patrick Hastings)
Messrs. Christopher Johnson Publishers Ltd.:	*The Power of Poison* (John Glaister)

PRINCIPAL CHARACTERS

Robert Tertius Campbell, of Buscot Park, Berks, and 37 Lowndes Square, London.

Ann Campbell (née *Orr*), wife of above.

Florence Campbell, The Priory, Balham; daughter of above: *b.* 1845; *m.* (*i*) 1864, Augustus Lewis Ricardo, Captain, Grenadier Guards; (*ii*) 1875, Charles Delaunay Turner Bravo, Barrister-at-Law.

Alexander Lewis Ricardo, Captain Grenadier Guards: *s.* of John Lewis Ricardo, M.P. (decd.) and Lady Catherine Ricardo (née *Duff*); *b.* 1843; *m.* 1864, Florence Campbell; *d.* 1871.

James Manby Gully, M.D., of Great Malvern and Orwell Lodge, Balham.

Jane Cannon Cox (née *Edouard*), widow; lady companion to Florence Ricardo.

Joseph Bravo, West Indian merchant, of 2 Palace Green, London.

Mary Hougham Bravo, wife of above; formerly wife of Augustus Charles Turner (decd.)

Charles Delaunay Turner Bravo, Barrister-at-Law: *s.* of Augustus Charles Turner (decd.) and Mary Hougham Bravo; *b.* 1845; assumed name of *Bravo* 1866; *m.* 1875, Florence Ricardo (née Campbell), widow; *d.* 1876.

Alice Turner, deaf-mute
Nellie Turner, mental defective
} daughters of Augustus Charles Turner (decd.) and Mary Hougham Bravo.

Hutchinson Royes Bell, F.R.C.S., 44 Harley St.
Ann Bell, sister of above
} nephew and niece of Mary Hougham Bravo.

Henry Smith, F.R.C.S., 82 Wimpole Street and King's College Hospital; brother-in-law of Mary Hougham Bravo.

Amelia Bushell, lady's-maid to Mary Hougham Bravo.

George Henry Brookes, senior partner of Messrs. Brookes & Jenkins, Solicitors, Godliman Street, Doctors Commons, London: legal adviser of Florence Bravo (née Campbell).

Doctors in Attendance upon Charles Bravo

George Harrison, surgeon, The Pentagon, Streatham.
Joseph Moore, M.D., Balham.

George Johnson, M.D., 11 Saville Row, London: Snr. Physician, King's College Hospital.
Sir William Gull, Bart., 74 Brook Street, London.

James Payne, F.R.C.P., 6 Saville Row, London, and St. Thomas' Hospital: performed autopsy.
Theophilus Redwood, Professor of Analytical Chemistry, Royal Pharmaceutical Society, 17 Bloomsbury Square, London: analyst.
William Carter, Her Majesty's Coroner for the County of East Surrey.

Servants at The Priory, Balham, appearing as Witnesses
Frederick Mark Rowe, butler.
Mary Ann Keeber, head housemaid.
George Griffith, coachman (dismissed).

Friends of Charles Bravo
F. H. McCalmont, Barrister-at-Law: shared Chambers with Charles Bravo at 1 Essex Court, Temple.
Carlyle Willoughby, Barrister-at-Law.
Jepson Atkinson   ,,   ,,   ,,
Edward Stanley Hope   ,,   ,,   ,,
John Reid   ,,   ,,   ,,

Court of the Queen's Bench
The Lord Chief Justice, Sir Alexander Cockburn, Bart.
Mr. Justice Mellor.
Mr. Justice Field.

Counsel at the Second Inquest
The Attorney-General, Sir John Holker, Q.C. ⎫
John Gorst, Q.C.   ⎬ Representing the Crown
Harry Poland   ⎭

Sir Henry James, Q.C. ⎫ Representing Florence Bravo.
John Biron   ⎭

John Patrick Murphy, Q.C. ⎫ Representing Jane Cannon Cox.
R. M. Bray   ⎭

George Lewis (of Messrs. Lewis & Lewis) Representing Joseph Bravo.

Serjeant Parry   ⎫ Representing James Manby Gully.
Archibald Smith ⎭

R. Burleigh Muir, Barrister-at-Law: Legal Assessor to the Coroner.

PREVIEW

OVER and above its psychological complexities which alone make the Bravo case one of compelling interest, over and above its mysteriousness, a haunting sense of fatality seems to beset the lives of those to whom it brought ruin and heartbreak.

It was a tragedy which descended in a split second; it was a tragedy of love, which is different from a love-tragedy; it was a tragedy of conscience; and in its climax there was a diabolical irony.

Its background was one of wealth and social position; its period 1876, when respectability was a cardinal virtue and immorality involved complete social ostracism. In such an atmosphere the Bravo case exploded like a bomb.

2

On 18th April, 1876—a date which was to become known as "the fatal Tuesday"—Charles Bravo, barrister-at-law, aged 30, caught the 4.7 p.m. train from Victoria station to Balham. Balham was then still largely rural, and the Bedford Hill Road along which he walked the three-quarters of a mile to his home on the edge of Tooting Common was a tree-embowered lane.

After greeting the beautiful and wealthy woman whom he had married only four months previously he rode out to exercise one of a pair of cobs they kept. An hour later he returned "much shaken and unnerved" to say that the animal had bolted with him. However, when he came downstairs dressed for dinner, and he, his wife and her lady-companion, Mrs. Cox, sat down to table at 7.30, he seemed none the worse, and not even the arrival of a letter which aroused his anger interfered with his copious appetite or prevented him from drinking his usual three or four glasses of Burgundy.

It was Mrs. Bravo's first appearance at dinner since an illness, and when she left her husband sitting by the morning-room fire at 8.45 and, with her companion to assist her, went upstairs to bed, there was no indication of the impending tragedy.

Since his wife's illness Charles Bravo had been occupying a separate room, and from the door of this, about sixty minutes later, he was heard "calling loudly for hot water". Before it could be brought he was seized with vomiting, and not many minutes afterwards collapsed and became unconscious.

Two local doctors were hastily summoned. Baffled by the patient's symptoms and alarmed at his grave state they asked for another opinion. A carriage was despatched forthwith to London with a letter to the stricken man's cousin—a Harley Street surgeon—requesting him to come at once bringing a physician with him.

Before their arrival the vomiting and purging of blood-tinged matter had proclaimed the fact that he was suffering from an irritant poison, but no other poison than a bottle of laudanum and another of chloroform—both nearly empty—neither of which could have caused his symptoms, was found in his room.

From 3 a.m. on Wednesday, 19th, when he regained consciousness, until coma supervened an hour before his death at 5.30 a.m. on Friday, 21st, Charles Bravo was "in full possession of his faculties". Two more doctors—one of them the most famous diagnostician of the day, Sir William Gull—saw him before the end, but he "made no admission" of having taken anything to cause his death.

The outstanding peculiarities of the death are these:

1. *At no time from first to last did Charles Bravo ask a single question as to the cause of the agony he was suffering.*

2. *When told he was poisoned he shewed no surprise.*

3. *At no time did he shew suspicion that anyone had poisoned him: his attitude towards his wife was demonstratively affectionate, and to Mrs. Cox perfectly friendly.*

4. *While he refused the ministrations of a clergyman, he prayed frequently and indulged in passionate outbursts of weeping.*

The analysis of ejected matter made on the assumption that

arsenic had been swallowed proved negative. The general analysis following the autopsy revealed that death had been due to a single dose of between 20 and 30 grains of antimony.

3

The inquest, perfunctorily conducted by a coroner over-anxious to "spare the feelings of the family", resulted in an open verdict, though the coroner himself in his address to the jury indicated that he expected one of *felo de se*. This theory of suicide was, however, passionately rejected by the dead man's own family and friends who declared that not only was he the "last man on earth to commit suicide", but, as a keen student of medical jurisprudence, would never, had he intended to kill himself, have chosen a medium so uncertain in its action and productive of such agony as antimony.

From Balham, meanwhile, there emanated a story that before her marriage to him Charles Bravo's widow had had a love affair with a retired doctor named Gully, still living close by. Simultaneously it began to be rumoured that the dead man had made up his mind to dismiss Mrs. Cox. Soon suspicion was being voiced that murder had been committed. Public excitement was enormous, and the demand that the inquest should be quashed and a fresh one ordered became too insistent to be ignored.

4

Concerning the new inquest, which opened at Balham on 11th July, 1876, and was extended over twenty-three days, Sir John Hall, Bart.—whose book, *The Bravo Mystery and Other Cases*, contains the most balanced and scholarly account of the case—has this to say:

"Never before or since have proceedings in a Coroner's Court been conducted under similar conditions. The Attorney-General was present in person and some of the most eminent members of the Bar held briefs on behalf of interested parties. Yet no judicial inquiry has ever in modern times been carried on so unbecomingly."

Since the first inquest had established that the cause of death was due to antimony, the second had only to concern itself with the question of how the antimony had found its way into the body of the deceased: in its efforts to do this it rapidly degenerated into what can only be termed a *trial by inquest*, with Florence Bravo and Mrs. Cox standing in the position of accused persons, yet deprived of those safeguards especially designed for the protection of accused persons in a criminal court.

In spite of the fact that no evidence was adduced to justify any other verdict than the open one which had been returned once already, the jury, composed of sixteen local men who could not fail to have been influenced by the gossip rife in the neighbourhood and by the unsubstantiated rumours produced as evidence, returned one of Wilful Murder, adding that "*there was not sufficient evidence to fix the guilt upon any person or persons*".

But no charge was ever preferred against anyone, and so, as Mr. William Roughead has said, the Bravo mystery "keeps its proud position as the prize puzzle of British criminal jurisprudence".[1]

But one man at least was convinced that he had solved that puzzle. Before me lies a private letter written on 1st December, 1923, by Sir Arthur Channell, Judge of the High Court and member of the Judicial Committee of the Privy Council. At the time of the tragedy he had already attained prominence in his profession: he had known Charles Bravo well, and though not himself engaged in the case his opinion upon it was sought by one of those "eminent members of the Bar" who was appearing for an "interested party". After much thought he arrived at a conclusion which his colleague unhesitatingly adopted. Unfortunately it came too late in the proceedings for him to base his case upon it, but he called an expert witness to support it, to whose evidence was probably due the fact that Florence Bravo and Mrs. Cox were not actually named in the verdict.

That great lawyer, Sir Travers Humphreys, has written:

"Of Mr. Justice Channell it is a commonplace to say that

---
[1] *Malice Domestic*—William Roughead.

wherever and whenever lawyers meet to discuss law a judgment of that learned Judge commands the deepest respect. It is his reported judgments, particularly perhaps his considered judgments, which are most illuminating and will always cause him to be placed in the very front rank of English Judges."[1]

5

In Part I of this book—which is, to the best of my belief, the only one to be devoted in entirety to this poignant domestic drama—I chronicle the life-stories of the principal characters up to the eve of the tragedy; Part II forms a study of their conduct from the time of Charles Bravo's fatal illness up to the opening of the second inquest; Part III records as much of those proceedings—a tragedy in themselves—as space permits in order that the reader may follow for himself the gradual emergence of the story within the story which Sir Arthur Channell perceived; Part IV sums up the evidence and carries the conclusion a stage further than that which Sir Arthur himself reached.

[1] *Criminal Days*—Sir Travers Humphreys. Sir Arthur Channell (1838–1928), the only child of Sir W. F. Channell, Judge, was educated at Harrow and Trinity College, Cambridge. Two of the best-known cases tried by him were those of Richard Price for the murder of the actor William Terriss (1898), and John Williams, "the hooded man", who shot and killed a police constable at Eastbourne in 1911.

Part I

ANTECEDENTS AND BACKGROUND

CHAPTER ONE

FLORENCE CAMPBELL

I

DR. HANS GROSS, Professor of Criminology at the University of Prague and a pioneer in criminal investigation, said in regard to human actions that "not one of them happens by pure chance unconnected with other happenings, none is incapable of explanation; they are the fruits which must of necessity develop under the influence of nature and individual culture, fruits whose formation is explained by the organism producing them. They are attached to the individual as naturally and surely as the fruit emanates from the tree. We do not look to gather grapes from thorns or figs from thistles."

Thus the only line of approach to a mystery so profound as this one is through an intensive examination of the antecedents, background, temperament and development of those concerned in it.

2

Only a few months separated the births of Florence Campbell and Charles Bravo, but the history of her family is as well authenticated as that of his is obscure. In the year 1825 her grandfather, Robert Campbell, left his native Argyllshire to seek his fortune in Australia. Taking up a great tract of land about a place which bore the name of Canberra he stocked it with sheep and built himself a solid stone homestead which he called Duntroon after the castle of the chief of his clan. He prospered exceedingly, and the subsequent history of the family is bound up with the growth and expansion of Canberra into the Federal capital.[1]

[1] Today Robert Campbell's stone homestead serves as the Officers' Mess of the Royal Military College, and within its walls Queen Elizabeth II was entertained in 1954. The Governor-General's residence, which Her Majesty occupied during her visit, was also built by a member of the family at a later date.

His son, Robert Tertius Campbell, married Miss Ann Orr, a lady of good birth, good looks, sense and charm. Florence, their second child and eldest daughter, was born in 1845, and within the next ten years, three more sons and two more daughters.

With the purchase of Buscot Park in Berkshire, Robert Tertius Campbell took his place among the landed gentry who, although their day was passing, still dominated politically and socially the life of their respective neighbourhoods. He followed the example set by the best of them and maintained their tradition of public service and private benefaction.[1] He was a pioneer in the cultivation of sugar-beet, and expended a fortune in the process. Except for the few weeks of the Season he and his family spent little time at their London house, 37 Lowndes Square: Buscot Park was their home and there were centred their interests.

In this world of wealth, leavened with piety and a sense of duty, and combining rural occupations with metropolitan fashion and interludes of foreign travel—when a courier went in advance to smooth the way and the family *entourage* included maids and valets, a tutor and a governess—Florence Campbell spent the first nineteen, and the only entirely happy, years of her life.

In our days it is not always realized how close-knit family life usually was a century ago. The Campbell children, lively, intelligent and affectionate, their characters moulded by a mother whose warm-hearted sensibility united them still more closely, grew up free from inhibitions. Florence herself possessed that appealing, thoroughly feminine, type of beauty which Greuze made famous: from a face of soft contours and transparently clear complexion, framed in glorious chestnut hair, a pair of violet-blue eyes looked out with tender gravity. Sensitive and affectionate, the romantic and the practical warred in her for supremacy, making her words and actions often appear contradictory, yet never masking her sincerity.

While contemporary sentiment declared marriage to be made in Heaven, contemporary materialism required it to bring both social and pecuniary advantages; and when Flor-

[1] He served in the office of High Sheriff of Berkshire in 1863.

ence made her début in 1863 her parents must have felt confident that so lovely and accomplished a daughter, with so generous an endowment in the background, could hardly fail to make a satisfactory match. The following spring, when she accompanied them to Canada, they must have thought their fondest hopes fulfilled, for Captain Alexander Lewis Ricardo, quartered at Montreal with a detachment of the Grenadier Guards, fell deeply in love with her.

Great-nephew of David Ricardo[1] and son of the late John Lewis Ricardo, M.P., he came on his father's side of a family of millionaires while his mother had been Lady Catherine Duff, sister of the fifth Earl of Fife.[2]

Captain Ricardo gave his bride a first life interest on £40,000; Robert Campbell one of £20,000, at the same time entering a bond to pay her the interest upon it. Samuel Wilberforce, Bishop of Oxford, officiated at the wedding, which took place in Buscot Church on 21st September, 1864, before a concourse of London fashion and county magnates, and after the wedding breakfast the bridegroom of twenty-one and the bride of nineteen drove off for their honeymoon in a barouche drawn by four horses.

3

No marriage could have held promise of greater happiness. The honeymoon, spent on the Rhine, was followed by a round of country-house visits, and then the young couple went to Hockham Hall, Norfolk, of which Captain Ricardo had taken a lease. But they spent little time there and it was soon given up, for Captain Ricardo was addicted to London where all too soon a propensity towards "over-indulgence in spirits" manifested itself. After each bout he was abjectly repentant and vowed never to yield to the temptation again. "When he was sober," Florence was to state, "we were very happy together." But these halcyon periods grew fewer and further between: by the spring of 1870 he was rarely, if ever, sober, and, shortly

---

[1] 1772–1832: author of *The Principles of Political Economy and Taxation*.
[2] Whose son, the sixth Earl and first Duke of Fife, married Princess Louise, eldest daughter of the Prince of Wales, later King Edward VII.

after the death of his mother in December of that year, he suffered his first attack of *delirium tremens* in which he became so violent that a male attendant had to be engaged. In the five and a half years of her marriage Florence had known all the disillusionment and suffered all the humiliations of a drunkard's wife: now she wrote asking her mother's advice.

For the past twenty-five years people had been flocking to Great Malvern to place themselves in the care of the celebrated Dr. Gully, and Mrs. Campbell's suggestion that her son-in-law should do likewise was warmly approved by his family, for Dr. Gully enjoyed a tremendous reputation, not only as a physician, but also for the almost hypnotic influence he could exercise over difficult and refractory patients such as Captain Ricardo seemed likely to prove.

On 8th April, 1871, therefore, Florence, leaving her husband in the care of his uncle and his man, Field, who combined the duties of nurse and valet, and accompanied by her maid, went into rooms at Great Malvern while she looked about for a furnished house. Three weeks later she moved into Orwell Lodge, where her husband, contrite and sober, joined her with Field in attendance. But this state of grace was of short duration: the power of the bottle proved greater than that of the physician, and after a fortnight of discreet but steady soaking, without a word to anyone he took train to London, leaving no address. It was the wife, not the husband, who was destined to succumb to Dr. Gully's hypnotic influence.

4

Field, despatched to find and retrieve his master, discovered him in rooms in Wigmore Street, and in the throes of a second attack of *delirium tremens*. Florence hastened to London; their house, 24 Chester Square, was hastily got ready and Captain Ricardo taken there in such a "shocking condition" that the doctor warned Mrs. Campbell that "the coatings of his stomach were seriously affected and he would not survive another such attack".

By August he was sufficiently recovered to return to Malvern and this time his reformation lasted a month before the inevitable recurred. "Although he constantly promised to mend his ways," said Florence, "without absolutely using physical violence his conduct towards me was most unkind." All through September and October she endured a crescendo of strain and misery; then in November she wrote imploring her mother to come "because she was afraid to stay in the house on account of his drunken violence".

Before this letter reached its destination it would appear that a scene of unprecedented vehemence had taken place between husband and wife; for on her arrival at Malvern Mrs. Campbell found Captain Ricardo in a state of sodden oblivion and Florence, accompanied by her sister, Mrs. Chalmers, staying in Dr. Gully's house vowing she would never see her husband again and would apply for a legal separation. Mrs. Campbell ordered her daughter's things to be packed forthwith and carried her off to Buscot.

5

The question as to what can have reduced the young husband to such a condition is one that has never been asked. The Ricardos were Dutch Jews of great culture and intellectual power, and on his mother's side Captain Ricardo was related to an old and distinguished Scottish family: he had married a girl with whom he had fallen deeply in love and who loved him in return—in short, there was everything to induce him to take his appointed place in society. Yet so rapid was the progress of his vice that at twenty-four it was incurable.

The cause here suggested was impotence.

To have children constitutes the pride and happiness of every normal couple, and with the Jews it is a mystic duty: later Florence was to conceive three times, but there is no hint that she ever did so during her first marriage: she had married —as girls so often did—knowing nothing of the facts of life and would imagine that such intimacies as took place between her husband and herself were normal. He, however, would know the truth, after marriage if not before it, and his wife's increasing disappointment at her failure to have children would make his pitiful secret harder to bear. There is no evidence that he had relations with other women—at least not until five months later when, in the course of a third attack of *delirium tremens*, he died in the house of a woman in Cologne.

It seems not improbable that it was the sudden discovery of his secret which drove Florence to leave him and demand a separation.

CHAPTER TWO

FLORENCE RICARDO AND DR. GULLY

I

JAMES MANBY GULLY, who, with Florence and Mrs. Cox, was to be suspected of having brought about the death of Charles Bravo, was born in Jamaica in 1808. The son of Daniel Gully, a wealthy coffee planter, the first eight years of his life were spent in running wild, like other planters' children. Then, from a preparatory school near Liverpool he went on to the École de St. Barbe in Paris, and thence to Edinburgh as a medical student. But before taking his degree he returned to Paris for a year at École de Médecine.

A liberal allowance from his father's estates and the expectation of an ample inheritance enabled him to travel freely, imbibing a wide knowledge and cosmopolitan culture; which, combined with a great admiration for the Continental school of medicine and great faith in his own powers, made him critical of the orthodoxy which he considered was hampering medical practice on this side of the Channel. For their part his British colleagues regarded askance both his self-confidence and the translations he was publishing of the works of the more advanced French specialists[1]: neither did he nor his associate, Dr. James Wilson, endear themselves to their profession by openly expressing the opinion that "the existing routine of medicine was effete and inefficient, if not positively harmful", and declaring their intention "to search for a better one". Confident that the answer lay in homoeopathy and hydropathy —the new theory of the water-cure which the Bavarian, Preissnith, was advocating and with the wonderful properties of which Dr. Wilson returned from a course of study "filled to the brim"—they established themselves in partnership at Malvern in 1842.

[1] He also tried his hand at drama, and in 1839 a play of his, based on Dumas' novel, *Mademoiselle de Belleisle*, was produced at Drury Lane.

Although Malvern had long been a spa, it had never been a flourishing one; but now in an extraordinarily short time people were flocking there from all over the kingdom, among them such celebrities as Tennyson, Dickens, Bulwer Lytton, Charles Reade, Bishop Wilberforce and Mr. and Mrs. Thomas Carlyle, to allow themselves to be packed in wet sheets, immersed in plunge baths, subjected to douches and frictions, to adhere docilely to rigid diets and swallow obediently the homoeopathic potions which the partners prescribed.[1]

Although the idea had originated with Dr. Wilson, the phenomenal success of the venture was due to the personality of Dr. Gully. It was *his* fame which made the town blossom into prosperity: he "made" Great Malvern, and in return Great Malvern rendered him homage. Though he throve upon his success and developed into a polished man of the world whose lively wit flowed from a well-stored mind; though he became an epicure who surrounded himself with beautiful things, he remained unsapped by complacency. The intensity of his gaze gained in benignity, but lost none of its penetration; the ironic twist which his smile had acquired enhanced rather than diminished the natural sweetness of his expression. His charm was as fresh as ever, his sympathy with suffering still as sensitive—for he was a born healer, the touch of whose really beautiful hands brought exquisite solace. The powers resident within him were greater than the man himself.

2

When she had been twelve years old Florence and her sisters had accompanied their mother to Malvern. Since then she and Dr. Gully had never seen each other, but the memory of the happy tea-parties he had given for them at his house formed a basis for friendship as soon as they met again, though by now he had grown rotund and bald, while on the black silk cord about his neck *pince-nez*, to which he frequently had occasion to resort, had replaced his former monocle.

[1] In August 1857, after a serious breakdown when she was thought to be dying, Florence Nightingale spent a month at Malvern, returning for another course of treatment the following year. Previously Dr. Gully had cured her father of eye trouble by hydropathy.

In 1876 a determined attempt was made to prove that adultery had taken place at Malvern while Florence and Captain Ricardo had been Dr. Gully's patients. But, though spruce and dapper, he was no figure to awake romance in the heart of a young woman thirty-seven years his junior. What he did possess were those comforting and sustaining qualities of which she stood urgently in need—wisdom, consideration and kindly masculine strength. And as in those first weeks at Malvern the wreckage of her marriage called forth his understanding and protectiveness, so that of his touched her own heart. In 1832 he had married a woman seventeen years his senior: three years later she had borne him a son; then her mind had begun to fail and he had ceased to live with her. Thus it was that between Florence Ricardo and Dr. Gully there flowered a love rooted in mutual sympathy: a love of the self-same quality as that which had linked the ageing Lord Melbourne and the youthful Queen Victoria; or Anthony Trollope and Kate Field—the lovely and intelligent American girl, young enough to be his daughter, who illumined his prosaic life. Such a love, compounded of lover-like devotion and paternal solicitude, can exercise a great and subtle power over a man who has reached the stage of life when physical desires are waning. It was not until the following spring that a sudden conjunction of circumstances overcame the seasoned logic which had hitherto governed Dr. Gully's life: it was not until then that Florence's tempestuous reaction to a threatened act of coercion on the part of her father placed her at a critical moment in her life under the full power of that fascination which Dr. Gully knew so well how to exert.

3

It was an age of masculine supremacy in which women enjoyed no legal status: before marriage a woman owed obedience to her father, after it to her husband. So when, in January 1871, Captain Ricardo wrote begging his wife to forgive and return, Robert Campbell insisted that it was her duty to do both. Florence's refusal angered him, and when a second and more urgent letter arrived their difference flamed into conflict—and no conflict can be so bitter as that between parent and child. Indignant at her flouting of his authority Robert Campbell foolishly threatened to withhold the interest on her settlement. With equal indignation she retorted that if he did so she would leave his house and take proceedings against him in Equity; then, as the quarrel grew in intensity, she fled precipitately to London.

Straight to Doctors Commons she went and into the ears of her sedate and elderly solicitor, Mr. George Henry Brookes, of Messrs. Brookes & Jenkins, Godliman Street, she poured the story of her troubles. He was dismayed at the predicament of his lovely young client, and for the better part of a year she became the guest of himself and his wife at their home in Streatham.

4

Dr. Gully spent part of each winter on the Continent, where he had as many friends, and interests, and enjoyed as great a reputation, as in England. He was sixty-three; he was comfortably off, and the idea of retirement with freedom to travel where and when he listed—including a visit to the island of his birth—and with more time to devote to contributions to the journals of the various medical societies of which he was a distinguished member, grew increasingly attractive.

Florence's departure from Malvern nearly coincided with his usual date for going abroad, and although his feelings for her may also have influenced his ultimate decision, he pondered the question for another month before writing to give his partner a year's notice of his intentions; and the fact that he announced at the same time that he would dispose of all his possessions suggests that he had made up his mind to sail for Jamaica as soon as the year was up.

As it was—perhaps because of the Franco-Prussian war, or perhaps because he had heard of Florence's flight from home—he was back in England in February, and to Mr. and Mrs. Brookes it doubtless seemed a most natural thing that this elderly and distinguished physician, who had attended Mrs. Ricardo's family for the past twenty-five years, and her husband and herself during the last twelve months, should

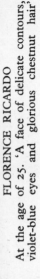

CHARLES DELAUNAY TURNER BRAVO
Barrister-at-Law. At the age of 25

FLORENCE RICARDO
At the age of 25. 'A face of delicate contours,
violet-blue eyes and glorious chestnut hair'

'Hydropathy'
JAMES MANBY GULLY, M.D.
From a *Vanity Fair* cartoon, 1876. 'The ancient lover'

frequently come to see and advise her at this critical tide in her affairs. Mrs. Campbell, however, who had thought that her daughter was falling too much under Dr. Gully's influence when she had carried her off from Malvern, became increasingly uneasy. Her only consolation was that to Malvern he must soon return, and then, perhaps, she might bring about a reconciliation between Florence and her father, and persuade her to abandon the idea of a legal separation from her husband. Her dismay was great, therefore, when at the end of March she learned that a Deed of Separation had actually been completed—with Dr. Gully's signature as one of the witnesses. This was bad enough, but worse was to follow.

Two weeks later a telegram announced Captain Ricardo's death at Cologne, and, since he had not revoked his Will, instead of the allowance of £1,200 a year which Florence would have received under the Deed of Separation, the £40,000 he had settled upon her at the time of their marriage became hers absolutely, while widowhood set her free from all legal control. She was only twenty-six, beautiful and wealthy, and on the verge of ruining her whole life for a married man thirty-seven years older than herself.

"We became aware," Mrs. Campbell told the Court, "of the frequent visits of Dr. Gully. That intimacy met with our entire disapproval. I remonstrated with her over her infatuation for Dr. Gully—but all to no purpose."

A further shock was in store. "On the advice of others," Florence stated, "I entered a charge against my father in the Court of Chancery." The "others", besides Mr. Brookes, could only comprise Dr. Gully, and the knowledge that such an action must inevitably lead to a total rupture with her family is indicative both of his power over her and his determination to consolidate it whatever might be the ultimate cost to herself. It clinched Mrs. Campbell's resentment and disgust and altered her conception of the man she had formerly held in such high esteem. It aroused Robert Campbell's wrath to its fullest and he issued an ultimatum: Florence must either sever all connection with Dr. Gully or he would forbid any member of his household to have any further communication with her.

Dr. Gully's own evidence epitomizes the story:

Dr. Gully: "I know she discarded her family for me in the spring of 1871."

Counsel: "You knew she had given up for you her home and her family?"

Dr. Gully: "I knew she had been given the choice of giving me up and had refused."

5

Florence Ricardo was essentially guileless and strangely immature, and in some ways she remained so all her days. She was also essentially single-minded and where she gave her affection she gave her complete trust. Dr. Gully's wife was eighty and a chronic invalid: it was therefore a logical deduction that the span of her life was drawing to a close. When, therefore, he asked Florence to regard their attachment as an "engagement" and voluntarily pledged himself to release her should she grow to care for anyone else, she entered into the compact in complete good faith. For the next year at least their conduct was compatible with that of a couple who were "privately engaged".

In that time she became a friend of Dr. Gully's son and daughter-in-law, and godmother to their little girl whom they named after her. That September she accompanied them— and took the Brookes' two daughters with her—to Malvern to bask in the reflected glory of the parting tributes, civic in character, being paid to Dr. Gully, and in January, after spending Christmas *en famille* with the Brookes, she spent six weeks with them in Italy.

Before leaving England she had taken the lease of a furnished house in Leigham Court Road, no great distance from the Brookes. But when on her return the latter learned that Dr. Gully had taken a house directly opposite, their eyes were opened and Mrs. Brookes spoke her mind with such vigour that Dr. Gully threatened to bring an action against her for slander.

CHAPTER THREE

MRS. JANE CANNON COX

I

"An article as necessary to a lady as her brougham or her bouquet is her companion," writes Thackeray in *Vanity Fair*. "Even those who are so bold . . . one might fancy they could face anything, dare not face the world without a female friend." Voicing this need to Lord Steyne, Becky Sharp said: "I must have a watch-dog," at the same time assuring him: "but he won't bark at you."

In Florence Ricardo's circumstances a lady companion was particularly necessary—a watch-dog who would not bark at Dr. Gully. Mrs. Jane Cannon Cox, at present employed as daily governess to the Brookes' younger daughter, might have been specially designed to fill the rôle—and she did so to the satisfaction of all parties, including herself.

At first sight there was something about Mrs. Cox which was apt to arouse mistrust, and even antipathy. On better acquaintance, however, people were usually so completely won over by the way in which she identified herself with their interests that they came to repose the greatest confidence in her. Antipathy towards her charged the Court when she faced it in 1876, and it has charged in some degree every account of the case since. The reason lies in the fact that she was devoid of sex appeal, possessed certain rather disagreeable characteristics and an unfeminine capacity for looking after herself. But the more one studies her story, the more one must admire the doggedness with which she refused to accept defeat.

From the day she was born until she became companion to Florence Ricardo her life had been a ceaseless battle to maintain her foothold in the world. Like Dr. Gully she had been born in Jamaica, but in a stratum of society divided from his by the impenetrable barrier of the colour-bar. French and Asiatic blood was mingled in her in about equal proportions.

The latter shewed itself in the coarseness and abundance of her straight black hair; in the compact formation of her head and the taut way in which her skin—the colour of old ivory—was stretched over her high cheekbones—skin which, about her sloe-black eyes, attained a dusky hue, while the eyes themselves, behind steel-rimmed spectacles, were unblinking and expressionless.

The art of insinuation and a native craftiness were bred in her blood; that of dissimulation had been fostered by her circumstances, which had also taught her to make a virtue of necessity and a fetish of gentility. All this expressed itself in a faintly unctuous demureness. Her slow utterance—the result of extreme caution—gave the impression of a tardy intelligence and a general disinterestedness: actually her mind was needle-sharp and nothing escaped her notice. She took no step without careful forethought, and if genius be the infinite capacity for taking pains, then Mrs. Cox possessed it.

On the other hand, one must not forget her virtues which have been too often overlooked. She gave constant and cheerful service to those who employed her: in a sick-room she was efficient, soothing and tirelessly selfless: she was even loyal and trustworthy, and if these transcendent qualities finally suffered extinction under the supreme test, let it be remembered that she was fighting not only for her life, but also for the future of her three little sons who were wholly dependent upon her and upon whom all her love was concentrated.

2

Only some six or seven years older than Florence herself and having been sufficiently well educated to fill the post of governess in an average household of the day, Jane Edouard, while still in her teens, scraped up enough money to come to England, where she found employment in the family of the Reverend John Papillon, rector of Lexden, Essex. In 1861 she returned to Jamaica as the wife of a compatriot whom she described as an engineer, but she was back again in 1867, widowed and determined to achieve an English education for her three little boys despite the fact that her total capital was under £500. While the two elder were reaching school age and the youngest emerging from infancy she opened a dame-school in Suffolk. After a couple of years, the venture having met with little success, she went to London to seek the advice of Mr. Joseph Bravo, another of her compatriots and head of a flourishing mercantile business who, on the rising tide of fortune, had a few years previously established an office in the City. He was close on sixty years of age, and the blood which coloured his complexion and tinted the whites of his eyes even more noticeably than her own was African; but that which had elevated the bridge of his nose and bestowed on him the shrewd brain which had brought him to affluence was of Jewish-Italian origin.

Mrs. Cox and her affairs were well known to him, and Mr. Solomon, his partner in Jamaica, had been her husband's executor and acted as agent for the "small property" owned by the late Mr. Cox's aunt. He now suggested that, as an investment, she should lease a vacant house he knew of in Lancaster Road, Notting Hill Gate, furnish it—which should not cost her more than £200—and re-let it. To supplement the small income this would yield, she could obtain a post as a daily governess. With the residue of her capital he advised her to purchase votes to secure the entry of her elder sons into St. Anne's Asylum School for the Sons of Impoverished Gentlefolk—an institution at Streatham in which he took a benevolent interest. He would, he added, be prepared to advance her an additional sum for this purpose should she need it.

Mrs. Cox put into practice both these suggestions and struggled punctiliously to repay by instalments his loan of £60, living meanwhile an arid and threadbare, but genteel, existence in one room at Streatham, from the window of which her youngest child could watch his mother's small, purposeful figure daily forging its way in fair weather and foul to and from the commodious residence overlooking Tooting Common where she taught the younger of Mr. and Mrs. Brookes' two daughters.

In June 1872 she abandoned this cramped and comfortless existence to share the roomy luxury of Florence Ricardo's home, discarding at the same time the threadbare dresses she had darned and sponged and refurbished for those of superior cut and quality, provided gratis by her employer.

She had become Florence Ricardo's watch-dog, and far from barking at Dr. Gully fawned upon him.

3

In their respective houses on opposite sides of Leigham Court Road, Florence Ricardo and Dr. Gully did all they could to observe the strict conventions of the period. Dr. Gully often crossed the road to dine at "Stokefield", but he never overstayed the sixty minutes which etiquette permitted a guest on rising from the table. Florence also crossed the road to dine with him, but unless others were present Mrs. Cox always accompanied her. If they drove up to London or took an airing in the surrounding countryside Dr. Gully would stroll by pre-arrangement down some quiet lane, where Florence would stop her carriage and pick him up. They observed discretion, too, whenever they travelled, both at home and abroad: they stopped at the same hotels, but always booked separate rooms in their own names, and each took their own servant. Indeed, so ceremonious was the attitude of the debonair old gentleman, who, though bald and stout, wore his three-score years like an orchid in his buttonhole, towards the girl whose beauty expressed a sweet and candid devotion unblemished by boldness or sophistication, that seeing them together the world might have judged them guardian and ward rather than lover and mistress—which is what in fact they had become since Florence had left the Brookes' house.

In the late summer of 1872 they went to the German spa, Kissingen, and from there Florence wrote Mrs. Cox a letter which is quoted in full because it serves emphatically to contradict two major misapprehensions which have appeared in accounts of this case and which, by dint of giving an entirely false impression of the character of the relationship between them, have done injustice to both.

The first of these is that Florence Ricardo, lazy, extravagant and self-indulgent, allowed the management of her household to pass from her incompetent hands into the competent ones of Mrs. Cox. This letter clearly demonstrates that the former was practical and firm in her housekeeping, and also—what a moment's reflection should have rendered obvious—that the impecunious Creole was helpless when confronted with the class-conscious snobbery of the English servant, and was contemptuously flouted when she endeavoured to assert a vicarious authority.

The second error has led to insinuations that a homosexual relationship existed between these two women—a charge which did not arise in the cleanlier minds of their own generation and was therefore mercifully not added to the load of suffering and humiliation they were called upon to endure. It claimed that from the beginning a state of familiarity and unreserve prevailed with the use of Christian names on both sides. In fact, it was not until after circumstances had placed Florence under a debt of gratitude to Mrs. Cox that they began to call each other by their Christian names, and it was not until September 1875 that Florence confided any of her more intimate affairs to her companion, while down to the very end of the story, although the latter was accorded various privileges, her position very definitely remained that of an employee.

"Kissingen,
"August 23rd.

"My dearest Mrs. Cox,
"Many thanks for your kind letter and parcels just received; please do not send any more flowers or forward any more letters.

"Will you tell Rance[1] that I have no intention of building a greenhouse, and will have nothing ordered from Mould or elsewhere without my order. I only wish for a few bulbs of each sort got for the house, and will leave the quantity in each pot to his judgment.

"I told McGrath[2] that he was not to sleep in the house, and *my order is to be obeyed*. Please tell him this. Will you

---

[1] Gardener.   [2] Footman.

write Mrs. ——[1] for me and demand my recipe book back; it is in a green watered cover, and tell her unless she returns it I will write to her mistress. Her address is 'care of Mrs. Goswell, The Abbey, Herne Hill'. Will you find out if she comes to Stokefield, as I gave strict orders she was not to come at all, and you can tell Barton[2] that it is as much as his place is worth if she comes to my house. I never gave Anna[3] permission to have her sisters and am writing to her about it.

"If all is well I shall be home on 24th or 25th September. Will you kindly get me eight laying hens of the Brahma breed by that time from *Exchange & Mart*—hens that will lay through the autumn and winter.

"I have such horrid baths now—peat-soil containing iron is mixed with mineral water, just like liquid manure. It is for soothing the nerves, but it is horrible, and one has to take a hot bath afterwards to get clean. Then I have three glasses of cold mineral water from 7 to 8 in the morning, and another glass at 6 p.m. I feel quite wearied out by 8.30 and am glad to get to bed. If it does me good I shall not mind, but it is not agreeable.

"I am sorry to hear you are suffering from your head, but hope by this time you are feeling better.

"Will you in the course of next week compare Pegg's prices for coals with Pigott's, as I should like the cellar filled before I return. I am anxious to hear of the safe arrival of the cheque I sent you; please acknowledge it at once, and if it fails to reach you, write at once to the London & County Bank, Great Malvern, to stop its payment at the Worcester Bank. As I have endorsed it anyone could cash it, but I hope you will get it safe.

"Please see Mould for me and tell him to take no orders from anyone but me. I am glad all the dogs and horses are well. I often wish Bruce[4] was here. Humphries[5] is very well and going on all right. Rance must manage as well as he can about the cuttings for next year; he has more shelves than

---

[1] This name for some reason has been suppressed.   [2] Butler.
[3] Housemaid.   [4] Dog.   [5] Lady's-maid.

he had last winter. I am getting on well with the lace for the mantelpiece.

> "With kindest love,
>> "Yours affectionately,
>>> "Florence Ricardo.

"P.S.—Please give the enclosed to Anna."

4

The West Indian islands cast a spell over, and create a life-long bond between, all who have been born, or have dwelt for any length of time, in them; but the allegiance Mrs. Cox gave Dr. Gully sprang from an affinity deeper than this, for within her resided a spark of those self-same powers which he himself generated, and the magnitude of his awed her and won her veneration. This secret little woman, who trusted none, confided the whole story of her life to him.

All the qualities they both possessed were taxed to the utmost some six weeks after he and Florence had returned from Kissingen. In that time Florence's face daily grew more pinched and wan, while her blue eyes widened with anxiety. Strain and anxiety also marked the usually urbane countenance of Dr. Gully.

Let Florence Ricardo tell the story in her own words as through her tears she answered the questions of her Counsel.

"There was at one time an improper intimacy between Dr. Gully and myself. That intimacy was in 1873 on the visit to Kissingen; there were intimacies on the occasion of that visit —more than one. In the November of that year I suffered from illness and I was then attended by Dr. Gully."

Counsel: "That illness was a miscarriage?"

Florence: "It was, and I did my utmost to conceal the fact from everyone about me. . . . I owe my life to Mrs. Cox's attendance upon me. I had acute physical suffering. . . . That terminated my improper intimacy with Dr. Gully. . . . Upon my oath there was no improper intimacy after that."

An instinctive piety had been vanquished by the temptations of the flesh; and the physical agony she now endured was accompanied by spiritual anguish that the life of the child for

which she hungered must be sacrificed to save her respectability. As she slowly regained her strength at Torquay the
romantic idyll perished and the realization of all she had lost
confronted her. As Frank Swinnerton has written:

> "It has always been the object of the English to be
> respectable, and at no stage in their history has this been so
> paramount as in the mid-nineteenth century. The loss of
> respectability was an insupportable punishment, amounting
> almost to physical torture."

So with Florence Ricardo: as a result she suddenly matured
and, well knowing Dr. Gully's power over her and her own
weakness under it, she took practical measures to safeguard
herself from both—from now on, wherever they went, Mrs.
Cox went too and shared her bedroom: the watch-dog was now
expected to bark at Dr. Gully. This sharing of the same bedroom has been cited by those eager to establish a homosexual
relationship as evidence in support of their theory; but the
truth is that, as soon as they returned to Streatham, Mrs. Cox
reverted to her own room on the top floor.

In the need to express her gratitude for all her companion
had done, Florence now initiated the use of Christian names
between them, and Mrs. Cox and her children were treated as
though they were members of the family. But another year
was to elapse before she made of her companion a confidante.

CHAPTER FOUR

THE PRIORY, BALHAM

I

SOME three-quarters of a mile from Balham station, at the point where the Bedford Hill Road emerges on to Tooting Common, there still stands The Priory, where this tragedy was enacted. Alas, this perfect example in miniature of the Gothic revival, built at the beginning of the nineteenth century when that style of architecture was still "in its sedate and gentlemanly phase—a charming fashion, not a crusade",[1] has been shorn of the ten acres of grounds and gardens which formed its setting: today, standing on a tea-tray of unkempt land above which garments flap from crazy clothes-lines, it seems to keep its gaze averted from the back premises of the houses that hem it in and to fasten it in mournful pride on its one remaining vista over the Common.

Until a few years ago a crimson rose which Florence had planted still clung to the wall, and nodded its blooms, below the window of the room wherein the tortured spirit of Charles Bravo left his stricken body, but the wisteria which was there in her day has managed to survive and still drapes the entrance front.

The leases of the two houses in Leigham Court Road were due to terminate at Lady Day, 1874, and the preceding autumn Dr. Gully began to search for a place which he could furnish to his own liking. About halfway between Balham station and the Common he found what he sought in a terrace of six semi-detached houses which had recently been built—the first instalment of the suburbia so soon to destroy the leafy tranquillity of the neighbourhood. Sentimentally naming it Orwell Lodge, after the house which Florence had occupied when first she had stayed at Malvern, he "furnished it from top to bottom".

[1] *2000 Years of England*—John Gloag.

The Priory was also to let at this time, and Florence went to view it.

Turning in at gates between two Gothic lodges, she beheld, for the first time, that unique little estate which "Mr. Cook of St. Paul's Churchyard" had brought into being to form a portion of his daughter's dowry. She was enraptured with it. The house with its crenellated roof and airy little turrets, its casement windows opening on to orchards, lawns and paddocks, and the sylvan prospect of the Common, looked as ephemeral as a poet's dream and deserving Horace Walpole's description, a "little plaything house", far more than Strawberry Hill to which he applied it. But Mr. Cook and his architect had not neglected practical issues: the well-proportioned rooms, though large enough for elegance, were not too large for comfort, and, facing south and west, caught the maximum of sunshine. And while they had provided a pleasaunce laid out in landscape fashion with walks shaded by fine trees, nooks screened by rare shrubs and little hedges, and sweeps of lawns bordered with flower-beds all to please the eye, they had also provided kitchen gardens, melon pits, pineries and vineries to provide delicacies for the table.

Florence's whole being responded to that mingling of the aesthetic with the practical, and with the ecstatic delight of one who has found the house of her dreams she took a long lease of the property from its owner "the Hon. Mr. Byng". With that typically English material, rose-garlanded chintz, and her collection of rare Venetian glass and china, she made the house harmonious and bright. She had striped sun-blinds with scalloped edges fixed above the windows, and when these were lowered on sunny days they lent the "little plaything house" a delightful air of frivolity.

The garden was her special delight and she bought scores of roses which she massed together in great beds. She bought fowls and ducks and geese to roam the orchards, fantail pigeons to strut the lawns and preen on the crenellations, and when she took possession in the spring of 1874 there were chicks and ducklings and goslings to which to carry titbits, and fantails to take grain from her hand. With her big dog, Bruce, and her two Skye terriers, Meg and Mrs. Dot, she would ramble on the Common, or else she would drive out in her phaeton behind a mettlesome pair of "handsome-actioned" cobs, handling the reins adroitly. Every eye would follow her then as she sped by, a gallant and lovely figure in a tight-fitting coat, and with a plumed hat on her bright hair, Mrs. Cox in mantle and bonnet sitting demurely beside her and a liveried groom with folded arms perched behind. On Sundays, with her companion in her pew and her servants filling another, she attended Service at Streatham church as had been the family custom at Buscot.

It was a life more in keeping with her character than any she had lived since she had driven away from her home with her bridegroom at the age of nineteen. She had never possessed social ambition and never cared for frivolity; there can be no doubt that, had she been able to live at The Priory in wedded respectability with the man who so well understood her and gave her the tenderness and support she needed, with a child or two to love and reunited with her family, she would have asked no more from life.

Indeed, her very love of The Priory deepened her craving for these things. Her brother William and his wife, Augusta, were the proud parents of three children: they had disregarded Robert Campbell's veto and sometimes came to see her—as did her widowed aunt, Mrs. Tom Campbell—but the happiness their visits brought was followed by a sense of loss and isolation even more acute, for which nothing could compensate.

Dr. Gully had apparently reverted without difficulty to the rôle he had originally occupied of affectionate mentor, and, indeed, the life he led could hardly have been better adjusted to suit his age and tastes. Pritchard, his butler-valet, ran his establishment at Orwell Lodge precisely to his liking; undisturbed in his study, he could compose his articles and essays in tranquillity; a warm welcome always awaited him at his son's house in Bayswater, and with a key to the entrance-gates of The Priory in his pocket he could stroll up the drive to lunch or dine there, or, on summer evenings, sit beside the woman he loved in the peace of her garden. He was too astute a man, too conversant with the moods and tenses of her sex, not to have noted and drawn inferences from the change in her. If he needed further evidence of this, it was provided in the autumn of that year—1874—when he and she, with Mrs. Cox as watchdog, were together in Paris after a tour of Italy. Suddenly she announced her intention of returning home, and, with a reluctant "Janie" at her heels, departed, leaving him to enjoy Paris on his own.

2

At Lexden Rectory the lessons of Mrs. Cox's pupils had been shared by the daughter of a Mrs. Harford, to whom she had made herself helpful and agreeable. During her short married life in Jamaica, she had kept up an assiduous correspondence with Mrs. Harford and had hastened to call upon her at Norwood as soon as she herself had found employment nearby, with Mrs. Brookes at Streatham. Mrs. Harford and her daughter—now the wife of a Mr. Fowke—had bestowed a kindly patronage upon the genteel widow who was having so hard a struggle to sustain that gentility. That patronage had warmed into friendship when, as lady-companion to the wealthy Mrs. Ricardo, she had acquired the self-assurance which good living and the rustle of silk petticoats bestow. Mrs. Cox was to make good use of that friendship in the difficulties which were to bestrew her path.

On her return from the Continent she hastened to Norwood to regale these two ladies over a cup of tea with an enthusiastic description of her travels, and so frankly did she speak of Dr. Gully's fatherly attachment to the young Mrs. Ricardo that neither of them doubted the relationship was other than *comme il faut* and were consequently flattered to be invited to The Priory; had she had any inkling of its true nature, Mrs. Harford was to tell the Court, nothing would have induced her to enter Mrs. Ricardo's house.

Mrs. Cox's next call was upon Mrs. Joseph Bravo, for which she seized the opportunity when Florence was driving to London for Christmas shopping to ask for a lift to Kensington. Mr. Joseph Bravo's increasing fortune had enabled him in recent years to move from the undistinguished house in

Lancaster Gate which he had formerly occupied into that very distinguished one of rose-red brick which Thackeray had so gladly built for himself and his two daughters at Palace Green in 1861 and in which he had drawn his last painful breath in the early hours of Christmas morning, 1863.[1]

When Florence returned to pick up her companion that cold December day, the butler came to her carriage to say that Mrs. Bravo begged Mrs. Ricardo to do her the honour of entering; and drawing her furs more closely about her she went to meet the woman who was to become her implacable enemy.

It was a brief and formal encounter, but Charles Bravo unexpectedly entered his mother's drawing-room in time to be introduced and to escort Florence politely downstairs. It is very unlikely that Florence gave the rather too fleshy and curiously pallid young barrister a second thought, but no man could overlook her beauty. Charles Bravo, besides, had a keen eye for values, and the jewellery she wore, together with the whole costly perfection of her *toilette*, would not have escaped his observation.

[1] Writing to a friend of 2 Palace Green, Thackeray says: "The house is delightful. . . . There is an old Palace" (Kensington Palace) "and magnificent trees before the window at which I write. I have a most delightful study, bedroom and so forth. . . ." The house is now the Israeli Embassy.

CHAPTER FIVE

THE CROSS ROADS: 1875

I

In April 1875 occurred two events which were closely to influence the respective destinies of Florence and Mrs. Cox. The first took the form of a letter which Mrs. Cox received from her aunt, Mrs. Margaret Cox, asking her to return to Jamaica with her boys and take charge of the "small business", which they would ultimately inherit, as she was now too old and frail to manage it herself.

This letter put Jane Cox in something of a quandary, but after careful reflection she wrote pointing out that it had cost her considerable sacrifice to send her elder boys to St. Anne's—where she hoped by saving to send her youngest as well—and she neither felt justified in cutting short their education and bringing them to Jamaica, nor could she maintain them at school if she gave up her post at The Priory and came alone.

The second event was a visit from Mrs. Tom Campbell, who brought Florence the news that her mother was seriously ill. She reminded Florence that her mother had never ceased hoping for a reconciliation and that, if only she would give up Dr. Gully, the whole family would welcome her back. The thought that her mother might die without their being reconciled caused Florence acute distress, and though it would be like tearing her heart from her body to part with Dr. Gully, she came to the conclusion that such a course was inevitable. But while summoning up her courage to "break" with him she heard that her mother was better; yet, though her anxiety was eased, her resolution remained unshaken. Dr. Gully was planning a trip to the Continent, but when he spoke of it to Florence, her lack of response chilled him; when he asked her what the trouble was, she shrugged away his questions; finally, losing patience, he threatened to go with a party of friends. She advised him to do so—and he did.

It had been her intention to write at once and "break off with him", but, as she told the Court, "I put it off because I did not want to spoil his holiday". Since her mother had now left to take a cure abroad, she decided to do nothing until October when both would have returned.

She spent the summer quietly at home, but in September she and Mrs. Cox went to Eastbourne—and there she admitted her companion so far into her confidence as to express her longing "to be reconciled with her family—particularly her mother". Meanwhile the destinies of them both were hanging upon the point of a schoolboy's pen.

His school, wrote Mrs. Cox's eldest son, was going to Brighton to compete at sports against a school there; good-naturedly, Florence suggested that they move to Brighton for the event; the jubilant mother hastened away and took rooms in King's Road—and their fates were sealed.

2

The introduction by the railway of return fares at 3s. 6d. had changed the Brighton season. In the summer months it was thronged with members of the proletariat, and Society consequently absented itself until these had returned to their labours. Then in September and October, in the sunshine of St. Luke's summer, it regained its former glory as a fashionable resort, and every afternoon a galaxy of distinguished visitors could be seen taking the air along the front in a cavalcade which rivalled in brilliance that of Church Parade in Hyde Park during the Season.

On the afternoon of their arrival Florence and Mrs. Cox joined the strollers on the Promenade, and as they turned their steps towards Hove, Mr. Charles Bravo, staying there with his people, turned his towards Brighton. They met face to face.

He raised his hat. Florence extended her hand. She gave him permission to walk with them, and when he was parting with them at their door he asked to be allowed to call next day and pay his respects.

He called next day, and the next, and the one after that; he escorted them to the school sports; in the words of Mrs.

Cox: "Mr. Bravo was very attentive to Mrs. Ricardo." Florence found it such a pleasant experience to walk and talk with this lively and well-dressed young man, whose every glance proclaimed his appreciation of her elegance and charm, that all her troubles—even the approaching ordeal of "breaking off with Dr. Gully"—melted like the mist that sometimes veiled the horizon. And although Charles Bravo returned with his family to Kensington the following week, it was surprising how often he found himself able to spend a day at Brighton during the next fortnight.

A woman's instinct seldom fails to inform her when a man is thinking of asking her to be his wife. Nothing could so completely re-establish her respectability as marriage, but she knew only too well that as an "unchaste woman" she had forfeited all right to man's respect, let alone love. But whether Charles Bravo proposed or not, she knew she must break off with Dr. Gully.

Although she dreaded the necessity, she felt she owed it to him to explain in person how urgently she had been longing for a reconciliation with her mother and her family, and she therefore wrote asking him to come and see her as soon as possible. She met him at the station, but, perhaps because they passed Charles Bravo as they drove to her lodgings and Dr. Gully asked her who was the young man whose bow she was returning, her nerve failed her. But no sooner had he gone than, deploring her weakness, she wrote and told him that ever since her mother's serious illness in the spring she had known she could never be happy until they were reconciled, and "since that could never happen so long as their attachment lasted, there was nothing to do but end it".

Charles Bravo called that same evening and, somewhat obliquely, both referred to the question of marriage. Charles said that since his mother "wished him to stay at home and not to marry anyone" it would be difficult to gain her consent to his becoming engaged. Florence in her turn said that "she had a devoted admirer, at which he laughed and asked how old Dr. Gully was". The long and short of it was that she now knew for certain he was seriously contemplating marriage with her and she was faced with the urgent question—when he proposed, should she confess or conceal her past? The irony of the situation was that the only person who was competent to advise her was Dr. Gully himself!

If she had cherished any illusions that the latter would accept his *congé* without protest, the return post shattered it. His letter opening diplomatically with the assurance that "if it were for her happiness that their attachment should end, then end it must", concluded with information which produced a nervous crisis in Florence—that he would come to Brighton next day but one and spend the night at an hotel near her lodgings. In her extreme agitation she did what so far she had refrained from doing: she took Mrs. Cox into her confidence concerning her intentions regarding Dr. Gully and the possibility of her marrying Charles Bravo.

Mrs. Cox, no doubt, had already weighed up the situation: if Florence were to marry, her own position at The Priory automatically became redundant and her children's future jeopardized. It was therefore in her interest to preserve the *status quo*. But apart from this she had known Charles Bravo for the past fifteen years—not intimately, but within the family circle—and she probably doubted—as her words and actions both now and later shew—his suitability as a husband for anyone so sensitive as Florence: a misgiving time was amply to justify. But she was too cautious, and too crafty, to express her opinion openly, and convinced by her faith in Dr. Gully that if only he could be put in possession of all the facts he would know how to nip the danger in the bud, she persuaded Florence that it would save pain both to him and herself if she —Mrs. Cox—were to meet his train at Croydon and prepare him on the way down for what was to come. A telegram was accordingly despatched giving him a particular train by which to travel and telling him to look out for "Janie" on Croydon platform.

From disjointed phrases in the evidence it would appear that after Mrs. Cox's departure Florence, fearful lest her fortitude should fail her when confronted with her lover, sent for a well-known local physician, Dr. Dill, who had attended her on former visits to Brighton, and "knew all about her attachment to Dr. Gully". Although Dr. Dill nowhere makes any personal appearance, he was indirectly to influence the course of events considerably, both now and at a later stage. Obviously one of those family doctors who acted as confessors and counsellors, as well as physicians, to their patients, he agreed with Florence that "it would be a good thing for the attachment to end" and, foreseeing that her resolution would be more likely to dissolve if the critical interview took place in the privacy of her lodgings, suggested the course which, fortified by *sal volatile*, she proceeded to act upon. When the travellers alighted from their train at Brighton they were astounded to find her awaiting them. With surprising coolness she dismissed Mrs. Cox to the station waiting-room, there to remain until retrieved, and led Dr. Gully to the public sitting-room of a nearby hotel. Here, among the antimacassars, potted palms and plush, she told him that, though Charles Bravo had not yet asked her to marry him, she believed he intended to do so; then, after reminding him he had voluntarily promised that if such circumstances arose "he would make no attempt to hold her to their engagement", she went on to say that "whether Charles Bravo married her or not, she had made up her mind that the connection between them must come to an end because she could no longer bear not to be reconciled with her mother".

The sweet reasonableness of Dr. Gully's attitude was such that when he pleaded to be allowed to lunch with her "for the last time" she was melted into consenting. But luncheon over and Mrs. Cox withdrawn there followed what Florence described as "a very painful interview".

"Are you engaged to Mr. Bravo?" Dr. Gully asked.

"No; he can fix nothing without his mother's consent."

Dr. Gully's next words suggest that they had been inspired by what he had learned from Mrs. Cox on the way down.

"I advised her," he said in evidence, "not to be in a hurry, but to be acquainted with him, *and especially with his family*,[1] for three or four months before she fixed her fate."

She assured him that she would "heed his advice" and he

[1] Author's italics.

then asked her "if and when Charles Bravo proposed, she intended telling him the truth about their attachment". She assured him that she did.

With that assurance Dr. Gully doubtless felt so sanguine about the outcome that when she asked him to leave Balham "in order to save her embarrassment" and offered, as she afterwards alleged, to take over the remainder of his lease, he replied evasively that "he thought of going back to his native island". He spent the night at Brighton, called at breakfast time next morning in a perfectly natural way, and kissed her hand on parting in his usual fashion. But when a few days later —Charles Bravo having made his proposal and Florence a partial confession—Mrs. Cox informed Dr. Gully privately in "a short note" that the two were engaged, he reacted with startling vehemence. He wrote Florence "a very angry letter" which brought him an equally angry reply in which she said she "must never see his face again": whereupon he summoned Pritchard and having told him that "Mrs. Ricardo had treated him very badly", gave orders that "if Mrs. Ricardo or Mrs. Cox ever came to his house, they were not to be admitted".

Having recovered somewhat from the shock, he wrote Florence a more kindly letter. Excusing her lover's previous outburst, Florence told the Court:

"He had lost me, and naturally he would say angry things when he heard I was to be married."

Counsel for the Crown (alluding to the parting scene at Brighton): "But he had lost you before."

Florence: "But perhaps he then looked forward to the hope of regaining me, which he would not do if I married."

Which indicates that she fully realized he had expected Charles Bravo to repudiate her on learning of their intimacy.

CHAPTER SIX

CHARLES DELAUNAY TURNER BRAVO

I

IN the case of a suspected murder the spotlight falls first upon the personality of the victim, and under the impact of the shock his friends tend all too readily to lose sight of his shortcomings and exaggerate his virtues: the moment a suspect appears, the spotlight is diverted to them and a reverse process takes place, their failings leaping into prominence and their merits fading into oblivion. So it was in the Bravo case. But whereas in most cases the victim's personality recedes into the background once a suspect appears, in this one the dead man's personality acquired an increasing importance and mystified the public as much as the manner of his death.

The failure to solve the problem presented by the latter lies largely in the fact that hitherto no attempt has been made to solve that presented by the former; for the evolution of Charles Bravo forms a striking example of the influence of heredity, environment and upbringing in shaping a character for good or ill. If one could penetrate the obscurity which enshrouds the life and death of the father, a revealing light might be shed on that which enshrouds those of the son; but except that he is entered on his son's marriage certificate as *"Augustus Charles Turner, gentleman"*, nothing whatever is known about him.

Florence stated that Charles, before their marriage, "promised to tell me after it who his father was, but he did not do so". It seems probable that he was domiciled in Jamaica, since Joseph Bravo married his widow soon after his death, while Charles was still quite small. Both Joseph Bravo himself and probably Mrs. Cox must have known something about him, but neither was questioned on the subject. Henry Smith, F.R.C.S., who had married Mrs. Bravo's sister, denied all knowledge of him; while, since Mrs. Bravo herself took to her bed on the day of her son's death and never left it until she was carried away in her coffin a year later, no information was obtained from her.[1]

But more positive reasons than these exist for suspecting that the career of Augustus Charles Turner reflected no credit upon those connected with him. Such was the heritage he bequeathed his three children that only Charles was in possession of his faculties. Of his two sisters, Alice was a deaf-mute, while Neuy was a helpless imbecile confined in an institution.

Since respectable Englishwomen did not in those days marry coloured men, one may assume that the widow of Augustus Turner was in such financial straits that the colour of the coin in the hand offering her marriage was of more importance than that of the hand itself. To Joseph Bravo, no doubt, the *kudos* of marrying a white woman afforded sufficient compensation for her penniless and encumbered condition.

As Charles was not sent away to school and his mother ever displayed a morbid anxiety over his health, it is likely that he was a delicate boy. It was suggested at the Inquiry that he was subject to fits. What is certain is that upon him was expended the whole of Mrs. Bravo's fiercely possessive maternal love. Solicitously she watched every change in his expression; her instinct forestalled his every wish; her hands flew to attend his smallest want: rewards were lavished to pacify when they should have been withheld to correct. Charles was the apple of his mother's eye and the best was scarcely good enough for him, but, on the other hand, he had grown to manhood as the dependant on the bounty of a self-made man—a man absorbed in the pursuit of money who to his way of thinking had treated his stepson generously in sending him to Oxford, yet could not bear to relinquish one iota of that control over him which his money gave; so although he opened a banking account for him, instead of making him a regular allowance he instructed the manager to notify him whenever Charles' credit fell below £100. By this means he not only kept himself *au courant* with his stepson's expenditure, but placed him under the obligation

---

[1] As the story unfolds, peculiarities will be noticed in the behaviour of Mrs. Bravo herself.

of rendering thanks every time a fresh sum was paid to his credit. It was a position guaranteed to foster deceit and resentment.

Having from childhood imbibed his stepfather's mercenary and materialistic outlook, the acquisition of money, and the power it could bestow, became an obsession with Charles and inspired his every thought. When upon coming of age he deferentially suggested that he take the name of Bravo, he may have hoped that his stepfather would reciprocate by making a settlement upon him. If so, he was disappointed and, though Joseph Bravo appeared pleased by the compliment, he continued to pay the allowance on the same invidious terms as formerly. Yet there can be no doubt that he was fond of Charles.

The majority of Charles' friends described him as high-spirited, happy-natured and possessed of excellent health. But there is also evidence that moods of dark depression succeeded the occasions of his greatest gaiety; that he was liable to irrational and violent outbursts of temper, and subject to neuralgia and rheumatism; while the *post-mortem* revealed that the condition of his liver, spleen and kidneys was only "fairly natural".

It was claimed that he was open and truthful in all he did. As will be seen, money was his only abiding passion and he was actually leading a double life. In fact, Charles Bravo could exercise a certain charm, which, because it was quick and vivid, gave the impression of being spontaneous and natural; he had a glib and persuasive tongue, a sprightly humour and a gay laugh which made his company superficially stimulating and amusing; but his laughter was apt to ring out too frequently, too loudly, and to verge upon the hysterical, his humour to degenerate into facetiousness, and his *bonhomie* to become bombastic and wearisome. The truth is he sought popularity as strenuously as he sought gold, and strove always to hold the centre of the stage.

The paradox of his character was demonstrated in his features. When exerting his powers to please he appeared almost good-looking; but in repose the full lower lip thrust out aggressively, the long, thin upper one clipped down upon it in a formidable line, and grooves formed from nostrils to mouth which were suggestive of a snarl. His eyes were too prominent and stared too glassily, while in anger his sallow complexion grew livid, his voice shrill, and he would repeat his words with hysterical reiteration.

Two of his colleagues, who knew him well, described him as "a sharp young barrister"; the *Daily News* said that he possessed "ordinary ability and more than ordinary ambition"; the friend with whom he had shared rooms at Oxford, visited Paris, and was sometimes invited for a night or two to his home, stated that he "possessed a great deal of sound common sense and very little sentiment". He himself knew his limitations too well to imagine that he would ever attain fame and fortune at his profession; but he felt that with his ready tongue, agile mind and good address he could make a success of a Parliamentary career to which the Bar was a useful and recognized stepping-stone. Unfortunately, such a career was costly and needed influence and social backing. But he had no private income, and outside the City Joseph Bravo was of no account. Through marriage with Florence Ricardo, who was rich and charming and whose people occupied the privileged position still accruing to the landed gentry, his problem would be solved. Furthermore, so brilliant a marriage should not only reconcile his mother to the idea of losing him, but even compel his stepfather to make a settlement upon him; while by setting him up in a household of his own it would free him from the former's domination and doting solicitude, and the latter's too inquisitive concern in his affairs.

With all the charm he could command he set himself to captivate Florence Ricardo.

CHAPTER SEVEN

THE ENGAGEMENT OF CHARLES BRAVO

I

THE plethora of questions put to Florence and Mrs. Cox in examination and cross-examination by the various Counsel in their endeavours to elicit the exact date upon which the former made a full confession of her past to Charles Bravo, complicates the issue instead of clarifying it. But the following would appear to be the order of events.

Shortly after Dr. Gully had accepted his *congé* Charles called and made Florence some form of proposal of marriage, at the same time making it clear that until he had obtained his mother's consent their engagement could not be "ratified". Florence then told him that she had been "attached" to Dr. Gully and had seen him continuously from the time of Captain Ricardo's death, and that the attachment had led to an estrangement from her family; but that, having now "dismissed" him, a reconciliation was about to take place. In fact, she told him, not the whole truth, but enough to leave little room for doubt as to what the real nature of the relationship had been. It was only natural that she should withhold the story of the Kissingen visit and its result, for should Mrs. Bravo refuse her consent to the marriage Charles might wish to break off the "understanding between them", and she would then have put him in possession of a damaging secret to no purpose.

Charles aroused her admiration and gratitude by taking her disclosure with complete urbanity, and four days later she wrote him the following letter, which indicates that she was heeding Dr. Gully's advice to be in no hurry to "fix her fate".

"113 King's Road,
"Brighton,
"21st October, 1875.

"My dear Charlie,

"After serious and deep consideration I have come to the conclusion that if you *still hope* and wish to gain my love we must see more of each other, and be quite sure that the solemn act of marriage will be for the happiness of us both.

"This is what I think—you ought to *tell* your mother. I would never enter a family where I was not welcome. I have no fear of not gaining her affection, but of course she must see me and judge for herself. All I can *say* is that you have behaved in the noblest manner, and that I have no doubt oi being happy with you; but of course before giving up my present freedom I must be quite convinced that it will be for our mutual happiness.

"Now I must tell you that I have written to the *Dr.* to say that I must never see his face again; it is the right thing to do in every respect.

"Whatever happens, whether we marry or whether we do not, I shall ever have a great respect for you and take a deep interest in your welfare, for I think you are a very good man. Write and tell me what you think of this letter, and with every kind wish,

"Ever your sincere friend,

"Florence Ricardo.

"P.S.—Of course this is sacred. I remain here till Monday."

Sir John Hall, in an attempt to reconcile the irreconcilable, suggests that the differences between the words and actions of Charles Bravo were due to the fact that while his marriage may have been "actuated at first by material considerations" he "later rapidly grew very fond" of his wife. Certainly his reply to the above letter could scarcely have been less lover-like. But Charles, though a gambler by instinct and prepared to run big risks to attain his ends, was also a very astute lawyer determined never to consign to paper any statement which might irretrievably commit him.

A glance at a copy of Captain Ricardo's Will would shew him that Florence had at her absolute disposal capital amounting to £40,000, apart from which she had, as she had told him, an income of £300 a year from her grandfather's estate and the interest on the £20,000 settled on her by her father, the capital of which would also revert to her on his death. If, as he shrewdly surmised, she had been guilty of moral delinquency with Dr. Gully, then that, of course, put her beyond the Pale: it debarred him from even introducing her into his mother's presence—as for presenting her as his intended wife, such a thing would be unthinkable. But to Charles Bravo the prize, if somewhat tarnished, was enormous, while the risk of Mrs. Bravo ever learning the guilty secret was remote. So while he continued to ponder the problem he wrote Florence a temporizing letter, resorting to facetiousness to cover up its deficiencies.

"1 Essex Court, Temple,
"Oct. 22nd, 1875.

"My dear Florence,

"You are quite right. I approve thoroughly of what you say and do; and I may tell you that I am in danger of losing my chief jewel, my modesty, when I consider that you, whose opinion I most value, give me such high praise. It was only the other day that I was wishing that I knew where a commodity of good names could be bought—and now I have them free—given. I must, however, in common honesty tell you that it is my opinion that if all 'the very good men' in the world were like me they would be an uncommonly poor lot.

"As you take an interest in my welfare I must tell you that I earned five guineas yesterday, but that I was unfortunately unable to do anything for my client, who was as much in the wrong as he could well be. Since my overthrow in that matter I have been doing work for a friend. He will, as a reward for some two years' services, when he obtains a silk gown, give me a red bag (value 5s.) in consideration of which I will present his clerk with a guinea. That is how we juniors get on.

"If you are not delighted, from weariness of reading it, to see that this letter is nearly finished, you will at any rate excuse its brevity when you know that I have nothing more to say, except that I am your sincere friend,

"Charles Bravo.

"P.S.—I will be in Brighton to-morrow."

No doubt Charles, following hard on the heels of this letter, managed to dispel the chilly impression it must have created, in assuring her of the affection which he omits to express, and in providing an adequate reason for continuing to postpone telling his mother of their engagement. At least none of these things finds any utterance in the correspondence which she now initiated with her father, as the following letter, written after her return to The Priory, shews.

> "The Priory, Balham,
> "Oct. 30th, 1875.

"My dearest father,

"Your kind and affectionate letter gave me the greatest pleasure last night, and I look forward with sincere and heartfelt joy to meeting you all again.

"My past has been a sad one, but it will be for ever blotted out and forgotten, and believe me when I say how much I regret ever having caused you, or any member of my family, pain with regard to the last few years of separation.

"With best love to yourself and Mamma and all at Buscot,

> "Ever your affectionate child,
> "Florence Ricardo."

The whole family gathered at Lowndes Square to welcome her back "with the greatest affection", and when shortly afterwards Mrs. Campbell went to spend the day at The Priory, Florence could tell her with a clear conscience that "the attachment" was entirely broken off, for in the meantime she had destroyed all Dr. Gully's letters, returned every one of his presents and received back her own.

"I found my daughter," Mrs. Campbell stated, "surrounded by every comfort and managing her establishment with the assistance of Mrs. Cox."

2

On 1st November Charles Bravo informed Florence that he had obtained his mother's consent to the announcement of their engagement and Florence was now faced with the necessity of deciding whether to reveal or conceal the whole truth about her past. It apparently took her a few days to do so, but it does not surprise one that her decision was to reveal it, or that, when she did so, she accomplished the humiliating duty with dignity and restraint. What does surprise one is that she should not have suspected that the lack of emotion with which he received her confession was because he had already suspected it and weighed it carefully in the balance against her fortune. Let her tell the story of what took place in her own words.

"I told him that I had been constantly in Dr. Gully's company; I told him we had travelled abroad together, and in England. I told him all. I told him of the intimacy which had occurred between myself and Dr. Gully at Kissingen in 1873. I told him that I had had a miscarriage, and that if he still wished to marry me, he married me in full knowledge of that fact. I left the room for a while so that he should have the opportunity to think over what I had said."

She was absent about half an hour. "When I returned he said I had acted nobly and generously in telling him, and that he was still more certain from my having told him that I was still less likely to err again.

" 'I am satisfied to make you my wife,' he said, 'but, of course, you must never see Dr. Gully again.'

"He made me swear a solemn oath that I would not divulge to any human being what I had told him."

And now Charles had a confession of his own to make. For the past four years, he said, he had been consorting with a woman at Maidenhead, who had previously had a son by another man and now had a daughter by him.

"He promised to give her up. We made a solemn compact that he would never mention Dr. Gully's name, nor I this woman's."

Before they had left Brighton, Florence, who was now confiding everything to Mrs. Cox, had put to her a question which must have been long on her mind: she asked her if she knew the cause of her illness on her return from Kissingen. When an awkward question was put to her, Mrs. Cox had a trick of stroking some nearby object while she deliberated her reply. She did so now; then said:

"I have no idea of it."

That she, who had brought four children into the world,[1] should really have been ignorant of the true nature of Florence's illness is inconceivable.

"It was a miscarriage," Florence continued. "If Mr. Bravo proposes I shall have to tell him of it."

"It would be right to do so," agreed Mrs. Cox.

It had therefore seemed as incredible to her, as it had done to Dr. Gully, that "knowing all" Charles Bravo should still wish to make Florence his wife; and his complacent reception of the "full confession" aroused the most conflicting emotions in Mrs. Cox's breast. She knew full well the devastating scenes that would ensue if a whisper of such a scandal were to reach Mrs. Bravo's ears. Consequently, the first moment she found herself alone with Charles she told him that she had only recently learned the truth about the intimacy at Kissingen and its aftermath—previously she had believed the illness to be due "to an unnatural state caused by the baths" Florence had had there.

"Florence has told me all," he said shortly.

Smoothing a nearby object she hazarded:

"Might it not be advisable to acquaint your mother with the attachment?"

"No," he replied emphatically. "You know what the consequences of that would be—the marriage would be broken off."

She ventured to suggest that keeping the truth from Mrs. Bravo might lead to trouble later on.

"Oh, she'll be all right after it has taken place," he impatiently replied. "But I will not have her spoken to on this matter."

Mrs. Cox knew exactly where she was: from now on her own future and that of her children would be largely dependent upon Charles Bravo's good will, and she set about earning this with the thoroughness with which she did all things. She

[1] A daughter had died in Jamaica.

paid a visit to Palace Green and there sang Florence's praises:
Florence was "so good and generous", she told his parents; so
much attached to Charles; "would make him such a good
wife" and "would do everything to make him happy".

While Joseph Bravo could not help but be impressed with
the material aspect of the match, to the jealous mother it was
an added bitterness that not only must she give up her son to
another woman, but that woman, moving as she did in circles
so different from her own, would separate him all the more
completely from her. The old adage,

> My son's my son till he gets him a wife,
> My daughter's my daughter all her life,

surely echoed agonizingly in Mrs. Bravo's heart as she gazed
despairingly at poor Alice.

3

Florence, radiant with happiness at the thought of her
future with the man who had so nobly "blotted out" her sad
past, took the news of her engagement to her mother at
Lowndes Square. The first question Mrs. Campbell asked was:

"Have you told him of the attachment?"

"I have told him *everything*."

"He must tell his mother of it," Mrs. Campbell said at
once. But she had no idea of the full extent of that "everything",[1] and was consequently astounded at the vehemence of
Charles' reactions when, meeting him a few days later at her
sister-in-law's house at Kingston, she took the matter up with
him.

"I have learned from my daughter," she said, "that she has
told you all the circumstances of her life which have been the
cause of her estrangement from her family."

"Florence has told me everything and I am quite satisfied,"
Charles assured her with an air of finality.

"But," she persisted, "you must inform your mother, and

[1] She did not learn the whole truth until after the opening of the second
inquest.

FLORENCE BRAVO
From a photograph taken on her honeymoon at Brighton

THE PRIORY,
BALHAM
'A perfect example
in miniature of
early 19th-century
Gothic'

JANE CANNON
COX
At the age of 30.
'Her strain of
Asiatic blood was
clearly apparent'

your stepfather, too—but especially your mother—so that there may be no recriminations or unpleasantness afterwards."

"My mother's temper," protested Charles, "is as changeable as the wind. To tell her would only create a scene and do no good to anyone. She is set against my marrying in any case and wants me to remain at home."

The speciousness of this argument did not impress Mrs. Campbell.

"It is your duty to my daughter and to your mother to tell her," she insisted.

"Sooner than do that," declared Charles, "I would leave the country and you would never see me again."

Accustomed as she was to her husband's irascibility, and knowing though she did the lengths to which men would go to avoid domestic scenes, she was nevertheless startled by Charles' vehemence. His pale face had grown livid and his words had been uttered in tones of "excessive temper". Seeking a compromise, she therefore suggested that Mrs. Cox, as an old friend of the family, might undertake the duty for him.

"No," he replied sharply, adding the argument which sounds reasonable enough to modern ears but was a novel interpretation of filial duty in 1875: "Florence has behaved nobly in telling me all. We are old enough to judge for ourselves. The name of Dr. Gully will never be mentioned by me again."

Mrs. Tom Campbell now intervened, pointing out the trouble that might arise should his mother learn of the attachment from some outside source, but Charles refused to consider the eventuality. Making a final effort Mrs. Campbell said earnestly:

"You will marry my daughter knowing everything, but I think your mother should know too. You will be happier if you tell your mother the whole truth."

Once more "his face grew livid" and Mrs. Campbell brought the interview to an end. But so disturbed was she that when she got back to Lowndes Square she wrote confidentially to Mrs. Cox, asking her "since she had known Charles so long to use her influence with him to induce him to change his mind". But discretion was ever the better part of Mrs. Cox's valour.

4

Throughout the fifty-four hours when he lay dying Charles
Bravo held at bay the urgent questions of six anxious and
bewildered medical men and the anguished entreaties of his
distracted wife and relatives by the sheer power of his will and
the advantage which his state gave him over them. Some in-
sight into this formidable achievement is afforded by the
methods he used to demolish the obstacles in the way of the
speedy marriage which he regarded as essential lest gossip
reach Palace Green and blow the whole splendid structure of
his plans sky-high.

It was the prerogative of the bride and her mother to name
the date of the wedding, and one shortly after Easter—which
fell on 16th April—was chosen. They were surprised when
Charles protested vigorously against so long a delay, and
positively aghast when he urged a date before Christmas. A
wedding after a betrothal of only six weeks! What would
people think?

Charles exercised the full range of his persuasiveness
and charm: under it Florence forgot the delay Dr. Gully had
urged "before she fixed her fate", and even Mrs. Campbell
wavered.

And what about the time needed to draw up the Settlements? the Campbells asked. With a laugh Charles dismissed
the whole tradition of legal procrastination and explained
just how expeditiously the thing could actually be done.
Almost before they realized it he had gained their consent
to the wedding taking place on 14th December, and arrangements were made for the banns to be published at All Saints'
Church, Ennismore Gardens: invitations were hastily
printed and set out; orders given for the wedding breakfast
at 37 Lowndes Square, and Florence immediately plunged
into a delightful orgy of fittings up and down Bond Street.

While these affairs were engaging the attention of the ladies,
the Settlements were engaging that of the men. Charles
Bravo's financial affairs are of the greatest importance and
must be continually kept in mind. All Mr. Bravo himself

appears to have known of them was that his stepson possessed a security valued at £500—which he held for him—and was earning—so he believed—about £200 a year at the Bar. He now arranged to give him a first life interest in £20,000 with a second life interest to his bride, the capital to pass to the survivor after his own and Mrs. Bravo's deaths, and entered a bond with Florence's trustees to pay the interest on the capital —about £800 a year—to his stepson in the form of an allowance which, with his professional earnings, would insure him an income of about £1,000 a year.

No sooner had this Deed been concluded than beneath the cloak of Charles Bravo's charm appeared a glimpse of the cloven hoof.

On 12th November Mr. Brookes wrote asking Charles to name his attorney so that he could discuss with him Mrs. Ricardo's Settlements. One can imagine the eyebrows of that meticulous family lawyer lifting incredulously at the reply he received: Mr. Charles Bravo was employing no attorney; he would call upon Mr. Brookes himself. "That he should not employ a solicitor to discuss his marriage Settlements," writes Sir John Hall, "seems in itself to imply a certain want of refinement, while a stronger term might be used about his behaviour at his first meeting with Mr. Brookes."

It might indeed!

When Mr. Brookes rose to his feet and offered his congratulations, Charles, ignoring the proffered hand, rapped out with outrageous rudeness:

"Damn your congratulations! I've come about the money."

Mortally offended, as well he might be, Mr. Brookes brought the interview to a speedy close and delegated to his partner the future duty of receiving Charles.

In that age of male supremacy a woman was a chattel and everything she possessed—including the very clothes she wore and even the money she might earn herself[1]—was legally the property of her husband unless secured to her by Deed. Mr.

---

[1] Mrs. Gaskell, for instance, received a small allowance from her husband out of the proceeds of her own books.

Brookes accordingly wrote to Florence and pointed out that, unless included in the Settlement, all the furniture at The Priory, her horses, carriages and personal effects would automatically become her husband's on her wedding day. Florence replied by telegram instructing him to take action accordingly, and returned to the affairs of that absorbing and happy little world of which she was the centre and out of which she was soon to be so rudely jolted. "Mr. Charles Bravo," wrote Mr. Brookes on 25th November, "wished the furniture, horses, carriages and everything about the house settled upon him, and Mr. Campbell thought she would be justified in meeting his wishes."

This letter had been the outcome of a meeting at Mr. Brookes' office between Charles and Mr. Campbell, at which the former had declared emphatically that he could not contemplate a marriage which put him in the position of having to sit upon a chair or at a table which did not belong to him: in such circumstances he would not be master of his own house. Mr. Campbell, understanding this masculine point of view, agreed after some consideration that the matter should be referred to his daughter.

Most of us have a strong sense of ownership, especially with regard to things we have collected and brought home to enjoy: they are the expressions of our own personalities. The pride of possession was strong in Florence, and she was aghast to think that the man who professed to love her should insist on depriving her of them; aghast to think that her very furs and jewellery, even her phaeton and cobs, would be hers no longer, and could be disposed of by her husband at any time and in any way he wished. Charles came to see her that day and she handed him Mr. Brookes' letter. He read it, handed it back, and with all trace of the lover gone told her bluntly:

"I cannot contemplate a marriage which doesn't make me master in my own house. I cannot place myself in the position of having to sit at a table or upon a chair which doesn't belong to me."

Though hurt and repelled she realized that this was the masculine view, but when he added: "Unless things are so settled I cannot marry you," her indignation flamed—and with justification, for though he might be too proud to use furniture which belonged to her, he was not too proud to obtain possession of it by threats and coercion.

"I was angry," she told the Court, "for it seemed to me that he was going to marry me for my money and not for myself."

All her instincts and wounded pride urged her to have done with him then and there; but her anger turned to chill fear: he could afford to issue this ultimatum because her reputation was in his hands, and if she rejected it and him he could apprise all the world of the fact that she had been Dr. Gully's mistress. She trembled at the thought of the scandal which would ensue, and its effects not only on herself, but on Dr. Gully, too. She must see him and consult him without delay.

Down the drive to the lodge at its gates she hastened—she had had that drive made and that lodge built, and it was to those gates that Dr. Gully had formerly held a key. Mrs. Griffith, the coachman's wife, who had been her maid, opened the door to her knock, and she despatched her with a verbal message to Dr. Gully asking him to come and see her at once; then fell to pacing agitatedly beneath the arching trees whose fallen leaves were forming a carpet beneath her feet. She continued her pacing until he had entered the lodge, when she joined him in the little parlour while Mrs. Griffith busied herself in the kitchen.

Wide-eyed with distress and tense with emotion, Florence poured out the story to him. Details of that interview did not transpire: all we know is that it lasted only some ten minutes; that Dr. Gully "advised her not to squabble about the furniture with Mr. Bravo" and reminded her that "her fortune was secure".

Then, as he raised her hand to his lips in farewell a sardonic note must have crept into his voice as he uttered the words:

"It is a small price to pay for happiness. I hope it turns out well."

From the door of the lodge, where he paused for a kindly word with Mrs. Griffith, he watched her go, walking slowly as

though with a heavy heart, her hair matching the burnished
leaves that were spinning down about her—a lonely figure.
He never saw her again.

"So in fact," said Counsel for the Crown sarcastically eight
months later, "so in fact it was Dr. Gully who made the match
at last!"

CHAPTER EIGHT

"MARRIAGE HAS TEETH"[1]

I

CHARLES BRAVO, having so far won each round of the game, now went farther: enfolding himself in the mantle of his fascination, professing such ardent love to his fiancée, making himself so charming and agreeable both to her parents and his own, he gained the consent of all parties to advancing the wedding date by another week.

Meanwhile, nothing could have been more dissimilar from the pattern of life led by the Campbells than that led at Palace Green. At Buscot and Lowndes Square it was kaleidoscopic in its brightness and variety, and made gay and warm-hearted by a large and affectionate family. Money was taken for granted, and though its importance was appreciated, it was valued as a means, not as an end.

At Palace Green, the rooms which had once heard the light steps and laughter of Thackeray's daughters and witnessed his own great-hearted hospitality were now drab and lifeless. Both by birth and temperament Joseph Bravo was alien to such surroundings: his interests were purely commercial, his social circle narrow, his outlook Philistine: with him money was an end in itself and to spend it on objects that gave pleasure, simply because they gave pleasure, was extravagance.

From her perfectly shod feet to her perfectly dressed hair Florence was the personification of everything of which the Bravos disapproved and at the same time envied. Her warmth of heart and generosity were an affront to their bleak parsimony, and when she spent the week before her wedding as their guest she found the experience dispiriting. Not all her efforts could thaw their chilly aloofness or discover a point of contact.

Mrs. Cox's presence was a boon to all: with artless persistence

[1] West Indian proverb.

she threw genteel little conversational bridges over the chasms of silence that began to yawn the moment Charles' voice or laughter ceased to sound. She had her reward: Joseph Bravo made her a further loan of £15 towards buying votes to get her youngest boy into St. Anne's Asylum School with his brothers, while both Charles and Florence assured her that their marriage "would make no difference to her situation at The Priory".

"I do not want you to leave us," Charles said.

"We have made up our minds for you to stay," Florence confirmed.

The matter was clinched by Mrs. Bravo:

"I do not want you to leave. Charlie is not strong, and it will be nice for Florence to have a lady friend. You will be useful to her."

After that pronouncement there could be no doubt.

As far as one can discover, Charles Bravo had been as successful in quieting the Campbells' anxiety that his mother should be told of Florence's former attachment as he had been in advancing the wedding date. Except for a solitary reference to the matter in conversation with Mrs. Cox, the subject seems to have been dropped.

"A woman who has gone wrong," he told her, "is more likely to go straight in future than one who has never strayed. We have exchanged a solemn promise never to allude to these things again."

"You have been wise to be so frank with each other," she murmured obsequiously.

The extremes to which Mrs. Bravo was prepared to carry that temperamental "uncertainty" of which Charles had warned Mrs. Campbell were now to be demonstrated: at the last moment she suddenly refused to accompany her husband to the wedding of her son.

2

It speaks much for Florence's will to be friendly with her husband's mother that she forgave this gratuitous insult and kept a promise made previously to stay again at Palace Green between returning from the honeymoon and going to Buscot for Christmas. And one evening when Mrs. Cox and herself were sitting together over the fire in Florence's bedroom Charles burst in upon them. His voice was shrill and his face livid as he thrust a sheet of notepaper under his wife's eyes and cried:

"If you had not told me before our marriage of your acquaintance with Dr. Gully I should have been on the sea tonight."

Startled, Florence took the letter: written anonymously, it accused Charles of marrying Dr. Gully's mistress for her money.

"It's a vile letter! Burn it, Charlie. Don't let it upset you."

Ignoring this, and regardless of the insult implicit in his action, he plucked it from her fingers, and passed it to Mrs. Cox, demanding:

"Is that Dr. Gully's handwriting?"

While Florence hotly repudiated the implication, Mrs. Cox quietly replied:

"I do not think this is Dr. Gully's handwriting."

In Court Florence stated: "It was only then that I learned that my husband had spoken previously to Mrs. Cox on the subject of my intimacy with Dr. Gully."

Counsel for the Crown: "Were you not very surprised to find that, after taking a solemn vow from you not to speak to a living soul of your intimacy with Dr. Gully, he had talked of it with Mrs. Cox?"

Florence: "No; I never extracted a promise from him not to speak of it. I looked upon him as a gentleman. I suppose he thought she knew of it and there would be no harm in speaking of it."

3

Life at Buscot revealed a new world to Charles, and if he needed further proof of the power of money, and the prestige it could bestow, he found it there. At Lowndes Square the Campbells were of no greater consequence than any of their neighbours, but at this great house Charles Bravo's father-in-law was a magnate whose word was law over several thousand

acres, and whose family was greeted wherever they went by a
pulling of forelocks and bobbing of curtseys. It was a life made
up of public engagements and private amusements, in the
performance of which everyone seemed happy, confident and
assured, while over all presided the sane and kindly presence of
Mrs. Campbell, who awoke in Charles what was perhaps the
most genuine and disinterested sentiment of his whole life.

He entered strenuously into all that was going on: he
laughed and joked and talked, and was demonstrably affectionate to his wife, but underneath lay a carking care that had
haunted him ever since the arrival of the anonymous letter: he
dreaded lest at any moment its author might send another,
this time to Palace Green. In private he plagued Florence with
the subject: he was even driven to discuss it with his mother-
in-law.

"It was a vile letter," he told her.

"All anonymous letters are vile, you must disregard it,"
she said.

"Dr. Gully wrote it."

"Burn it," Mrs. Campbell advised, sensibly declining to
discuss its problematical authorship.

Another time he told her that he thought Florence was too
fond of wine. "I have a horror of ladies drinking too much
wine," he said, and seemed particularly to object to her drinking a glass of sherry while she dressed for dinner.

"That was her habit," Mrs. Campbell told him.

"I'll cure her of it," he said.

"You may do so by kindness and firmness."

Florence also had troubles to discuss with her mother:
Charles' temper, she said, was very uncertain, and he sometimes behaved like a spoilt child. That was a fact already
apparent to Mrs. Campbell: she advised patience and tact,
but grew concerned when Florence went on to say that in spite
of his solemn vow never to mention that name he had several
times "upbraided her about Dr. Gully". Mrs. Campbell had,
in fact, already heard from her sons that he had spoken to
them "in disparaging terms of Dr. Gully". There was yet
another trouble: "Charlie was shewing a very grudging dis-

position towards expenditure," said Florence, and cited an instance when he had objected to her ordering a load of peat for her roses. "He said he would give up gardening if it involved that sort of expense." His mother, moreover, "shewed a disposition to interfere with their household arrangements".

But Mrs. Campbell, observing that her daughter and son-in-law appeared none the less to be on very affectionate terms, expected that these little differences would gradually adjust themselves, It was the duty of a wife, she told Florence, to practise submission towards her husband and patience towards his family—especially his mother. The happiness of married life depended on it.

Charles and Florence left Buscot on 5th January, 1876.

CHAPTER NINE

"MAN IS AN EMBODIED PARADOX, A BUNDLE OF CONTRADICTIONS"[1]

HITHERTO Charles Bravo had possessed neither stick nor stone of his own and had lived all his life in the house and upon the bounty of his stepfather. Now for no more than the price of a ring and a licence he had not only made himself heir to £20,000 from Joseph Bravo and master of a "liberally run establishment",[2] but had gained a wife with an income of £4,000 a year and £40,000 in her own right. He had also obtained release from the fixed routine and rigid supervision to which he had been compelled to submit at Palace Green, for at The Priory—with Rowe to help him on and off with his overcoat, hand him his hat and gloves when he left and relieve him of them when he returned—he came and went as he pleased.

The speed with which he was putting on flesh perturbed him, and he made a practice of always walking to and from Balham station, and from Victoria to Westminster, where the Courts still sat as they had done from time immemorial. For the same reason, though an indifferent horseman, he energetically rode the cobs when at home, and perambulated every corner of what he proudly referred to as "my estate".

When work at his Chambers or in the Courts did not detain him, he would spend an hour or two at the Junior Carlton Club, or visit either his cousin, Hutchinson Royes Bell, F.R.C.S., in Harley Street, or his uncle by marriage, Henry Smith, F.R.C.S., at 82 Wimpole Street, often accompanying the one or the other to King's College Hospital to watch them at work in the operating theatre. He was well known to the staff there, for his stepfather was a Governor of the hospital. He took a keen interest in medicine and surgery and was regarded by his colleagues as an authority on medical jurisprudence. But

[1] C. C. Cotton.   [2] Rowe, the butler, in evidence.

whenever he was in London, no matter what his engagements or inclinations might be, at some time or other during the day he was expected to pay his respects at Palace Green, and that was a duty he was careful to perform.

To all his friends he was eloquent on the happiness of his married life and on the amenities of "his estate"—the cobs, the carriage horses, the garden, even the very fantails, were all referred to possessively as "his". Upon all his friends he pressed invitations to come and dine or stay with a persistence which at times they found embarrassing. For instance, meeting his colleague, Mr. Carlyle Willoughby, he invited him down for the approaching week-end. Mr. Willoughby regretted, but he had to go to Norwich.

"Well, come the week-end after."

Mr. Willoughby was sorry, but he would be in Paris then.

"Well then, come the week-end after that!" urged Charles.

Mr. Willoughby capitulated.

"His friends," stated Florence, "mostly young barristers like himself, came frequently to dine at The Priory. I always received them and made them welcome as his friends."

Through the eyes of Mr. McCalmont—with whom Charles shared Chambers at 1 Essex Court in the Temple—of Mr. Edward Stanley Hope[1] and Mr. Jepson Atkinson one catches glimpses of Charles as the generous host and happy husband. All were impressed by the affection existing between his wife and himself, and by the "good terms on which he was with Mrs. Cox". They marvelled at the consideration shewn her. "She was treated like one of the family", and "all called each other by their Christian names". No fly was discernible in the amber of their friend's life: he appeared so fit, so energetic, so "full of fun", that all pronounced him a man to be envied.

This charming picture of Charles Bravo in the intimacy of his own home was displayed to the eyes of the world to add poignancy to the shock and mystery of his death. It remained intact and unblemished up to the early stages of the second inquest. Then cracks began to appear and its pigment to undergo a change which dimmed its glossy perfection. It seemed

[1] Later Sir E. S. Hope.

that entertaining tongue had had a bitter edge to it and had been employed to taunt his wife with a name he had vowed never to utter; that his mirth could turn to moroseness almost before its echoes had died away, and that "violent ebullitions of temper" could, on the most trivial pretexts, displace his good humour. It was also revealed that this young barrister, so outwardly presentable, had some uncouth habits and was so lacking in personal fastidiousness that he did not clean his teeth and would use the same bath-water twice; that he would drink straight from a jug instead of using a tumbler; that he apparently thought nothing of smoking his pipe in his wife's bedroom when she was ill; and he would jump up from the dinner-table and drink her wine when he thought she had had enough; and that he would thrust aside a dish he did not like and fling himself out of the room until besought by his wife or Mrs. Cox to come back "because of the servants". Furthermore, he appeared so obsessed with a passion for economy, and so indifferent to his wife's feelings, that he had no scruples about coercing her into giving up those very things from which she derived most pleasure and satisfaction: things which her money had purchased in the first instance and was continuing to maintain.

It is essential to examine this last point. For six years before her marriage Florence had run her house on precisely the same lines as she was doing now. Out of doors she employed three gardeners, a coachman, a groom and a stable-boy: the indoor staff consisted of a butler, footman, lady's-maid, two housemaids, a cook, kitchen-maid, and Mrs. Cox— not an excessive establishment by the standards of 1876. She lived well, dressed well and travelled freely, and the only criterion that can be applied to her mode of life is that of economics, concerning which it was established that she lived well within her income. Her marriage to Charles Bravo in no way altered this fundamental fact, yet he immediately began to press for wholesale retrenchment, putting forward each new proposal as coming from his mother.

"*My mother* thinks a lady's-maid an unnecessary extravagance."

"I have always had one since I was a child," Florence protested.

Then again:

"*My mother* thinks three gardeners excessive. If we grassed over some of the flower-beds we could get rid of one gardener."

"I could not see the reason for this retrenchment," Florence told the Court, adding that she had greatly resented Mrs. Bravo's interference. There had arisen, however, a cogent reason for preserving her own peace of mind and her husband's good humour, for by mid-January she knew herself to be pregnant: so "to please Charlie" she dismissed her maid, and Mary Ann Keeber, the head housemaid, assumed the duties of lady's-maid in addition to her own. She took, however, a firm stand on the subject of the garden. "Gardening was my particular hobby," she explained: nor did Charles' passion for economy in this direction prevent him from laying out a lawn-tennis court to minister to his own pleasure.

Meanwhile his sole contribution to the upkeep of the establishment of which he had made himself master was, by his own request, the payment of the stable bill. As he had quoted his mother over housekeeping costs, so he now began to quote "Father Joseph" in order to reduce the stable expenses. "Father Joseph" thought they should sell the carriage horses and job a pair in their place. Florence objected until Charles told her that, since his marriage, he had not had a penny from his stepfather. For his sake, therefore, she agreed; so Charles sold the carriage horses and pocketed the money, while a jobbed pair took their place in the stables. At the same time, "because she did not want him to be short of money", she promised to pay over to him the interest due from her father on her first marriage settlement as soon as this came in.

Charles also grew voluble over the fact that three firms of solicitors should be drawing fees for managing his wife's affairs[1]: of these the first were Captain Ricardo's solicitors, the trustees of the first marriage settlement; the second had been appointed by the Court of Chancery after her action against

[1] Paragraph 4 of his letter to Mrs. Campbell quoted in Appendix I indicates his feelings on the subject.

her father; and, thirdly, there was Mr. Brookes. Charles argued that all these fees would be saved if her affairs were placed in his own hands, but she declined to make any change; perhaps the possessive attitude he had already shewn towards her property warned her not to allow more of it to pass into his control.

Whether as a result of these stresses and strains or from some other cause Florence had a miscarriage at the end of January, and Charles shewed himself curiously unsympathetic. "I put his conduct down," she said, "not so much to want of kindness as want of knowledge. He was so accustomed to being waited on by his mother that he did not know what it was to wait upon a lady." Augusta Campbell—William's wife—who was recuperating at St. Leonards from a similar mishap, wrote inviting them both to join her there, as the change would be good for Florence. Charles could not accompany her on the day arranged, and since Florence insisted on going by herself he vented his irritation by asking maliciously as he was seeing her off at the station:

"Is Dr. Gully going too?"

Sir Henry Sidney, writing about 1564 to his son, the future Sir Philip, then a boy at school, adjured him to avoid "biting woordes to any man, for a wound given by a woorde is oftentimes harder to be cured than that which is given by the sword". Still suffering that spiritual and physical malaise which afflicts a woman at such a time the wound left by those "biting woordes" indeed proved "harder to be cured than that which is given by the sword", and when in a day or two Charles joined the little party in the gayest of moods, and was affectionate and charming towards her, Florence realized with a contraction of the heart that the charm which had captivated her was wholly superficial: something to be turned on and off like a tap, and gushing at its fullest only in the presence of an audience.

The Joseph Bravos' attitude also caused her distress and bewilderment. She had not permitted her mother-in-law's odious behaviour on her wedding day to influence her, but had done everything to win her liking. Yet, except for paying a formal call after she and Charles had returned from Buscot, they had neither invited her to Palace Green nor accepted her own invitations to The Priory.

All the evidence points to the fact that Charles was deliberately fostering dissension between his parents and his wife. While on the one hand he complained bitterly to the latter that Joseph Bravo had only paid him £100 of the promised allowance, to the former he was protesting that his wife was hopelessly extravagant and inundated with bills.

As soon as she realized that her household management was the object of the Bravos' criticism, she declared that she would see Mrs. Bravo and explain that she lived strictly within her income. But each time she did so Charles would first warn her of the scene which might ensue, and then, if she persisted, create one himself, ending invariably with the threat that he would leave the house and never return.

For the sake of peace she would give in: for the sake of peace she endured her mother-in-law's increasing animosity until mid-February, when, as she told the Court, "she insulted me through my father". The nature of this insult we do not know, but stung past endurance, Florence declared that she would go to Palace Green and "have it out" with Mrs. Bravo, whereupon Charles, finding all his expostulations and threats of no avail, sped thither himself as though to guard it against assault, leaving "Janie"—who had quickly slipped into the rôle of mediator—to exert her soothing influence on Florence and dissuade her from her intention.

In this she was largely successful: at least Florence did not go to Palace Green; instead, she took her indignation and wounded feelings to Buscot, where William and Augusta were in charge during Mr. and Mrs. Campbell's absence in Rome.

CHAPTER TEN

PARTINGS AND PERSUASIONS

CHARLES' complacency was badly shaken: his usually pliant wife had not only threatened to go to Palace Green and "have it out" with his mother, but had shewn herself quite capable of carrying out that threat. He knew by experience, however, that by appealing to her affections he could soon win her back, and this he now proceeded to do in daily letters, the flamboyant style of which comes strangely from the pen of a man whose wife, scarcely a month before, had added the following postscript to a letter he had written her mother: "Charlie writes tersely as all barristers do: you must imagine twice the amount of affection, as I had to do when he wrote me love-letters, which, by the way, nobody would have recognized as such, as they were as cold and undemonstrative as possible."[1]

It is upon those letters, examples of which follow, that Sir John Hall bases his suggestion that though Charles Bravo was "actuated at first by material considerations" he "rapidly grew very fond" of his wife. Sensing the story within the story, yet unable to grasp its nature, he poses the question: "Was there a secret in the lives of these people which the investigations failed to discover?"

On the day after Florence reached Buscot—15th February—Charles wrote from Palace Green:

"My darling wife,

"Looking back on the weeks of our marriage I feel that many of my words, although kindly meant, were unnecessarily harsh. In future my rebukes, if it is necessary to say anything, which God forbid! shall be given with the utmost gentleness. . . .

"I hold you to be the best of wives. We have had bitter troubles, but I trust that in times to come the sweet peace

[1] See Appendix II.

of our lives will not be disturbed by memories like these.
. . . I wish I could sleep away my life until you return.
. . . Come back as well as you can to your devoted husband,
"Charles."

In another letter he says: "I miss you, my darling wife,
dreadfully. When you come back I will so take care of you that
you will never leave me again."

These letters softened Florence's heart: others in the same
strain melted it and took her back to The Priory, though still
resolved that the situation between themselves and the Joseph
Bravos must be cleared up if she and Charles were to hope for
any married peace. And so from Brighton—where he had gone
on behalf of a client—Charles wrote the day after her return:

". . . I have been thinking all this morning of the sweet old
girl I left behind me. . . . Although I passed the day in the
fresh air I am not happy, neither shall be till I regain you.
You will find me the best of husbands. . . ."

He regained her, but alas! it was only a lull between
storms.

To recoil from having one's private affairs discussed by
others is an instinctive form of self-protection. Eighty years
ago "scandal" was more to be feared than death, and a Victorian precept says: "Servants talk: gentlefolk discuss things."
Servants, indeed, presented an array of eyes, ears and tongues
to see, hear and repeat everything that went on in their
employers' lives. Charles and Florence took the utmost pains
to preserve a façade of wedded bliss before their little world—
with Mrs. Cox as their ally. Resentment, which might have
smouldered all day beneath exchanges of civilities, only
found an outlet when guests were gone and servants out of
earshot in their rooms at the top of the house. As Florence herself observed when giving evidence concerning the conflicts between Charles and herself: "If this inquiry had not
taken place no one would have heard of these things, except
Mrs. Cox."

Soon after her return from Buscot she began to suffer from

depression accompanied at times by nausea. As this state persisted she told Charles that, unless she got better, she would take a house at Worthing "for a change of air". He set his face against the idea, and must have voiced his feelings at Palace Green, for, said Florence, "Mrs. Bravo wrote and objected to my going on the score of expense." That night at dinner, under the eyes of Rowe and the footman, a façade-preserving small-talk was maintained, but as soon as the household—including Mrs. Cox—had retired to the top of the house the most violent quarrel of their brief married life took place.

"I was angry," stated Florence, "and upon going up to bed that night he" (Charles) "shewed signs of temper. I said I would write her such a letter that she would not interfere with us again; that she did not find the money and that she had no right to interfere with us or any of our affairs. He was angry with me for saying that. He jumped out of bed saying, 'I will go and cut my throat!' He rushed into his dressing-room and I rushed after him. . . . His temper was like a frenzy. . . ." In that frenzy he struck her.

Turning now to Mrs. Cox's more detailed account of the same incident, Florence went up to her room and told her that "she and Charlie had had some words on the subject and that Mr. Bravo had struck her". The blow had hurt her, she said, and added that Charles was now dressing and repeating his familiar threat that "he would go away and they would never see him again".

In Mrs. Cox the dread of scandal was almost pathological. Hurriedly she threw on some clothes. "I went downstairs and saw Mr. Bravo with his hat and coat on. He told me he was going away, took the bolt off the door and went down the drive. I followed him and begged him to come back again. I told him what a scandal there would be. 'What would the world say?' I asked him.

" 'Some will say it is her fault, and some will say it is mine,' he replied.

" 'What will your mother say?' I asked.

" 'My mother! She will be only too glad to have me back at any price!' "

Redoubling her persuasions, she "took him by the arm" and coaxed him indoors, promptly rebolting the door "so that the servants should notice nothing unusual" and no crack be detected in the façade. Then she fetched Florence downstairs. "He told Mrs. Bravo how sorry he was for having struck her. . . . She said she would forgive him and they were reconciled. His temper, though violent, was soon over. . . . I cannot recall that Dr. Gully's name was mentioned."

But the peace she had patched up did not survive the night, and the quarrel ended on that 7th March as it had on 14th February. Florence sought sanctuary at Buscot and Charles retired to Palace Green, whence once more he plied her daily with eloquent letters, in the first of which—8th March—he seeks to soften her feelings towards his mother.

> "My dear old Florence,
> "My poor mother is glad to have me back with her, and I am sure if you heard the kind way she speaks of you, you would not mind my being with her. . . . Without you I feel as if I was at Brighton in lodgings by myself, I cannot be happy in the absence of my best of wives. My only object is to make you happy. . . ."

Again his letters had the desired effect: she suggested that he joined her at Buscot, but in his reply, after alluding to his love for her as "an exceeding great love", he laments that to his "great regrets" he is engaged in a "dreary cause" which "precludes me from the much-longed-for pleasure of seeing you. . . . How I hate this vile profession which gives me so much toil and no pay."

A still more typical Carolean touch illumines the letter written three days later:

> ". . . I miss you dreadfully, and I would willingly give £100—if times were not so hard—to have you here now. . . ."

He closes with the assurance that "I will always try to please you and justify your choice of me as a husband".

She had never been able to harbour ill-feeling, and now the

discovery that she was again pregnant—which seemed to solve
the puzzle of her attacks of sickness—softened her towards
everyone, even her mother-in-law, while the longing for her
husband, her home, and the comforting ministrations of Mrs.
Cox echo in this hasty note:

> "Buscot Park,
> "Lechlade,
> "Glos.,
> "March 12th.

"My dearest Janie,
  "I sent you a telegram this morning saying I was
returning to-morrow (Monday). As Charlie cannot come
down I had resolved to come home, being miserable without
him and you, as I am weak and ill. . . .
  "With best love,
> "Affectionately yours,
> "Florence Bravo."

Charles, engaged upon a case, and having promised to see
his mother and "Father Joseph" off to St. Leonards for a
couple of months, delayed his return until 16th March. A letter
of his written on the 15th illustrates the Bravos' determination
to force "retrenchment" upon Florence, and is an example of
his own methods: sandwiched between endearments come
suggestions which he cannot fail to know will cause her distress:

". . . As you make sunshine wherever you go, your presence
here is much needed, for we have rain, snow and sleet. . . .
Father Joseph has promised to give us the barouche on
condition we put down the cobs. By giving up the cobs and
Mrs. Cox we can save £400 a year and be as comfortable.
But I only want your love, and without your love, riches
and honours will be as nothing. . . ."

CHAPTER ELEVEN

"EVIDENCE OF INTEREST": MRS. COX, MRS. CHARLES BRAVO AND DR. GULLY

I

CRIMINAL poisoning is not a matter of sudden impulse: the poisoner sets about the construction of his crime well in advance, and with the utmost craft and cunning in order to avoid suspicion and detection. From 16th March a gradual and subtle alteration is perceptible in the atmosphere at The Priory, and we cannot do better than pause and consider the course of events as they relate to the three persons who were to be suspected of causing the death of Charles Bravo; and this can be done most tellingly in the light of "those three important points" which, at the trial of F. H. Seddon and his wife in 1912 for the murder by poison of their lodger, Miss Barrow, the Attorney-General, Sir Rufus Isaacs,[1] stressed in his opening speech to the jury. These are: (i) *the interest* of the suspects in the immediate death of the victim; (ii) *the opportunity* of administering the poison; and (iii) *the conduct* of the suspects "both immediately before and immediately after, and for some little time after the death".[2] But in this particular case it is also essential to consider the *conduct* of the victim himself.

Both Mrs. Cox and Florence Bravo had equal *opportunity*. Mrs. Cox's *interest in the immediate death of the victim* was based on the supposition that he intended to dismiss her from his household, and what substance there was in this theory we will now examine.

It will be recalled that in April 1875 she received a letter from her husband's aunt in Jamaica requesting her to return to that island.[3] During the ensuing year a correspondence arguing ways and means shuttled across the Atlantic until on 8th

[1] Later first Marquess of Reading (1860–1935); Lord Chief Justice, 1913–1921; Viceroy of India, 1921–1926.
[2] It was Seddon's conduct during the last days of his victim's life and immediately after her death that led to his conviction.   [3] See page 48.

March, 1876, Mrs. Cox got a letter written by a friend on be-half of her aunt which met the objections she had advanced against giving up her post and taking her boys away from school with this suggestion: "Could you not leave the boys and come for a few months? Mrs. Cox thinks it would be to your advantage to be here as you understand business so well. *Decide quickly*."

Mrs. Cox had so far mentioned to no one the possibility of her having to go to Jamaica; now, however, under the neces-sity to "*decide quickly*", another problem faced her: Mrs. Mar-garet Cox had agreed to forward the money for the outward passage, but had said nothing about the return fare at the end of the visit, and Mrs. Cox determined that she would not leave the shores of England until that had been deposited as well. She would have to write a tactful letter and she wished she could have advice on how to compose it, but on that date—8th March—Florence had sought sanctuary at Buscot after her first major quarrel with Charles, and he himself was at Palace Green. Fortunately for herself she made up her mind to con-sult Mrs. Harford and Mrs. Fowke, with whose aid she wrote the necessary letter and posted it forthwith, resolving not to mention the matter at The Priory until an answer came. About a week later she called upon Joseph Bravo at his office in the City—perhaps to pay off an instalment of the loan he had made her in December—and in the course of conversation she casu-ally mentioned that her aunt had been ailing. The effect of this chance observation on Mr. Bravo was astonishing, for he immediately began to urge upon her the advisability of return-ing to Jamaica without delay. Mrs. Cox surprised was Mrs. Cox suspicious, and she immediately assumed an air of passive resistance.

"I expressed," said Joseph Bravo in evidence, "a very strong opinion as to the propriety of her going at once to the island. She urged that it would be inconvenient—that she did not know what to do with her boys. I told her that it was for her boys' future welfare that she should go; that it was her duty to her boys as well as to her aunt that she should go. . . . But all in vain."

She must have known him too well to imagine that his insistence sprang out of altruism, and as she made her way back to Balham her active brain must have been much occupied as to the reason for this sharp change from the patronizing pleasure displayed the previous December at the thought that she was to remain at The Priory. Let it be remembered that at the date of this interview Charles was still at Palace Green and that shortly after it he wrote to Florence: "Father Joseph has promised to give us the barouche on condition that we put down the cobs. By giving up the cobs *and Mrs. Cox*[1] we can save £400 a year and be as comfortable."

But evidence that Charles was not seriously considering "giving up" Mrs. Cox comes from two disinterested witnesses —Mr. McCalmont and Mr. Edward Stanley Hope. The former stated that after dinner at The Priory towards the end of February he asked Charles point-blank why he retained Mrs. Cox. He replied: "She is very useful in doing household work and I owe her something because she used to urge my suit," adding that "*he had no intention of dismissing her*". They seemed, continued the witness, "on the very best of terms".

Mr. Hope testified that when he had dined at The Priory on 22nd March—that is to say, exactly a week *after* Charles had written the letter just quoted—he had noticed "the consideration with which Mrs. Cox was treated", and that Charles told him on this same occasion that "he found her very useful, and she was sent in the carriage to do shopping. . . . His references to her were always complimentary."

On the other hand, evidence that Mrs. Cox *was* intending to go to Jamaica, and quietly making preparations to do so, comes from Mrs. Harford, who vouched for the fact that she had assisted her to compose the letter asking her aunt to deposit the money for her return as well as her outward passage; and also from Dr. Gully. The latter deposed to having seen her at Balham station one day in March when she had told him of her aunt's request that she should go to Jamaica "which she expected to be doing shortly", and had asked him for the homoeopathic "treatment" for Jamaica fever.

[1]Author's italics.

To complete the argument we must take a brief glance ahead. On 11th April—seven days before the fatal Tuesday—Mrs. Cox received an urgent letter from her aunt, which must have crossed the one she had written with Mrs. Harford's assistance, telling her to "hurry up and come" and saying that Joseph Bravo would be asked to advance her outward fare, and the money for her return would be deposited with his partner, Mr. Solomon. This communication sent Mrs. Cox straightway upstairs to read it aloud to Florence, who then said: "Charlie must hear it." He, having done so, said:

"It seems you will have to go. I will take care of the boys while you are away and I shall be happy to see you on your return."

Then, and then only, *when her departure had been accepted as inevitable*, is there reliable evidence that Charles gave the matter serious thought.

"I saw him," Mr. Hope deposed, "on April 11th"—that selfsame day—"in the Exchequer Court. He had a pen in his hand as if calculating something, and he said: 'After all, Mrs. Cox must be costing us £300 a year.' I said in reference to that, laughing: 'You might keep another pair of horses for that.' "

Particularly in connection with her children's welfare during her absence abroad, Charles Bravo *alive*—and with Florence at his elbow—could be of immense value to Mrs. Cox. But Charles Bravo *dead*—even from natural causes—would delay her departure and involve her in complications, and perhaps even loss should Mrs. Margaret Cox die before she reached Jamaica. In fact, it is exceedingly difficult to discover any grounds whatever for *interest in the immediate death of the victim* on the part of Mrs. Cox.

2

"What," writes Professor John Glaister,[1] "are the most common reasons for one person to poison another? Looking to such cases, one finds that there is a range of divergent reasons,

[1] *The Power of Poison*—John Glaister.

but that out of sixteen of these . . . no fewer than eight of them had a sex background and seven were prompted by gain."[1]

Florence Bravo's *interest* in the immediate death of her husband can be ruled out on both these scores: the money all belonged to her and Charles had given her no cause for jealousy. The sex motive, therefore, could only exist if it arose out of her desire to marry another man. But as there had never been any other man in her life than Dr. Gully, *and his wife was still alive*, that too can be ruled out; while, as Sir John Hall says, "it is incredible that Mrs. Bravo can have killed her husband in order to return to 'the ancient lover' whom she had discarded only a few weeks before."

In Dr. Gully's case evidence of *interest* is equally lacking. Although he may have felt a natural jealousy towards the man who had supplanted him, there is nothing to suggest that it ever attained homicidal proportions. Although he could, as a medical man, have been in possession of the poison, or have readily obtained it, without the complicity of Florence or Mrs. Cox he could not have administered it, and if neither of these had a motive to aid and abet him, his *opportunity* was non-existent.

[1] In the majority of them the poisoner was a person of good education and social position.

CHAPTER TWELVE

CRIMINAL CONDUCT

IF Dr. Gully had made towards the woman who had "given up for him her home and her family" the generous gesture of giving up Orwell Lodge—as she averred she asked him to do —or even if he had adhered to his own resolution to have nothing more to do with her or Mrs. Cox, suspicion for complicity in Charles Bravo's death would never have fallen upon him.

Soon after Florence had "dismissed" him he had gone away on a round of visits, and except for a couple of fleeting returns to replenish his wardrobe, during the first of which he had yielded to Florence's request to meet her at the lower lodge, he had remained away until the middle of March. But from then until Charles Bravo's death he was continuously in residence, and during that time a series of far more damaging encounters took place between him and Mrs. Cox.

One afternoon in March, as he was strolling to Victoria station to take his train home, he heard a diffident greeting, but instead of merely raising his hat and walking on when he saw that it was Mrs. Cox he made the mistake of falling into step beside her and travelling down to Balham in the same compartment. Doubtless his better judgment was vanquished by the temptation to speak to the woman who not only linked him with the island of his birth, but through five years of close association with that other woman whom he loved. A few days later, as Dr. Gully was buying his ticket at Balham station, she again appeared, and, the ice being now broken, they travelled up to town together. She chatted freely with this man whom she admired and trusted more than any other: she told him she was busy preparing her house in Lancaster Road for a new tenant; she told him of her aunt's illness, and in expectation of sailing "shortly" for Jamaica begged him to send her a "treatment"[1] for Jamaica fever. This he promised to do forthwith. Then in her artless way she mentioned that Charles had had an anonymous letter—the previous December—which had annoyed him very much and of which he believed him—Dr. Gully—to be the author: a suggestion Dr. Gully "positively" repudiated.

In this connection Mrs. Cox was to describe a curious incident which occurred soon afterwards: Charles, she declared, called her attention to a notice in *The Times* inserted by a firm of solicitors offering a reward of £100 for information which would lead to the conviction of the writer of certain anonymous letters "which for some time past have been sent to a lady in Palace Gardens, Kensington, reflecting on the character of her near relations".

As she handed him back the copy of *The Times* he declared "furiously" that Dr. Gully had been sending his mother anonymous letters—"a wicked thing for the old wretch to do"—and insisted that the notice had been inserted on Mr. Bravo's instructions and "Palace Gardens" substituted for "Palace Green" because "since there was only one other house besides Mr. Bravo's in Palace Green people would know whose house was referred to. He said it was very decent of 'the Governor' not to mention it to him."

Mrs. Cox claimed that she refuted this ingenious argument and told him that, having met Dr. Gully, she had asked him point-blank if he had sent the anonymous letter Charles had received.

"He denied having done so—positively."

"Do you believe that?" asked Charles contemptuously.

"Yes; he would not have been so positive otherwise."

Charles' response is illuminating.

"You should not let Florence believe that, because she will think him an injured man."

Mrs. Cox apparently did not notice the date of the paper which contained the advertisement. It had appeared twice, *on*

---

[1] The word "treatment" seems to have been used indiscriminately in homoeopathic circles to denote both a prescription and the instructions for applying it.

11th and 17th of January; but the incident just related did not occur until the middle of March, so Charles' exhibition of fury was either unduly delayed or else faked.[1]

One of his habits was to take the letters from the postman himself, open and read those addressed to his wife, and scrutinize those for other members of the household. On 25th March Mrs. Cox had left to go to London before the post arrived when she was overtaken on her way to the station by Charles with two letters addressed to her.

"One of them, he said, was from Dr. Gully, and he insisted I should open it before him. I was annoyed as he had no right to do such a thing, but I complied."

Of the three sheets of notepaper she drew out one contained the following "list of drugs to be obtained" for the treatment of Jamaica fever, and the other two directions for their use.

> "Aconite (tincture), tartar emetic, arsenicum alb., nux vomica, ipecacuanha, 3d decimal potency, cheva. No other tinctures. Belladonna tincture 3d decimal. Half an ounce bottle of each."

All these Charles "took and looked through carefully". The fact that this list contains tartar emetic—a salt of antimony—might appear highly suspicious, but the quantities involved, as in all homoeopathic "treatments", are infinitesimal, and since the Crown accepted without demur Mrs. Cox's statement that she had never procured any of the drugs, it must presumably have satisfied itself that the prescription was harmless.

Fortunately for herself she was "so indignant" at Charles' behaviour—and who can blame her?—that on going to tea with Mrs. Harford and Mrs. Fowke that same day she told them "of the episode"—as Mrs. Harford related in Court. That evening, writing to thank Dr. Gully for the "treatment" and to ask him for another for yellow fever, she recounted the incident and begged him to leave the new prescription at her house to avoid a repetition of it. He complied with this request.

Two further encounters were to take place between Dr.

---

[1] As was afterwards established, the advertisement did not refer to the Bravos.

Gully and herself which will be related in due course, but meanwhile we must take a glance at what was going on within The Priory itself.

Until Charles' return from London on 16th March life within it, to all outward appearance, had been uneventful and humdrum. He had gone regularly to his Chambers and, apart from bringing one of his friends home to dinner occasionally, and having his sister Alice, or his cousin Ann Bell, or one of the Campbells to stay for a few days, there had been little entertaining. But after that date there was a marked change. He seldom went up to London, but busied himself instead about "his estate" and shewed an increasing disposition to fill the house with guests. "There has been a great slaughter of cocks and hens and pigeons for the feast," he tells his mother in one of his letters; and in another: "We are expecting half-a-dozen people and, with children, shall have 31 guests in the house." Florence, in her letters, describes him as "looking the picture of health", and "walking about with a book under his arm as happy as a king".

After the tragedy there were plenty of witnesses to vouch for these outward manifestations, but only Florence and Mrs. Cox could vouch for the change which had taken place behind the façade. Both women testified that, before 16th March, Charles had relentlessly harassed his wife on the subject of retrenchment; had given vent to sundry "ebullitions of temper", while his habit of "continually upbraiding" her about her past and his complaints about "the proximity of Dr. Gully" had grown so insistent that in desperation she had written to her landlord for permission to terminate her lease. Charles, however, had refused to move elsewhere. But all this discord suddenly ceased as soon as he had seen his people off to St. Leonards, and Florence attributed the harmony which ensued to the removal of their influence. "With the exception of the first three years of my first married life," she stated in Court, "this time of my marriage with Mr. Bravo formed the happiest part of my life."

But though Charles ceased to press retrenchment on his wife, there is ample evidence that the subject of money continued to occupy the forefront of his mind. Rowe stated that he frequently spoke to him of stocks and shares, Mr. Meredith Brown testified that he was throughout indulging in Stock Exchange speculations, while his letters to his step-father are mainly concerned with financial matters.

The first hint of a still stranger change in life at The Priory emerges from a brief remark of Charles' in a letter dated 26th March: "Florence is not strong." Accustomed for the past six years to summon Dr. Harrison, of Streatham, for the most trivial complaint—he had attended her in January—it is surprising to find that, though continuing to feel "weak and ill" as when she wrote to Mrs. Cox from Buscot, he was not called in. In that same letter of 26th March Charles says of himself that, though otherwise "unusually well" he was troubled by "twinges of rheumatism", and in his next one, of 31st March, he says: "Royes came down to dinner. He prescribed for my rheumatism and ordered me to stay at home which I was glad enough to do. My walks have been confined to my own estate which begins to look finely under the influence of the sun."[1] In neither of these letters is there any further reference to Florence's health and he does not appear to have taken the opportunity to consult his cousin about it. Moreover, in view of the fact that he had seldom gone up to London since 16th March, his statement that Royes Bell now "ordered him to stay at home" is, at least, curious, especially when taken in conjunction with a passage in another letter of 3rd April in which he says "I am well again now. . . . Tomorrow I return to work", for apart from attending the Brighton Sessions on 5th and 6th April he does not appear to have left Balham before 11th—the day on which Mr. Carlyle Willoughby met him in the Exchequer Court.

On the evening of 6th April Florence again miscarried. Charles moved into another room, and one would have expected that now at least Dr. Harrison would have been sent for; but though she had severe pain and vomiting all the following day and night, she remained without any other

[1] Royes Bell prescribed a liniment, regular doses of Epsom salts, and the wearing of flannel over the affected parts.

attention than that of Mrs. Cox. That this caused Mrs. Cox the
greatest concern cannot be doubted, but perhaps her fear of
offending Charles restrained her from urging—at any rate too
strongly—the obvious course. So when on the 8th, despatched
to London on some errand, she chanced to meet Dr. Gully on
Balham platform, it is plain that she hailed the encounter with
relief, even though she seems to have been rather less than
clear as to the cause of Florence's condition. According to Dr.
Gully's account she told him that "Mrs. Bravo was suffering
from pains in the back and sleeplessness" and asked his advice.
"I suggested sitz baths and compresses," he said, and added:
"She did not tell me that Mrs. Bravo was suffering from a miscarriage until later."

On her return that evening Mrs. Cox found that Charles,
still ignoring the proximity of his wife's customary physician,
had sent all the way to London for Royes Bell—a surgeon.
What Bell prescribed does not emerge, but we know that
when Mrs. Cox told Florence of her chance encounter with
Dr. Gully[1] and the advice he had given, she eagerly adopted
it and passed a better night.

On Sunday, the 9th, Royes Bell again saw Florence and
noticed the improvement in her condition. None the less he
recommended that Dr. Harrison should see her, and that as
soon as she was well enough she should go to the seaside to
recuperate. Charles concurred in the latter suggestion, but
the former he ignored.

Meanwhile Dr. Gully, "knowing that Mrs. Bravo was driven
frantic by opiates", had "bethought" him of laurel-water, and,
as his "allopathic knowledge was rusty", had, on his return to
Balham that same evening, called at the local chemist's and
asked to see the Pharmacopoeia; whereupon he bought a two-
ounce bottle of laurel-water which the chemist labelled with
the prescribed dosage and on which he stuck a *Poison* label to
comply with the regulations. Next day—Sunday, 9th April—
on his way to visit his son in Bayswater, Dr. Gully left the
bottle at Mrs. Cox's house in Lancaster Road, where she had
told him she would be calling on Monday.

[1] "It was," said Florence, "the first I had known of these meetings."

H.B.D.—4

These events were to take on a sinister complexion when every action of Florence, Mrs. Cox and Dr. Gully became charged with suspicion. Then Mr. George Lewis, for Joseph Bravo, strove hard, though unsuccessfully, to prove that the encounter between Mrs. Cox and Dr. Gully had taken place before 6th April; that he had suggested the compresses and sitz baths to procure an abortion for Florence, and that the bottle of laurel-water had contained the poison which killed Charles Bravo.[1]

During Mrs. Cox's absence that day Charles wrote two letters; one from his wife's bedside at her dictation—with interpolations of his own—to Mrs. Campbell just returned from Italy with her husband; and the other to his mother at St. Leonards.

"The Priory, Balham,
"10th April, 1876.

"My dearest Mamma,

". . . Will you tell Augusta, with my love, that it was like her own dear self to write me such a kind letter, and that as we are intending to take a small furnished house at Worthing, and to take the servants and carriages, it would be a wise plan if she came to us, as she is going to the seaside? (*Mrs Cox will cater, so we will have nothing to do but kick up our heels and get well.*)[2] It will give me real pleasure to have her with us. We think of starting to-morrow week.

"I am sorry Papa has been so ill. I hope he will soon be better. . . . Charlie is very well, and equally happy. (*He is not. The quality of the tobacco he is smoking has been impugned and his pipe ordered to be extinguished*).[2] He has been so good and kind to me while I have been ill. Mrs. Cox is pretty well and

[1] In this connection it is interesting to recall that in 1781 Captain John Donellan was tried and convicted of the murder of his young brother-in-law, Sir Theodosius Boughton, Bart., of Lawford Hall, Warwickshire. He poisoned him with prussic acid distilled from laurel leaves and administered in medicine which, as Mr. William Roughead neatly puts it, "the lad was taking for a specific ailment precociously contracted at Eton".

[2] Interpolations by Charles, the first of which confirms the view that nothing was further from his thoughts than the dismissal of Mrs. Cox. It was the next morning—11th April—that she got the letter from her aunt agreeing to her terms for returning to Jamaica.

has been all kindness to me. I do not know what I should do without her. I eat more than I did, but I am weak. My back is very painful. . . . It will be some time before I am able to get about as usual. . . . I will not answer for any of Charlie's additions to this—he is a buffoon. . . .

"With our best love and plenty of kisses,
"Your loving child,
Florence Bravo."

The following is the casual manner in which Charles announced his wife's miscarriage to Mrs. Bravo. Nowhere is there an expression of regret for the loss of the child, or a word of sympathy for his wife's disappointment and suffering.

"The Priory, Balham,
"10th April, 1876.

". . . Florence thanks you for your letter and sends her best love, and will answer it as soon as she can sit up. She lost Charles the Second on Thursday, a youth of great promise. Royes declares that he had the Hougham cast of countenance. Royes will tell you his other characteristics when he sees you. He looks ill, but is very kind as he always is. Florence likes him very much. Trade is dull and I came home early to sit with my better half during Mrs. Cox's absence in town to get me some things. . . . I am remarkably well, so well that I shocked Royes with the quantity I ate yesterday. I am quite sorry to think that Florence will have to go to Worthing when she is better. I am going to take a tiny house for her, and she will take her retainers to wait on her, and Augusta, who is ill and obliged to go back to the sea. . . ."

We have now scrutinized the *conduct* of all the parties concerned up to and including 10th April—eight days before "the poison entered the body of the victim". Before examining still further the *conduct* of the victim himself, one finds oneself agreeing with the sentiments expressed by *The World* in a leading article at the close of the case.

"It seems curious that a young husband whose letters to his wife breathe a spirit of generous and disinterested affection should inform a professional friend that he doesn't want congratulations, but the money, and should, according to his wife's shewing, be as happy as a king, and fondness and happiness itself, and yet at the same time be perpetually taunting her with a subject to which he had pledged his word he would never advert, and carry what would appear to be a groundless jealousy to violent extremes. He is said to have possessed a remarkable fund of animal spirits; and the letters written by him and read in Court certainly have about them much coarse boisterousness, and do not impress one favourably as to his taste and refinement. . . ."

CHAPTER THIRTEEN

CONDUCT: CHARLES BRAVO

Up to this point we have observed the conduct of Charles
Bravo vicariously through the eyes of witnesses; now we must
study it more directly, and this is best done by turning to the
subject which dominated his life and upon which the story
within the story hinges—money.

When he became engaged to Florence he promised to sever
all connection with the "establishment at Maidenhead"; but
that it was never completely severed is clear from the following
letter which, though the name was suppressed, was stated in
Court to have been addressed to his mistress' sister.

> "Junior Carlton Club,
> "March 20th, 1876.
>
> "My dear ——,
>
> "If I repay you the £500 you lent me, you will not
> get more than £30 a year for it. I will, if you like, keep
> your money another year, or repay you in June. Perhaps,
> unless you doubt my ability to pay, you will be wise to
> leave the money with me—you get more interest and your
> capital is not very unsafe.
>
> "I am afraid you thought me unkind when I met you
> yesterday. I assure you I did not mean to be so.
>
> > "Give my love to ——, and believe me,
> >
> > "Ever yours truly,
> >
> > > "C."

Two letters from this woman, the first prompted by the
meeting referred to by Charles and the second in answer to his
own, indicate that she was ready to leave the money in his
hands.[1] It had evidently been borrowed some years previously
and used by Charles to open an account with a firm of stock-

[1] These letters are quoted in Appendix III.

brokers in which a friend of his, Mr. Meredith Brown, was a partner.

Now, although Joseph Bravo, his eyes moist with emotion, was to swear in Court that "the closest confidence and affection" united his stepson and himself, it scarcely surprises us that he knew nothing of the Maidenhead connection, while for the very good reason that "Stock Exchange operations" of any kind—let alone with the borrowed savings of an "unfortunate woman"—were anathema to him, Charles kept this discreditable business a closely guarded secret.

As we have seen, Joseph Bravo at the time of his stepson's marriage settled £20,000 upon him, and "entered a bond" with Florence's trustees to pay him the interest. The phrase is Mrs. Campbell's: in reality he seems to have *pledged his word* to make Charles an allowance of £800 a year which would represent the interest upon that sum. An Englishman's word was proverbially as good as his bond, but not a drop of English blood flowed in Joseph Bravo's veins, so when Mrs. Campbell and Florence both swore in Court that Charles "had only brought £100 to the marriage" it seems they spoke the literal truth; for Mr. Brookes stated: "Mr. Bravo brought nothing to the marriage and would have brought nothing to the marriage until the deaths of both his parents."

At the inquiry Joseph Bravo was the first witness to be called, and swore that between his stepson's marriage and death he "had *given* him £1,100". Under cross-examination, however, it became abundantly clear that all he had actually *given* Charles was the £100 mentioned by Florence and Mrs. Campbell, the truth about the remaining £1,000 being as follows:

(i) While Charles was staying at Palace Green between 8th and 17th March he requested his stepfather to sell the security of £500 which he held on his behalf and place the proceeds to his credit on the books of the firm: which Mr. Bravo did. (ii) On 26th March, Joseph Bravo having come up to town for the day from St. Leonards, Charles called upon him at his office and asked for a loan of £500 on, stated Mr. Bravo, "the joint security of himself and his wife" to be repaid on 8th April. (iii) On 29th March Charles wrote to his step-father saying he required the money derived from the sale of the £500 security. "I sent him a cheque for it," stated Mr. Bravo, adding rather vaguely for so exact a business man, "either on the 1st, 2nd or 3rd of April." (iv) On 2nd April Charles wrote to his stepfather concerning the *loan* made on 26th March, saying: "As the day on which I promised to repay the £500 is only a week off I may as well ask you if you approve the plan of deducting the amount from my allowance," an inquiry which provides further evidence that he had not yet received any of the allowance which Joseph Bravo had undertaken to make him. The latter stated that he replied telling Charles to "let it lie"—a statement which remains un-confirmed since none of his letters appeared in evidence.

Five questions now arise:

(i) What lay behind Charles' monetary transactions with his stepfather?

(ii) Why did Charles, whose wife had an income of £4,000 a year, persistently endeavour to induce her to "retrench"?

(iii) Why did the Joseph Bravos exert themselves to the same purpose?

(iv) Why did Charles react with such violence when Florence wished to "have it out" with her mother-in-law?

(v) What was really Charles' financial position at this time?

To take the last question first, Mr. Meredith Brown stated in Court that at this time Charles had a credit of £1,196 with his firm, of which £500 was, as we know, owing to his lady-friend; but the astonishing thing, which did not come to light until after the proceedings were over, was that he had a far greater nest-egg secreted elsewhere, for probate was granted on £14,000!

To question (i) the answer probably is that Charles hoped that these manœuvres would stimulate his stepfather into activity concerning the promised allowance; that to question (ii) is considerably more involved, but may temporarily be summed up in a phrase of Mrs. Campbell's—"He had a money-mania." Concerning question (iii) it seems tantamount to certainty that in order to extract money from his parents he led them to believe that Florence was hopelessly extravagant and systematically overspent her income, which in itself provides the answer to question (iv), for if she "had it out" with them the falsity of his representations would be exposed.

Support for this theory is supplied by the following letter from Charles to his stepfather:

> "The Priory, Balham,
> "April 9th, 1876.
>
> "My dear Father Joseph,
>
> "... Our financial position is steadily improving. We owe about £250 and we have in hand about £500. As soon as the Chancery dividends, due last January, amounting to some £260, are paid, we will be out of the wood. ... You may depend upon our not touching capital. ..."

Out of all this arises the pertinent question: *why* was Charles Bravo playing this exceedingly risky game of double deception? It would be obvious to the meanest intelligence that it could not be sustained for long—and Charles' intelligence was remarkably astute. The answer to this question will appear in due course.

CHAPTER FOURTEEN

EASTER AT THE PRIORY

I

On the evening of Wednesday, 12th April, Charles entered his wife's bedroom nursing his face and asked for something to relieve neuralgia. She suggested laudanum which, as an anodyne, then held the place now occupied by aspirin, and going to her medicine cupboard he selected from the vast array of homoeopathic remedies the familiar blue fluted bottle and bore it off to the spare room which he was still occupying—for Florence, though a week had gone by since her miscarriage, was still suffering from pain in her back and loins, weakness and nausea, in spite of which, and of Royes Bell's advice, Dr. Harrison had not been called in.

Later that evening Charles returned and complained that the laudanum had not relieved him—" he was very impatient of pain", stated Florence—whereupon she and Mrs. Cox suggested that he should rub his gums with chloroform and "he took the chloroform bottle". The laudanum bottle had been about half full; the chloroform bottle contained slightly less.

2

For the past week or so the weather had been unusually mild and sunny, but on Good Friday—14th April—it had turned stormy, and all that morning Charles perambulated the house irritable and restless, staring out at the rain from each window in turn. "He was in and out of his wife's room all the time," Mrs. Cox stated. However, by noon, when Florence was dressing to go downstairs to lunch for the first time since her illness, the sky had cleared, and Charles, having hurried out to inspect the tennis court, returned to announce that if the rain held off the court would be fit for play next day.

Luncheon over, he followed his wife into the morning-room where she wished to rest on the sofa, but, as Mrs. Cox said, "he made this impossible; he was in and out of the room, never in it many minutes."

"Why don't you go round the estate?" Florence suggested.

"I've been round it."

"Shall I put a match to the library fire?" asked Mrs. Cox.

"If you do, I shall put it out," he retorted roughly.

At last, exasperated by his lack of consideration, Florence "ordered him out of the room and he grew very angry". Mrs. Cox lit the library fire, and coaxed him there, but a few minutes afterwards he was out in the garden where she presently found him to tell him she "was going out". That night there occurred his last "ebullition of temper". Sir John Hall is of the opinion that Mrs. Cox when recounting it deliberately "magnified a trivial squabble into a serious quarrel" in order to drag in the theme of his jealousy of Dr. Gully. This may be so: none the less there is the ring of truth in her story, and Charles' mood, as she describes it, is consistent with his behaviour whenever he was bored or out of sorts.

When they were alone together after dinner "he was", she said, "still in a very bad temper with his wife for having ordered him out of the room. 'She is a selfish pig,' he said, 'I despise myself for having married her. I have made up my mind not to live with her. I am going away. I wish I were dead.'

"It was, I told him, very wrong of him to say such things, as God had given him life to do some good in. . . . 'What do you think will become of Florence if you go away?'

" 'Let her go back to Gully.'

"I told him that was very wrong of him; there was no reason. 'You know her every thought is for you,' I said. 'You know she does everything possible to make you happy.'

" 'I have felt a change coming over her for some time. She does not care for me or she would not have ordered me out of the room.' "

He went upstairs—not, as Mrs. Cox had urged, "to make it up with his wife", but to his room, where he locked himself in.

Instead of leaving him alone to recover his temper, Mrs. Cox
must needs go and knock on the door.

"He would not open it for some little time. I knocked again
two or three times. He then opened it, and I begged him not
to leave the house. He said he had quite made up his mind to
go; that he could not live with her any longer. I remained with
him a long time, but he seemed quite determined.

" 'You are a good little woman,' he said, 'I have no quarrel
with you.'

" 'I will ask Florence to come to you,' I said.

" 'If you do, I will turn her out.' "

All her persuasions were of no avail. Eventually he bade her
good night. "As I was turning to leave the room he kissed me
on the cheek. 'You love Florence and have done the best you
can for me. I thank you for what you have done. Good night
again.' "

On this note of pathos he shut his door, but still she could
not curb her officiousness. "I went and told his wife that she
had better go to him, as he was going to leave the house. She
got up immediately and went to him. I don't know what
occurred but afterwards she told me he was very angry. I
could not rest all night, as I feared he was going out of the
house."

Charles never had the slightest intention of "going out of
the house", as Mrs. Cox probably knew full well. He was
merely "playing up" Florence, as he had done time and again.
In relating the conclusion of the incident Mrs. Cox becomes
positively arch. Next morning, she said, Charles told her:

" 'We have made it up. Florence has admitted that she was
in the wrong.'

" 'Oh yes, I should think so!' I said, laughing. 'Very likely
indeed.' "

On the evening of Easter Sunday—forty-eight hours before
"the poison entered his body"—the doomed man wrote his
last letter to his mother. It shews him in the best of spirits:
there is no hint that two nights previously he was threatening
to leave the wife to whom he refers affectionately. Nor—
though he knows that his doting mother, who has devotedly

tended his most trifling ailments since babyhood, would pour out her sympathy—does he mention the neuralgia of which he complains each night to Florence.

> "The Priory, Balham,
> "Sunday, 16th April, 1876.

"My dear old Grannie,

"I passed the whole of yesterday most pleasantly. I rode Cremorne from 9.30 to eleven, and on Victor afterwards by the side of Florence while she took an airing in the family coach. We went to see if we could persuade the St. Anne's people to let Mrs. Cox's babes pass the holy season with us. We could not, but they are to come on Monday.

"After lunch I put up the lawn-tennis [net] with the assistance of Rowe and under the superintendence of Florence, and after that great work was completed I naturally had a game with Rowe, and later on a very vigorous one with Osman.[1] Mrs. Campbell [2] came over from Kingston, and Mrs. Fowke with her little girl (with whom I had another game) from Norwood. Altogether I loafed vigorously and enjoyed myself.

"The east wind made this day rather less enjoyable than yesterday, and lawn-tennis was avoided, partly from fear lest it might shock the good people of Balham and Tooting, and partly because Rowe was at church and in his Sunday clothes, and Osman was gone on a tour of visits to neighbouring gardens. . . ."

While Charles was writing this, Florence was writing to Mrs. Campbell in a similar façade-preserving strain.

". . . We hope Papa is gaining strength and that he will soon be quite well.[3] Auntie came over yesterday and is looking blooming. Uncle and Peggy[4] are coming tomorrow, and Charlie is looking forward to a game of lawn-tennis. I never saw him look so well. The country is life to him, and

---

[1] Head gardener.   [2] Mrs. Tom Campbell.
[3] He had been taken ill on returning from Rome.
[4] Mrs. Campbell's brother, Mr. Orr, and his daughter.

he walks about with a book under his arm as happy as a
king.

"We leave here (D.V.) on Thursday for Worthing, and
hope to return to welcome you and Papa here, and then
Ernie and Tot. I am getting stronger, but it is a long business. It seems ages before one feels really well, but by dint
of sitz baths and spinal washes I have wooed sleep back, one
of the most important steps to recovery.

"The flowers here are in great profusion and so lovely. . . ."

These letters had been posted and Florence was reading in
bed when Charles came to her room to complain that he was
again suffering from neuralgia. She recommended a hot toddy
of brandy and lemon, which he drank in his room.

3

"The inner life of the household" (stated an article in
the *Daily News* after the inquiry had been concluded) "was
one of affection, possibly, and even of hope, but assuredly
full of the petty tortures, and some of the greater torments, with which men and women lacerate each other's
hearts. . . .

"But with all these real or alleged motives for unhappiness there was surely little sign of a tragedy like that of
April 18th."

Indeed, nowhere in the British Isles could the sun on that
glorious Easter Monday of 17th April, 1876, have shone down
upon a more delightful scene or a more amiable little gathering
than that at The Priory. A balmy breeze stirred the scolloped
edges of the gay, striped sunblinds lowered over the windows,
and Florence and Mrs. Cox sat under a great oak while
Charles took on the Cox boys at tennis during the morning,
and in the afternoon conducted Mr. Orr and Peggy over the
"estate"—the expansive host, the happy and affectionate
husband. Promising to lunch with Mr. Orr at the St. James
Hall Restaurant in Piccadilly next day, he waved a gay farewell as they drove off. But when Keeber, after helping her mistress to bed, returned to ask what she would like for dinner,

she found Charles slumped in a chair by the fire, his face in his hands.

"Mary Ann," he said, "I feel very cross."

"Do you, sir? What is the matter?"

"I have toothache, like you do sometimes. What do you take for it?"

She replied that the last time the mistress had given her something for it, and asked:

"What are you doing for it, sir?"

"I rub my gums with laudanum, and sometimes chloroform," he replied, and Florence added that on Saturday night he had taken brandy and hot water—"I remembered seeing the tumbler and spoon in his bedroom," said Keeber.[1]

On that Easter Monday night the moon was drenching the world in her magic light, silvering the great oak and throwing in sable shadows the tracery of its branches upon the turf beneath. Under its radiance the garden with its wealth of spring flowers, and all the expanse of the Common beyond with its burgeoning trees, were still and silent as though under a spell, while the house with its dainty crenellations and airy little turrets was vested with an insubstantial quality as though it had been called into being by the wave of a fairy wand and might as easily be made to vanish away.

One by one the pointed casements darkened as its inmates settled down to sleep; and somewhere in one of those darkened rooms was a packet of crystals, as innocent in appearance as they were deadly in effect.

Before the moon again reached that point in the heavens they had done their terrible work.

[1] Evidence of Mary Ann Keeber.

Part II

THE TRAGEDY

CHAPTER ONE

THE FATAL TUESDAY—18TH APRIL:

9 A.M.–9 P.M.

I

THE writer on criminal cases derives immense assistance from the addresses to the jury by Counsel, who present and comment upon the evidence from the point of view of their respective clients, and still more from the Judge's charge to the jury, in which, with his trained mind, he marshals the essential features, smooths out the complexities and presents a balanced and lucid summary of the whole.

In the Bravo case, not only is one deprived of these invaluable aids, but confronted by so many side-issues and by the admission of so much irrelevant matter due to the conflicting interests involved and the extra-judicial character of the proceedings themselves, that one's path is bestrewn with difficulties that do not arise in the study of a regular criminal trial. Indeed, one's bewilderment at first is almost as great as that of the numerous witnesses, suddenly put up, who had to sustain, to their own confusion and that of the result, a veritable cross-fire of questions from a galaxy of legal luminaries.

Well within an hour of the poison entering his body there were two medical men at Charles Bravo's bedside: four hours later their number was doubled by the arrival of two London doctors, whereupon responsibility for the case passed from the hands of the former into those of the latter; while, when the crisis was at its height, two more London doctors saw the patient. All six gave evidence, much of which was conflicting, some of it acrimonious, and some inconclusive. Besides these, we have the evidence of Florence, Mrs. Cox, Rowe, Mary Ann Keeber, Mrs. Campbell, forming a more or less concordant

account against the opposing testimony of Joseph Bravo
supported by Ann Bell and Amelia Bushell.

It is fairly easy to give an account of events from the
morning of that fatal Tuesday until the case changed hands;
but from then onwards, except for sudden flashes, it is only
possible to present a composite picture cautiously constructed
from material salvaged from that verbal maelstrom in Court.
Yet it is essential to present it with an accuracy as meticulous
as possible, in order to demonstrate that all-important factor,
*the conduct of the two principal suspects and the victim himself
immediately before, and during, the fatal illness*. In order to point
the way to a final solution of the mystery the salient features
of the case are, where necessary, summarized in the form of
notes at the end of the chapters.

2

On Tuesday, 18th April, Charles Bravo awoke in a liverish
mood which was not improved by the sight of a dun sky holding the threat of snow; for, if it snowed, Florence, who had
promised to drive up to London with him in order to transfer
the £260 from her Chancery dividends to his account, might
refuse to go. Entering the dining-room he derived no pleasure
from the sight of Mrs. Cox finishing her breakfast and all
ready to set out for Worthing to make the final arrangements
about the house Florence was taking there. As he sat down he
tossed his *vis-à-vis* a letter from his mother in which she strongly
objected to the Worthing plan on the grounds of expense and
declared that "Florence would be better at home".

"Shall I shew it to Florence?" he asked.

Mrs. Cox read it and advised sagely:

"No; it will perhaps only lead to unpleasantness."

A few moments later she set off down the drive: a neat,
purposeful little figure, one gloved hand grasping a tightly
furled umbrella, the other the drawstrings of a black silk bag
in which reposed a case of sandwiches and a goodly flask of
sherry to sustain and cheer her on her pilgrimage.

At ten o'clock the landau, closed against the weather, drew
up at the door, and Charles was pacing the hall as Florence

came slowly downstairs.[1] Suddenly she clutched the banisters for support.

"What is the matter?" he asked.

"I feel faint."

"Then you had better stay at home."

But in a moment or two the faintness passed and they got into the carriage; as it started he continued sourly: "You had better go to Worthing alone. That would be better for your health."

"I shouldn't be happy unless you came too," she protested.

It had become her habit to look the other way whenever she passed Orwell Lodge. Instinctively she did so now.

"Did you see anybody?" Charles asked.

"No: I didn't look."

Then he began to "abuse" Dr. Gully. "He was angry before he started and then became worse in the carriage."

"It's no good," he said, "we shall never get over it. We had better separate."

"I was very much hurt," Florence continued, "and told him he was most unkind to talk like that; that he ought to have considered it all before he married me. I told him I was not always speaking to him about the 'establishment' he was keeping before he married. When he saw how deeply grieved I was he apologized, confessing he was wrong and I right, and asked me to kiss him. I said I was too much hurt then to kiss him—hurt, not angry.

" 'If you don't kiss me, you will see what I will do when I get home.' When he said this he looked quite brown in the face, and as if he were determined to do something violent." She therefore kissed him "because I was frightened".

Meanwhile they had reached Clapham Common and as it had begun to snow the coachman was ordered to turn back. But before they had gone far the sun was shining, and the order was given to turn about once more and they "drove quite amicably to London".[2]

[1] What follows is taken from Florence's evidence.

[2] The coachman and footman stated in evidence that they had heard no quarrelling; but it was unlikely that they would do so, seeing that the carriage was closed, unless voices were raised to shouting pitch.

They drove first to the bank in Stratford Place, then to Benson's, the Bond Street jewellers, where Florence paid a bill, and thence to the Turkish baths in Jermyn Street where she dropped Charles. From there she went to the Haymarket Stores, where she bought a bottle of special hair-lotion and some particularly choice tobacco as a peace-offering, after which she drove straight home.

3

After luncheon Charles and his host strolled along Piccadilly where they met Mr. McCalmont; and having parted from Mr. Orr in St. James Street these two friends walked together to Victoria station. Charles pressed Mr. McCalmont to return and dine at The Priory, and it is possible, if he could have done so, Charles' death would not have taken place. But he had another engagement, and promised to "go down and spend the day on the morrow instead".[1] So the train carried Charles, whom he described as being "in the highest spirits", to his doom.

"I lay on the sofa in the morning-room," stated Florence. "My husband came back about four o'clock. He came in cheerfully and affectionately kissed me and told me he had had 'a jolly lunch'. I said to him: 'Go up and see what I have got for you—in your bedroom.' He came down and said it was just like me—forgetting all about his unkindness in the morning and getting him the things he liked. He appeared on the best of terms with me and I saw no trace of the ill-temper of that morning."

Without, apparently, mentioning his meeting with Mr. McCalmont, Charles went out to the stables, where he was told that the cobs had not been exercised that day.

"I think I shall ride them."

"Which one shall I saddle, sir?" asked the groom.

"The worse one—Cremorne. Perhaps I shall be back in time to take the other out."[2]

Returning to the house he called to Rowe for his riding-

---

[1] Evidence of Frederick Hayes McCalmont.
[2] Evidence of George Younger, groom.

clothes and looked in to tell Florence he was going for a ride. When he returned at 6.30 the coachman was in the stable-yard. Charles climbed stiffly from the saddle looking "pale and haggard" and said:

"The cob has bolted with me. I'm all of a shake. You could knock me down with a feather."

"I told you he wasn't safe to ride on a snaffle, sir. You ought to have a curb for him."

"I'll get one. I should think he has galloped five miles with me. I can hardly lift a limb." [1]

On reaching the morning-room he slumped groaning into a chair and told Florence that "Cremorne had bolted with him all the way to Mitcham Common and back". He looked so exhausted and shaken that she suggested some brandy or a glass of wine. He refused both. She then advised a hot bath, and rang for Rowe to get one ready.

"Get a hot bath ready for the master, please, Rowe," she said.

"Shall I light the fire in his bedroom, Madam?"

"Yes, of course, Rowe." [2]

It was the day of hip-baths set before blazing bedroom fires, and when Rowe returned to say it was ready Charles, so Florence stated, "looked ill, very ill, and was so stiff that I had to help him out of the chair into which he had put himself".

She led the way upstairs to make sure the bath-water was properly hot, then went to her dressing-room to change for dinner—her first dinner downstairs since her illness; the last she was ever to have with her husband.

As Charles slowly mounted the stairs Rowe followed him. "He was evidently in great pain," the butler testified, "and he put his hands to his sides and cried out. He looked exceedingly pale—paler than he usually did, for he was generally pale."

"The cob," he told Rowe, "bolted with me all the way to Mitcham Common, and before I could get properly seated again he bolted all the way back."

"I hope he didn't throw you, sir?"

Charles smiled wryly.

[1] Evidence of Charles Parton, coachman.   [2] Evidence of Rowe.

"Oh no, he didn't throw me."

Emerging from his bedroom at 7.20 Charles encountered Keeber lighting the gas on the landing, and she, who was to prove an observant witness, "noticed nothing unusual in his appearance"; while, contrary to his usual talkative habit, he made no allusion to his misadventure, merely remarking before going downstairs:

"Don't take away my bath-water, Mary Ann; it will do for me in the morning."

This remark has sometimes been quoted to shew the lengths to which Charles was prepared to carry his passion for economy, but its real significance, especially when taken in conjunction with his invitation to Mr. McCalmont, lies in the fact that obviously nothing was further from his mind than the idea of death.

4

When Mrs. Cox, on getting back from Worthing at 7.25, bustled into Florence's dressing-room, she was astonished to find her dressed for dinner. "I knew she had been to Town," she said in evidence, "and I told her she ought to go to bed as she must be so tired. But she said she was anxious to sit up to dinner: 'Charlie says I can if I go to bed directly afterwards,' she said."

Dinner being punctually at 7.30 Mrs. Cox had no time to do more than run upstairs and take off her mantle and bonnet while Florence was joining her husband in the morning-room.

"How are you now, Charlie?" she asked him.

"I'm all right now," he said. "I feel much better."

Then Mrs. Cox appeared and Rowe announced dinner.

At Charles Bravo's elbow stood the Burgundy he always drank with his meals. For the ladies there was a decanter of sherry and another of Marsala. The menu consisted of fish, roast lamb, and an anchovy savoury.

An important incident now took place. Charles, refusing the first course, slit open a letter which the evening post had brought. It consisted of a communication from his broker, Mr. Meredith Brown, which had been addressed to him at Palace

Green, forwarded thence to St. Leonards, where it had been opened and read by Mr. Bravo, who now sent it on with a covering letter. Florence stated that as Charles read it "his face became quite livid. My husband was extremely angry, excessively angry, at the contents of his stepfather's letter and the opening of his own. He said he would 'tell him to attend to his own affairs and not to mettle'; he would write him 'a

SKETCH OF CHARLES BRAVO'S BEDROOM

shirty letter'. His face worked the whole of dinner and had such a strange yellow look. I thought he would go mad any minute, and if I tried to turn the subject he always went back to it."

Mrs. Cox, for her part, stated: "He went on and on about it. He said 'the Governor' had no business to open his letters or to write as he had done. He described his stepfather's communication as 'a shirty letter'."

Rowe attributed Charles' state to the effects of his ride. "During dinner that night Mr. Bravo seemed in great pain. He appeared greatly put out by everything. He said in the course of dinner something about a letter from 'the Governor' which he had had. Mrs. Cox shewed him a photograph of the house" (at Worthing). "He threw the picture down as if disgusted and said: 'The usual thing'. . . . He said: 'I shall not see it,' or, 'I shall not be there.' Mrs. Cox looked over her glasses and said: 'Oh!' "

He was a large eater, and as he talked he bolted his food.[1] Three times Rowe filled his glass with Burgundy. That he was thoroughly discomposed is further supported by Keeber's evidence: she, who at 7.20 had "noticed nothing unusual in his appearance", was shocked by it when she next beheld him at 9.15. Recalling the hair-trigger precariousness of Charles' financial dealings one cannot help wondering if Mr. Bravo's letter may not have given him cause for panic. We shall never know, for it vanished.

Questioned about it in Court, Mr. Bravo said that Charles had bought £1,000 worth of Caledonian Railway stock shortly before Easter at 119, and that Mr. Meredith Brown's communication contained a "sold note" which shewed that he had sold it at $117\frac{1}{2}$. "I heard from my son some days before that the stock had been bought for investment. Having learned from the 'sold note' of its sale I communicated with him on the morning of 18th April, sending him the 'sold note' and my remarks were that 'it was not a happy way of making money' and that 'I very much disliked Stock Exchange operations'."

It was strange that the letter of Charles' to which Joseph Bravo refers should not have been put into evidence along with so many of his others. But stranger still is the mystery surrounding Joseph Bravo's own. Two hours after Charles had received it the household was in confusion and no one gave it another thought. Next day, Joseph Bravo was himself at The Priory with unimpeded access to the library where Charles kept his correspondence. Neither his letter—the exact contents of which were known only to himself and the dying man —nor the 'sold note' was ever seen again.

---

[1] An hour later he vomited "a mass of undigested . . . mostly animal matter weighing 20 ounces." (Evidence of Professor Redwood, analyst.)

CHAPTER TWO

THE FATAL TUESDAY—18TH:
9 P.M.–MIDNIGHT

I

AT 8.30 Charles followed the ladies into the morning-room. At 9 o'clock he "told his wife she ought to go to bed" and, since Keeber was at her supper with the other servants, Mrs. Cox went with her to perform the duties of lady's-maid. At the foot of the stairs Florence turned and asked her companion "to get her a little wine and water". Mrs. Cox, taking the decanter of Marsala from the cellarette in the dining-room, "half-filled a small tumbler which always stood with a carafe of water on the sideboard", added water and took it upstairs.

When at 9.15 Keeber entered the dressing-room with a gleaming copper can of hot water, Florence, already undressed, held out the little tumbler, saying:

"Mary Ann, fetch me a little Marsala."

Having taken a similar can to Mrs. Cox's room, Keeber went to get the wine. As she came out of the dining-room with it Charles emerged from the morning-room opposite.

"I knew he was going up to his bedroom," she said, "and I let him go before me. . . . As he was going up he turned round and looked at me twice. He did not speak, but I remarked to myself how queer he looked—I mean very pale. I thought he was angry as he did not speak, for he had always spoken when he met me."

When she saw he was going to his wife's dressing-room, she turned aside into Florence's bedroom to await his departure. There was an inner and an outer door to the bedroom, the latter covered with baize, and when both were shut the room itself was virtually sound-proof. Keeber left them both open so that she could see her master go by. Meanwhile, "I heard voices in the dressing-room," she stated, "but I could not distinguish what was being said. I heard no angry voices, nor did I hear anything unusual."

Mrs. Cox deposed that as soon as Charles entered the dressing-room, "he said to his wife, speaking in French because he thought Keeber was following: 'You have sent downstairs for more wine; you have drunk nearly a bottle of wine today.' Mrs. Bravo made no reply. She was folding a compress for her back."

Florence, however, denied her companion's allegation. "I have no recollection of his speaking to me in French," she said, "or of upbraiding me for taking too much wine that day. . . . My husband came to bid me good night and left the room after he had done so."

Keeber went on to say that, having seen Charles go by, she left the bedroom. "I met Mrs. Bravo on the landing—Mr. Bravo had gone then and shut himself in his bedroom—and she asked me where the wine was. I said: 'It is in your bedroom.' Mrs. Bravo then went into her bedroom and I went into the dressing-room to put Mrs. Bravo's clothes away." This, Keeber reckoned, took her some five or six minutes, though Florence and Mrs. Cox considered it could not have taken her less than ten.

Before the bedroom fire the two Skye terriers were stretched: the room was warm, tranquil and reposeful. Florence got into bed at once, and Mrs. Cox drew up an armchair to sit beside her. In her low, soothing voice she described the house she had taken at Worthing, but before she had uttered many words Florence had drifted into sleep.

Keeber continues that, having tidied the dressing-room, "I went into Mrs. Bravo's bedroom. Mrs. Cox was there, sitting beside Mrs. Bravo's bed, as she often did . . . Mrs. Bravo's eyes were closed and she seemed asleep. . . . I asked Mrs. Cox, 'Will Mrs. Bravo want anything more tonight?'

" 'Have you brought up the little tray?'

" 'Yes.'

" 'Then that will be all. Take the dogs with you.' "

The important point—whether or not Keeber shut the outer door—was never satisfactorily cleared up. Florence stated that

Mrs. Cox shut both doors when they entered the bedroom, and since it was customary for both to be shut when Florence was in bed, the probability is that Keeber shut it. If so, this would explain why Mrs. Cox failed to hear the cry for help which Charles Bravo gave a few moments later.

2

The dogs followed Keeber unwillingly. One lolloped reluctantly down the stairs behind her; the other sat stolidly at the top. Halfway down she paused and called it. The next second she was startled by the sudden opening of Charles' door. For an instant she had a glimpse of him in his night-shirt. He called urgently, *"Florence! Florence! Hot water! Hot water!"* then, seeing her, beat a hasty retreat.

His tone, his distraught appearance, sent the girl quickly back to the bedroom. "Mrs. Cox was sitting as I had left her. I told her that Mr. Bravo seemed ill. She got up at once and went before me to Mr. Bravo's room."

Charles was standing at the open casement on the further side of his bed. Mrs. Cox went straight to him while Keeber stood uncertainly in the doorway. His face was grey and beaded with sweat as he turned and cried in a voice rising to a scream, *"Hot water! Hot water! Hot water!"* then, leaning from the window, was violently sick.

"Be quick! Fetch hot water!" ordered Mrs. Cox sharply.

Keeber ran to the kitchen; the errand, she thought, took her three or four minutes: when she returned Charles was seated on the floor beneath the window with Mrs. Cox, crouched beside him, massaging his chest above the heart.

"Go and fetch mustard—hurry!" she said.

Back to the kitchen sped Keeber; then in obedience to Mrs. Cox's instructions mixed some mustard with hot water in the basin from the wash-stand and lifted Charles' feet into it.

"Keep his feet in it. Rub them as hard as you can."

But Charles suddenly kicked out convulsively, then grew rigid, crumpled and collapsed inertly at full length.

"Wake, Charlie! Do wake!" implored Mrs. Cox—then

peremptorily to Keeber, "Mix some mustard with water in a tumbler—*quickly!*"

"How much?"

"Mix and make haste," she snapped, rubbing the stricken man's chest without pause.

"You had better do it yourself," said Keeber resentfully.

Her small dark face tense, Mrs. Cox hastily mixed the emetic and, supporting Charles' head, poured some into his mouth entreating him to swallow it. With difficulty he gulped down a little, but more overflowed on to his bare chest. "Mrs. Cox," said Keeber, "then told me to make strong coffee. But Mr. Bravo could only swallow very little. Mr. Bravo was then sick. I held the basin for him. Mrs. Cox told me to throw away the vomit, wash the basin and bring it back."

"Go to my room," Mrs. Cox next directed, "and bring my spirits of camphor," then with the swiftness of a lizard darted downstairs and broke in upon Rowe in his pantry. "Rouse the groom, Rowe, and tell him to go at once to Streatham and fetch Dr. Harrison—Mr. Bravo is ill." Upstairs again she darted to crouch once more beside the now completely unconscious man and resume her tireless massaging.

After a hurried search for the camphor, Keeber decided that Florence ought to be called.

"She was asleep. I wakened her. She looked at me and asked: 'What is it?' I told her Mr. Bravo was very ill. She got up at once, saying: 'What's the matter? What's the matter?' I helped her on with her dressing-gown and she went with me to Mr. Bravo. I then went again to look for the camphor, which I found."

So through the eyes of Mary Ann Keeber we have a clear and comprehensive view of Mrs. Cox's *conduct* during that first quarter of an hour after Charles Bravo was struck down; we also see the conduct of his wife when she was roused from sleep.

"When I went into the room," said Florence, "I found my husband lying on the floor near the window looking like death, and Mrs. Cox rubbing his chest."

At the sight of his inert body, his face grey-green and

glistening with sweat, his chest and night-shirt stained with vomit, coffee and mustard, she clasped his nerveless hand and burst into shocked, convulsive sobs, imploring him to speak to her. Then through her tears she asked:

"Has the doctor been sent for?"

"Yes," said Mrs. Cox.

"Which doctor?"

She was "horrified" when she learned that precious time was being wasted in sending two miles or more for medical aid when it lay close at hand.

"Why didn't you send for Mr. Moore? He lives nearer."

Not waiting for a reply, heedless that she was in her "night attire", she ran downstairs calling for Rowe, through whose eyes we have a further glimpse of her *conduct*.

"She was crying as she came," he stated, "and called out to me to fetch someone quickly. I told her Dr. Harrison had been sent for. 'Never mind,' she said, 'get someone! Get someone from Balham! I don't care who it is!' She screamed it at me."

He went off to knock up the Balham doctor, Dr. Moore, to whose questions he could only reply that he believed Mr. Bravo, who had been run away with by a horse that afternoon, had "had a fit".

Florence's first thought on returning to the sick-room was to get Charles off the floor. With Keeber's aid he was hoisted into an arm-chair, as the three women had not sufficient strength to lift him into bed. In readiness for the doctors' visit, Keeber now emptied away the bath-water and carried off the bath; Florence and Mrs. Cox contrived to change Charles into a clean night-shirt; then, leaving Mrs. Cox to stoke the fire and generally tidy up, Florence went to dress.

3

The account of Charles Bravo's illness now passes to Dr. Moore and Dr. Harrison. When the former—a complete stranger to the household—arrived at 10.30 Florence told him, "My husband has been taken ill; I don't know what is the matter with him," and went on to say that he had looked very upset after the cob had run away with him, but after a hot bath had seemed better and had eaten a good dinner. She added that her regular attendant, Dr. Harrison of Streatham, had also been sent for.

With Rowe's assistance Dr. Moore got Charles to bed; then, with everyone out of the room, he made his examination of the patient, whom he found "totally unconscious" and "with the pupils of the eyes dilated. The patient was breathing heavily; the skin was cold; the pulse almost imperceptible and, I was apprehensive, would cease at any moment. He looked like a person under the influence of poison, but I could not identify any poison which would correspond with the symptoms. Mrs. Bravo asked me if I thought his state was dangerous, and when I replied that I did not think he would recover she burst into a flood of tears. Her grief appeared to me altogether natural."

Mrs. Cox, with an instinctive distrust of strangers who might make "scandal", gave him the briefest possible account of the measures she had taken "to relieve the patient", meanwhile keeping her ears alert for the arrival of Dr. Harrison. As soon as she heard it she darted downstairs again to meet him at the front door and told him that when she reached Charles' side he had screamed for hot water and then vomited out of the window. "Dr. Harris, I am sure he has taken *chloroform,*" she said.

But Dr. Harrison could detect no smell of chloroform on the patient's breath. He and Dr. Moore were completely mystified by his condition, and the only conclusion they felt able to draw was that "a large vessel near the heart had given way".[1] They decided to administer brandy and water, which, since the jaws were locked, had to be injected. Dr. Harrison told Florence that he and Dr. Moore would like another opinion, at the same time informing Mrs. Cox that he "did not think Mr. Bravo would live an hour", in which Charles was to confound their expectations.

Florence at once suggested sending for Royes Bell. "He

[1] Mrs. Taylor, who was murdered by her son-in-law, Dr. Pritchard, with antimony (1865), was seen by the doctor called in lying fully dressed in bed and with "the appearance of having suffered a sudden seizure".

knows my husband's constitution," she said eagerly. "He has known him all his life. I know my husband's people would like him to be called in." While Dr. Harrison wrote a note to Royes Bell telling him that he and his colleague feared "a blood vessel near the patient's heart had given way and they would like the opinion of a physician and himself", the carriage was ordered; but the moment it was gone Florence bewailed the fact that she had not sent the cobs instead, "as they went so much faster than the carriage horses".

Dr. Harrison and Dr. Moore were to remain outside the controversy which ensued between the London doctors. Their evidence strikes one as being thoughtful, honest and impartial, and when Dr. Harrison, who knew Florence well, states that her *conduct* was "entirely natural under the circumstances", what he says carries conviction.

"She lay down beside her husband for a while imploring him 'Do speak to me, Charlie dear', and other endearing terms. I knew she had been very unwell. She became exhausted and fell asleep. I roused her as I was afraid she might interfere with the patient's breathing. She rose at once."

4

There was nothing more to be done but watch, and await the arrival of Royes Bell and the physician he would bring with him.

Charles Bravo lay upon his bed as though life had already fled. On one side sat Florence, her face tear-stained and wan with anxiety, on the other Mrs. Cox, her expression shuttered and remote, yet alert. The doctors sat together near the foot of the bed. Save for the faint hiss of the gas-lamp, the sudden stutter of a flame in the grate and the fussy ticking of a little clock on the chest of drawers, a silence heavy with calamity hung over them all. Side by side on the mantelpiece stood the blue fluted bottle labelled *Laudanum—Poison* and the white one labelled *Chloroform—Poison* which Charles had taken from Florence's cupboard a few days before; both were empty. There, too, stood the bottle of liniment and the package of Epsom salts which Royes Bell had prescribed. The doctors

examined them all and were satisfied that none could have
caused the patient's condition.

At 1 a.m., without regaining consciousness, the sick man
was purged and vomited, and the blood tinging both evacua-
tions confirmed the doctors in their suspicions that he was
suffering from an irritant poison. Now it is elementary knowledge that, if poison has been swallowed, its greatest concentration is contained in the matter first evacuated; yet these two
doctors committed the grave error of not only allowing this
matter to be thrown away but of continuing to ignore that
lying on the leads beneath the window—an error about to be
repeated by the two other medical men now on their way from
London. Later on little heed was paid to this blunder, attention
being focused instead on the fact that Mrs. Cox had ordered
Keeber to throw away the vomit in the basin—the inference
being that she had done so to destroy incriminating evidence—
while Dr. Harrison's admission that it was Mrs. Cox herself
who had drawn attention to the vomit on the leads was con-
veniently ignored. Subsequent writers on the case, in their
eagerness to fix the guilt on Mrs. Cox, have pursued the same
course.

Yet another grave error was committed by the medical men
that night: they neglected, as the *Lancet* pointed out, "the
need of at once impounding all bottles and glasses, searching
the rooms, the clothes, the belongings and surroundings of the
person dying at the time of his illness. . . ."[1]

NOTES ON CHAPTER TWO

1. Charles Bravo called in a voice of panic to *his wife* for
hot water. When Keeber went to fetch it he and Mrs. Cox were
left alone together—*and he did not call for his wife again.*

[1] In the Chapman case (1903) Mr. Justice Grantham similarly censured
severely the medical profession for failing to detect and frustrate the operations of the poisoner. On the other hand, in a case of poisoning the doctor's
position is one of great difficulty and delicacy: he can render little assistance
to the patient unless the latter actually accuses someone of attempting to
poison him. Very few poisoning cases have been brought to light at the
instance of the medical men engaged: exceptions are the Armstrong case
(Dr. Hincks) and the Richmond case (Dr. Julius and Dr. Bird).

2. Why did he call for hot water? Why did Mrs. Cox administer a mustard emetic? Dealing with these questions the *Lancet* said: "A mustard emetic . . . is by no means a remedy likely to be instantly applied, least of all in a family of homoeopathic proclivities. . . . The inference is forced upon us that either the patient made a statement to the effect that he had taken poison, or it was known or suspected by the person directing the use of the mustard emetic that he had taken something which would require to be removed from the stomach by a powerful stimulating appliance to produce vomiting. . . . The hypothesis that the patient himself knew or believed he had taken poison is further supported by the circumstance that he called loudly for warm water. . . ."

3. It is characteristic of poisoners that they delay as long as possible before summoning medical aid to their victims: Mrs. Cox sent at once for the family physician; Florence, immediately she was called, sent for the *nearest* medical man.

4. It is also characteristic of poisoners that they try to keep their victims' relatives from the bedside. When the doctors needed another opinion Florence herself suggested sending for Royes Bell, her husband's cousin and closest friend, and first thing next morning telegraphed for his family.

CHAPTER THREE

WEDNESDAY, 19TH: 2 A.M.–NOON

I

R OWE deposed that when he was called at 1 a.m. to assist in changing the sheets he heard Charles muttering: "No . . . laudanum; no . . . laudanum." During the next hour and a half the local doctors perceived signs of returning consciousness; at the end of that time the London doctors arrived, and after consultation all four returned to the patient's bedside. He was lying with his eyes closed. Royes Bell flicked his cheek, saying, "Charlie? . . . Charlie? . . . This is Royes," and when presently he opened his eyes asked him: "Do you know me?"

"Yes, you're Royes."

Indicating his colleague he asked:

"Do you know this gentleman—Dr. Johnson?" [1]

"Yes."

Then Florence entered the room and the sick man, in her own words, "looked up at me in the most piteous manner and said, 'Kiss me, my wife'."

Charles Bravo, in fact, shewed no trace of that bewilderment, surprise or consternation one would expect in the case of a man suddenly struck down by poison; the first thing that every patient asks his doctor is: "What is the matter with me?" and never from first to last did Charles Bravo put that question to anyone. In short, from the moment he opened his eyes until they were closed in death *he gave nothing away*.

It seems probable, therefore, that while he lay there in the small hours of the morning the recollection of all that had happened earlier returned to him, and having heard and understood what was said and done by those about him he made up his mind, before ever his cousin aroused him to speech, as to the course he meant to pursue. Always sharp-witted, ten years' experience at the Bar had taught him the value of silence and

[1] They had met once or twice.

how to answer questions in such a way as to avoid a direct commitment. Furthermore, as a sick man, he knew he had the advantage over those gathered anxiously about him, and, let it be remembered, he had made a special study of medical jurisprudence.

Dr. Johnson,[1] in an account of the case which appeared in the *Lancet* a month later, says that when he and Royes Bell entered the room the patient was "still unconscious, lying on his back, breathing rather deeply; his pulse was about 100, rather feeble; the sounds of action of the heart were normal and the pupils were then of normal size. The aspect of the patient was like that of one in the state of drowsiness following an epileptic fit. . . . Within a quarter of an hour of our arrival there were signs of returning consciousness. He began to toss about uneasily, and he soon recognized Mr. Bell and replied to his questions. He now vomited some mucus deeply tinged with blood, then made violent efforts to get out of bed,[2] and complained of severe pains in the abdomen."

Every thoughtful person who studies Charles Bravo's *conduct* from now onwards cannot but admit that it seems to be that of a man exerting all his powers to preserve a vital secret: a secret which tortured his mind even more than the fear of death—even more than the corroding poison was torturing his body—until, all passion spent, he paid in silence the final reckoning.

Dr. Johnson, who had now taken charge of the case, gave a morphia suppository to subdue the pain, and these continued to be administered as often as it returned. At about 3.30 a.m., when the patient seemed a little easier, Dr. Johnson asked him some questions. The nature of his answers is significant. To the direct question, "What have you taken?", he gives the indirect reply, "I rubbed my gums with laudanum for neuralgia—I may have swallowed some."

"Laudanum will not explain your symptoms."

---

[1] 1818–1896; Senior Physician, King's College Hospital; knighted 1892.
[2] He struggled so violently that Rowe, according to his own evidence, had to be summoned to help the three medical men restrain him—Dr. Moore had already taken his departure.

"If it isn't laudanum, I don't know what it is."

At this moment Rowe entered to say that Mrs. Cox wished to speak to Mr. Royes Bell. He went out to her in the dressing-room, and returning a moment later said to Dr. Johnson:

"Mrs. Cox has an important statement to communicate to you."

Dr. Johnson and Dr. Harrison accompanied him back to the dressing-room, where, according to the former, she said: "When I answered Charlie's cry for help he told me: 'I've taken *some of that poison*; don't tell Florence.' " [1]

"Did he tell you what poison he took," Dr. Johnson asked, "and why and when he took it?"

"No; nothing more than that."

Dr. Harrison then demanded why she had not told him this when she had met him on arrival.

"I did," she said.

"You did nothing of the kind!" he expostulated. "You told me he had taken *chloroform*."

Charles would probably have heard Rowe repeating Mrs. Cox's request to Royes Bell; he would have seen the solemnity of the latter's expression when he returned, and if he did not actually hear the words, "Mrs. Cox has an important statement to communicate", his mind was clear enough to guess their import. So when Dr. Johnson returned he would be prepared for what was to come.

"Mrs. Cox tells us that you have spoken to her of taking poison—what is the meaning of that?"

Charles' answer is a characteristic evasion.

"*I don't remember having spoken of taking poison.*"

"Have you taken poison?" asked Dr. Johnson directly.

"I rubbed my gums with laudanum; I may have swallowed some," Charles replied as before.

"Laudanum would not have caused your symptoms," Dr. Johnson repeated, whereupon Charles repeated in his turn, impatiently:

[1] Mrs. Cox, however, insisted that the phrase which Charles used, and which she repeated, was: "I have taken *poison*; don't tell Florence."

"If it isn't laudanum, I don't know what it is."

"Are there any poisons in the house?" pursued Dr. Johnson.

"Yes, several; chloroform, laudanum, and rat poison in the stables."

The next moment he was writhing and vomiting.

"It was quite evident," continued Dr. Johnson in his article in the *Lancet*, "that the symptoms were the result of some powerful irritant poison: there was violent pain in the abdomen, excessive tenderness on pressure, severe *tenesmus*, frequent passing of blood by stool and occasional vomiting of blood. The tongue, mouth and throat presented no appearance of abrasion. . . . We agreed to give cold milk as copiously as it could be taken, to foment the abdomen and give half a grain of morphia in a suppository as often as might be necessary to subdue the pain."

But it was not until Mrs. Cox had made her statement that some of the newly evacuated matter was kept for analysis; while, though Dr. Johnson's attention had already been called to the vomit lying on the leads, he took no action to collect it. The rising sun now shone down upon it: a rain-storm had swept much of it down into the gutter.

Dr. Harrison left about 4 a.m. About the same time Dr. Johnson, speaking to Mrs. Cox, referred in Florence's presence to her allegation that Charles had told her he had taken poison.

"Did he say he had taken poison?" Florence asked.

"Yes, he did," said Mrs. Cox.

Dr. Johnson, while conceding that her manner both before and after this incident struck him as "perfectly natural in the circumstances", was surprised that she "shewed so little astonishment at this". Mrs. Cox, however, pointed out that Florence was by then too exhausted to appreciate the significance of what was being said—"Soon after that I persuaded her to lie down for an hour"—while Florence herself stated that she understood the exchange to refer to the laudanum or chloroform which Charles had been using, and the question of his having "deliberately taken poison to kill himself" never entered her mind.

Dr. Johnson records that he left his patient at "5.30 a.m.,

and took with me some of the vomited matter for analysis. . . .
Mr. Bell remained with the patient throughout." From that
moment Royes Bell was with his cousin day and night until at
the same hour on Friday, the 21st, he drew his eyelids down
and pulled the sheet up over his still form. No man could have
shewn greater devotion; no woman greater tenderness.

Now, there were only three ways in which the antimony
could have got into Charles Bravo's body: (a) it had been
"laid" for him; (b) he had swallowed it accidentally; (c) he
had done so deliberately.

In the first case, while he would not have known what the
poison was, with his considerable knowledge of medical jurisprudence he would have realized that he *was* poisoned and
recognized the *nature* of the poison from his symptoms. If it
were a case of (b) or (c), then the poison must have been already in his possession and he would have known both its
name and nature. He would also have known how much he
had swallowed, at what time he had done so, and how soon
afterwards it had taken effect. He had seen for himself how
copiously he had vomited; he had known before he lapsed into
unconsciousness that Mrs. Cox had given him a mustard
emetic: while, therefore, it was obvious that enough poison
had been absorbed into his system to make him very ill, he
could hope that enough had been eliminated to prevent it
proving fatal. In this connection it is significant that, while he
failed to ask a single question as to the *cause* of his illness, he
asked Royes Bell several times in the early hours of Wednesday
morning "if he was *likely to recover*".[1]

The *Lancet* called attention to another factor: "Whether
antimony was taken alone—that is to say, without any other
drug—may be questioned. There are features in the attack
which seem to point to the presence of another poison." In
fact, the laudanum, which he had admitted taking.

2

Until 3 o'clock that afternoon—Wednesday 19th—when
Mrs. Bravo arrived from St. Leonards, the atmosphere of The

[1] Evidence of Hutchinson Royes Bell.

Priory was that of any normal household of the period in which there was a case of grave illness. Until then its members entered and left the sick-room without let or hindrance. But afterwards Rowe and Keeber, neither of whom had spared themselves in the service of their master, were excluded; afterwards Amelia Bushell stood on guard like a sentry, admitting with reluctance even the wife to her dying husband's side under the basilisk stare of her mother-in-law. Before Mrs. Bravo's iron curtain clamped down upon the scene, however, two intimate glimpses are afforded us.

The first is derived partly from the evidence of Royes Bell and partly from that of Florence. As soon as Dr. Johnson was gone she went to her husband's side, and as she took his hand he said:

"What a lot of trouble I'm giving you, Florrie! Kiss me. You've been the best of wives."

"Oh, Charlie, Charlie!" she cried brokenly, "what is the matter with you? What have you taken to make you so ill?"

At that "he screamed" in an anguished voice: "Lord, have mercy upon me! Christ, have mercy upon me!" and his head rolling upon the pillow, great sobs broke from his lips.

"Oh, Royes!" he gasped, "shall I recover?"

"I hope so, Charlie, but you are very ill indeed."

Then, stated Royes Bell, the sick man "tossed from side to side" in such marked agitation that, hoping to encourage "an admission", he asked him:

"Charlie, have you anything on your mind?"

"No," came the reply; then after a pause: "I have not led a religious life." Almost immediately he added, "Draw back the curtains; open the windows—the room stinks."

His bed faced a bow window: for several moments he lay, his face set and inscrutable, staring at the pattern of branches against the pale morning sky; then he said:

"Royes, I want to make a Will."

"Is it necessary, Charlie—to make a Will?"

"I want to make a Will," he insisted.

Rowe brought writing materials. In clear tones Charles dictated: "*I give all I possess to my wife, Florence Bravo, whom*

I appoint my sole executrix." Royes Bell and Rowe witnessed his signature, and as the former departed Charles sank back on his pillows with the request:

"Royes, will you read some prayers?"

Florence, weeping, fetched a prayer book, but when Royes Bell tried to read he broke down, and Charles, the tears streaming down his own cheeks, "offered up an extempore prayer" for mercy upon himself and upon them all, then recited the Lord's Prayer, which they repeated after him. As Florence rose from her knees he asked her to kiss him.

He grew calmer now and lay with eyes closed, but he was not asleep, and when a little while later Keeber, piquant and pretty in her fresh print dress, white cap and apron, entered with broom and dusters to tidy his room, he gave her a kindly greeting.

"How are you, Mary Ann?"

"I am very well. How are you, sir?"

"Not much better."

"I'm sorry, sir."

"We shan't have our trip to Worthing, Mary Ann."

"Oh, I hope we shall, sir."

"No; my next trip will be to Streatham churchyard."

Surveying the ravaged, tear-stained faces around his bed he held out his hand to his wife and said, "What a bother I am to you all."

"Oh, don't say so, Charlie," she besought him. "You're no trouble—is he, Mary Ann?"

"Of course not!" said Keeber stoutly.

"When you bury me, Florence, make no fuss over me. Don't have plumes, or any show whatever."

"Oh, don't talk like that, Charlie! But I won't if you don't wish it."

"Give Royes my watch when I am dead."

"Yes, Charlie."

When Keeber had gone, he said to his wife, "You must marry again. But next time, not a word of the past. Royes, if I should die before my mother comes, ask her from me to be kind to Florence. She has been the best of wives to me." Then his face grew contorted once more and he cried out, "Oh, Royes! shall I linger long in such pain?"

When the two local doctors called, his condition was a little easier and his pulse less irregular. Royes Bell informed them that the patient "had not admitted to taking anything", and that he expected Dr. Johnson back with the result of the analysis at 3 p.m.

Early that morning Florence had telegraphed to the Bravos at St. Leonards and her mother at Buscot. To the latter she said:

Charlie dangerously ill. Internal inflammation. Have telegraphed his mother.

Except for that single reference to "poison" made by Dr. Johnson at 4 o'clock that morning, the word had not been uttered to any members of the household. The term "internal inflammation" was being used to describe Charles Bravo's illness, and it continued to be so used for the next twenty-four hours.

Mr. Campbell was still ill, and William replied asking whether Florence would like him, his wife, or their mother, to come. The report of the local doctors, if not reassuring, was at least slightly more hopeful, and Florence replied:

Charlie rather better. Still very ill. Will telegraph should I wish you to come.

Before the descent of Mrs. Bravo's iron curtain we have one more fleeting glimpse into the sick-room. At 1 o'clock Rowe entered to tell Royes Bell that luncheon was ready. Mrs. Cox stated that he "followed Mr. Bell from the room", but Rowe stated that he lingered to collect some things and Mrs. Cox told him he could go.

She had not been alone with Charles for a single instant since he regained consciousness, and she stated that, the moment Rowe was gone, he upbraided her for telling the doctors he had taken poison.

"Why did you tell them I had taken poison?" he demanded. "You should not have told them."

"I had to," she replied. "I couldn't let you die."

"Does Florence know I have taken poison? Don't tell her."

"What have you taken, Charlie?"

"I don't know."

"He turned away impatiently," said Mrs. Cox, and before she could say more Florence entered the room.

NOTES ON CHAPTER THREE

1. Judging from his tears and prayers Charles Bravo was neither indifferent to life nor prepared for death. No effective antidote to antimony was known, but its effects were notoriously uncertain, many cases of recovery after large doses having been recorded. He was presumably aware of this: that he "made no admission" indicates he hoped for the best; that he made his Will shews he was preparing for the worst.

2. Why did Mrs. Cox send for medical aid only after Charles became unconscious, and omit to arouse his wife? Was she acting on orders from Charles?

3. Did Mrs. Cox delay to tell the doctors that he had said he had taken poison also because of his orders? And did she finally do so when it became apparent that he himself intended making "no admission" and she realized that, if he died, she might be suspected of having caused his death?

4. If the poison were not self-administered, Charles would surely have shewn suspicion towards someone and demanded an investigation. As the *Daily News* was to say: "The curious demeanour of the dying man . . . was so strange as almost to baffle even conjecture."

CHAPTER FOUR

WEDNESDAY, 19TH: NOON–THURSDAY, 20TH: 5 P.M.

I

A GLANCE at the plan of The Priory will shew the strain put upon the accommodation there when a telegram was received from St. Leonards to say that Mr. and Mrs. Bravo, Alice Turner, Ann Bell and Amelia Bushell would all be arriving at 3 p.m. Charles' dressing-room had been given up to the doctors' use, so Florence had the only spare room got ready for Ann Bell and Alice Turner, while she herself moved into her dressing-room and gave up her bedroom to Mr. and Mrs. Bravo. Should it be necessary to send for Mrs. Campbell too, she would have to give up the dressing-room to her and join Mrs. Cox on the floor above.

As soon as she set foot in the house Mrs. Bravo told her daughter-in-law in tones that admitted of no argument: "I have always nursed Charlie in his ailments. I should like to do so now. Amelia will help me." Her meaning was clear: she would take absolute control of the sick-room, giving place only to the physicians. Mr. Bravo appears to have seen his stepson only occasionally and to have had but the briefest of exchanges with him.

Ann Bell said in her evidence:

"Mr. and Mrs. Bravo took me into the sick-room. . . . My cousin asked me to kiss him. . . . He said to his sister, 'Alice, kiss me.' I interpreted it to her and she kissed him. I remained in the room a little while assisting my aunt, and then walked round the garden and into the conservatory with Mrs. Charles Bravo. . . . I conversed with her, and she never suggested that Mr. Bravo was jealous . . . or had any cause why he should commit suicide. She spoke of him very affectionately. She said nothing accounting for his illness. . . ."

Amelia Bushell stated that she was the wife of the Bravos'
butler and had been "confidential maid" to Mrs. Bravo for
fifteen years. Mr. Charles Bravo had recognized her, but did
not speak to her, when she first entered the room. His mind
was perfectly coherent. "I was with him from Wednesday
afternoon until he died excepting the times I left to get my
meals. He never in the slightest way said anything to me, or in
my hearing, accounting for his illness. . . . Mrs. Bravo, senior,
asked that she and myself should be allowed to take charge of
the patient. I do not know if Mrs. Charles Bravo made any
demur. She seemed pale and weak and could not sustain stop-
ping up all night. She appeared very distressed. . . . She came
to me—she was crying—and said: 'What a dreadful thing.
Amelia! The only way I can account for the illness is that Mr.
Charles took lunch at the St. James Hall and had something
cooked in a coppery pan which has disagreed with him.' . . .
Mr. Charles Bravo and Mr. Royes Bell were on most intimate
terms—like brothers. I am not aware of any reason why Mr.
Charles Bravo should not have frankly communicated anything to Mr. Royes Bell."

At 3.30 p.m. Dr. Johnson arrived and informed Royes Bell
and the local doctors that as "his impression had been that the
patient's symptoms had been caused by arsenic" he had had an
analysis made specifically to detect arsenic, but as this had
given a negative result he intended to take away further samples of ejected matter for a general analysis. The *Lancet* was
subsequently to comment:

> "It is impossible to disguise that a grave omission was
> made in not at once applying the proper chemical tests to
> the matter vomited and passed from the intestines. Had
> anyone been in a position to say pointedly to this poor man,
> who was conscious after his recovery from the first collapse
> up to within a very short period of his death, 'You have taken
> antimony', the truth might have been ascertained."

But even the fresh samples which Dr. Johnson now took
away did not include the matter lying on the leads, though as
he afterwards stated: "I saw it there . . . a mass of masticated,

undigested food. Anyone looking out could not have failed to see it there."

2

Nothing that the medical men were doing or thinking was communicated to the family, who were still allowed to retain the impression that the patient was suffering from "internal inflammation". But as a tiny escape of gas in one room will gradually percolate through a whole building with so faint an odour that its occupants absorb it unconsciously for some time before realizing what it is, so the notion of poison seeped gradually into the consciousness of the occupants of The Priory before it was formulated in an actual fear. It remained unexpressed for another twenty-four hours, but during that Wednesday night, as the patient's condition worsened, though the word still remained unuttered, the notion could no longer be subdued.

By dawn of Thursday, the 20th, all knew that death was approaching, and must soon overtake, Charles Bravo. Mrs. Cox had never once relaxed her vigilance: she had not even taken off the clothes she had put on to go to Worthing on the morning of Tuesday, the 18th; but though her complexion had taken on a yellower tinge and the dusky flesh about her eyes became duskier still, the eyes themselves behind her spectacles were sharp and wary. The house overflowed with Charles' kith and kin who, with family solidarity, supported each other in their anxiety and grief; but Florence had no one to turn to in hers but "Janie". First thing that morning she sent off a final telegram to her mother:

If you want to see my Charlie alive come at once, I fear the worst.

She then tried one last desperate resort.

Mrs. Cox was to claim that when before breakfast she hurried down the drive to knock upon the door of Orwell Lodge "like an ordinary visitor", it was with the object of procuring for Charles a homoeopathic "treatment" from "the cleverest doctor in the world". This was true, for the "treatment" was procured; but subsequent events suggested that Mrs. Cox also confided to Dr. Gully what Charles had told her, and his refusal to admit it to anyone else, for on her return Florence immediately took such skilful steps to evade, though not to flout, medical etiquette in order to bring to Charles' bedside the one man in all England who might be able to wring an admission from him as to prompt the belief that her action was inspired by a professional mind.

Taking pen and paper she carefully composed the following letter to a man she had only seen once before in her life, though he was the friend, and, from time to time, the medical adviser, of her father.

"The Priory, Balham,
"April 20th.

"Dear Sir,

"My husband is dangerously ill. Could you come as soon as possible to see him? My father, Mr. Campbell, will be so grateful if you can come at once. I need not tell you how grateful I should be to you.

"Yours truly,
"Florence Bravo."

She addressed the envelope: "Sir William Gull, Bart., 74 Brook Street, London." She did not seal it, but awaited Dr. Johnson's arrival at 9 a.m. When he had gone, looking perturbed and grave, she went upstairs to Royes Bell, then returned and added a postscript to her letter:

"Dr. Johnson is coming in the course of the afternoon. Mr. Royes Bell of King's College Hospital is with his cousin, Mr. Bravo, and acquiesces in my wish for you to come."

Within a few minutes Mrs. Cox was setting out for London in the phaeton with the cobs "which went so quickly" to deliver the letter.

At 2 p.m. Dr. Johnson returned, bringing Mr. Henry Smith with him, and upon learning that Florence had in his absence, though with Royes Bell's consent, sent for Sir William Gull, so far from shewing resentment he welcomed her initiative and set out for London almost at once to get in touch with Sir William and bring him to The Priory.

Including Mr. Henry Smith, Sir William Gull was to make the sixth doctor summoned to the case. *The Dictionary of National Biography* describes him as "a mystic" whose "sense of the mystery of the universe was deep", and says that he "possessed singular powers of penetration", exercising "a sort of fascination over his patients" by means of which he extracted from them all he wished to know; that he "loathed cant and humbug", and though "self-assertive and inclined to be sarcastic was generous and kind-hearted". He had established his reputation as the foremost diagnostician of the day in 1871 when he was instrumental in saving the life of the Prince of Wales by diagnosing typhoid after the symptoms had baffled the Court physicians. He had then been rewarded with a baronetcy.[1]

Surely this great man, with his mystical powers of penetration, his magnetic influence upon his patients, could not fail to extract from a man lying prostrate and upon the verge of death any secret that lay upon his mind?

Mrs. Campbell and William reached Balham station at 4.30 where Mrs. Cox met them with the news that "there was no hope for Charlie".

". . . I asked my daughter," said Mrs. Campbell in evidence, "what could have made him ill, and she said she thought the food at his luncheon might have been cooked in a copper vessel . . . I knew he had lunched at St. James Hall with Mr. Orr. . . . My daughter appeared very much distressed, especially out of his room. She did not desire to distress him and appeared composed before him, but out of the room, when she was with me, she was deeply distressed. I saw her kiss him several times and he returned her affection."

She saw Charles altogether five or six times. When she first entered his room he held out his hand in welcome and asked her to kiss him, saying: "You have been very kind to

[1] He also diagnosed as cancer the cause of Lady Beaconsfield's continued ill-health. He was appointed Physician-in-Ordinary in 1887; he died in 1890, aged 74, leaving estate worth £334,000 besides landed property.

me." Then turning to his mother he said: "Mother, will you be kind to Florence?"

"I am never unkind to anyone," Mrs. Bravo replied. "I assure you I will be kind to her."

With his icy hand between her own, Mrs. Campbell had spoken to him with the maternal solicitude she would have shewn to one of her own sons.

"Wouldn't you like to see a clergyman, Charlie? Won't you see Mr. Nicholas, the rector?"

Tears rushed into his eyes. "No," he said; then, with sobs choking his voice, he prayed fervently for mercy, and all knelt as he recited the Lord's Prayer.

CHAPTER FIVE

THURSDAY, 20TH: 6 P.M.–FRIDAY, 21ST: 6 A.M.

I

DR. JOHNSON, a man of middle age who had attained some eminence in his profession, was strictly orthodox in his outlook and methods, and therefore the antithesis of Sir William Gull. The former, for instance, had refrained from telling his patient, "*You are poisoned*," because he lacked actual proof of it; or, "*You are dying*," because that was contrary to the ethics of his profession. But the latter had no hesitation in telling him bluntly both these truths. "On my own responsibility and without previous consultation," he informed the Court, "I told Mr. Bravo he was a dying man."

While Dr. Johnson declared that on the way down to Balham he had given Sir William a history of the case and told him of Mrs. Cox's allegation that Charles had told her he had taken poison, Sir William contended that, having been summoned by the patient's wife, he had entered the sick-room in the expectation of finding a case of disease and that after he had emerged from it Mrs. Cox had herself spoken of her allegation: which caused Dr. Johnson sarcastically to observe that Sir William evidently paid more heed to a lady's note than to the report of the physician in charge of the case. But what probably injured his *amour-propre* still more was the fact that it was by Sir William's orders that the vomit on the leads was at last gathered up and despatched in sealed jars to Professor Redwood, who not only obtained from it the poison taken, but was able to estimate the quantity involved.

These two eminent physicians had reached The Priory at 6.30 p.m. and gone straight up to the sick-room, which was cleared of everyone except Royes Bell. Sir William went straight to the bedside where, with characteristic detachment and concentration, he fixed his penetrating gaze upon the man lying before him; then he made a swift examination of the abdomen.

"This is not disease. You are poisoned," he told Charles outright. "Pray tell us how you came by it."

He was, he told the Court, surprised that the patient shewed no astonishment at this. "If I were to tell a man he was dying of poison and he shewed no surprise, it would induce me to think that he knew of it. He was in full possession of his faculties." It has been argued that Charles shewed no surprise because he had already been told of it; but according to the evidence he had been asked "what was the meaning" of Mrs. Cox's allegation; *if* he had taken poison, and *what* he had taken: but had never been told categorically, "*You are poisoned.*"

Continuing his evidence, Sir William asserted that Charles replied:

"I took it myself."

"What did you take?"

"I rubbed my gums with laudanum and I swallowed some."

"You have taken much more than that. This isn't opium poisoning. If you tell us what it was, it might help us to find an antidote." Sir William checked himself. "No," he said solemnly, "that would not be quite fair, as I fear no antidote would do you any good. It is not for me to press a dying man."

And now Dr. Johnson uttered a solemn warning.

"If you do not tell us more than we know at present, some-one may be accused of being the cause of your death."

"I am aware of that," Charles said, "but I can tell you nothing more."

"Where was he sick?" Sir William asked, and the spot being pointed out to him, he looked down upon the matter lying there. "Let that be collected with a clean silver spoon and sealed in a jar."

The doctors had scarcely gone downstairs when Charles called out wildly:

"I want to see Dr. Gull! I want to see Dr. Gull!"

Ann Bell sped downstairs. "Charlie wants to speak to Sir William Gull," she said and, following them back to the bedroom, held the pillows to support Charles who was struggling to sit up.

"Am I dying?" he asked Sir William desperately.

"You are very ill and in all probability you have not very many hours to live, but of course as long as there is life there is hope." Then Sir William earnestly adjured him. *"Pray say what other poison was mixed with the laudanum.* You must consider the gravity of your situation."

"I know that. I took it myself."

"What did you take?"

"Before God it was only laudanum. Is there really no hope for me?" he asked again, as though unable to accept his fate. Sir William felt his pulse and heart. "There is very little life left in you. In fact you are heart-dead[1] now."

"Give me something to ease me," begged Charles, and burst once more into tears and prayers. Mrs. Campbell stated, "He repeated the Lord's Prayer after denying that he had taken anything but laudanum, and prayed very earnestly." Amelia Bushell confirmed this, saying: "Immediately after saying 'Before God I have taken nothing but laudanum', he commenced 'Our Father' and asked us all to repeat it after him, which we did."

The whole family now assembled downstairs and Sir William Gull, in the presence of the other doctors, informed them that Charles Bravo was dying of an irritant poison. As he left he handed Florence that "something to ease" him for which he had asked and told her gently that her husband could not live through the night.

After he had gone she turned to the other doctors and said: "Now that you have all given him up I, as his wife, will have my way. I have been recommended to try a treatment: small and frequent doses of *arsenicum*, mustard plasters on the spine and cold compresses on the stomach."

"That is a homoeopathic remedy," Dr. Johnson protested, "but nobody who saw your husband would imagine that he

---

[1] "Heart-dead" was the expression used as reported in *The Times*. Other organs of the Press gave it as "half-dead" and this has been commonly repeated since. "Heart-dead" seems the more probable phrase.

who wished to do so might enter, and that dining-room, where Mr. McCalmont had so recently enjoyed hospitality, transformed into a Coroner's Court.

The jury, led by Mr. Carter, filed upstairs to the flower-filled room, where the mortal remains of Charles Bravo lay in a coffin lined with white satin, with white lilies between his folded hands. Then downstairs they came and solemnly took their places around the dining-table, while Mr. Carter, seated in that chair at the head of the table which Charles had formerly occupied, picked up a pen and wrote the following preamble:

"Information of witnesses taken on oath at the house called The Priory, in the parish of Streatham, in the county of Surrey, on the 25th day of April 1876 before me, William Carter, one of her Majesty's Coroners for the said county, on view of the body of Charles Delaunay Turner Bravo then and there lying dead."

Having delivered himself of this, Mr. Carter's official zeal seems to have evaporated, for his record of the proceedings was so slipshod and incomplete that later on the higher authorities were compelled to amplify it from Mr. Reid's scribbled notes.

Mr. Joseph Bravo, the first witness called, stated that he had been summoned to The Priory by telegram on Wednesday, 19th April. His stepson had been conscious and had not complained to him of pain. Witness had seen all "the medical gentlemen" in attendance.

Mrs. Cox, the next witness, said that she had been called to deceased's bedroom by the servant and had found him standing by the window looking very ill. "He said as soon as I went to him that he had taken poison. I asked him how he had come to do such a thing, but he made no reply." Witness had seen the bottles labelled *Laudanum* and *Chloroform* on his mantelpiece: he had been using their contents for neuralgia and only a few drops remained in each bottle. She had not told Dr. Harrison what deceased had said. "I saw deceased continually until he expired, but he did not explain to me, or in my hearing, how he came to take poison. He was a person of good mind. He and his wife lived on good and affectionate terms.

He had no reason to commit suicide. Why he should have taken poison I cannot give an opinion."

Mr. Reid's notes contain the following amplifications of Mrs. Cox's evidence: "*He said to me, 'I have taken poison; don't tell Florence.' That was all he said. . . . He did not say which bottle; he merely said 'poison'. Most probably he took it medicinally. . . . He asked me afterwards why I had told.*"

Amelia Bushell stated that she had been in attendance upon deceased from the time of her arrival at The Priory until his death. He was conscious to the last, and appeared in great pain and was very sick. "He did not at any time account for his condition to me or to anyone in my hearing." She could not say what had caused his state, and "nothing in writing had been found to account for it".

Dr. George Harrison stated that he had found Dr. Moore with the patient when he had reached The Priory. The patient was in a complete state of collapse, almost pulseless, the pupils of the eyes widely dilated, his limbs flaccid, the muscles of his body inactive, and he was unable to swallow. "I did not detect the effluvia of chloroform or laudanum emanating from his breathing, only that of mustard, understanding that this had been given him as an emetic and that he had vomited. . . . He was treated for collapse. . . . The first symptoms were those attendant upon chloroform which is a poison. He vomited blood before becoming conscious and also passed blood from the rectum which gave rise to the idea that he was labouring under an acid poison."

Mr. Reid's notes included these additional statements: "*The symptoms were more like arsenic than anything, but I could form no opinion as to what it was. I had not been informed that he had admitted to any ingredient. We all repeatedly asked him. He denied having taken anything. His mouth was not excoriated.*"

At this stage the inquest was adjourned until Friday, 28th April, to enable Professor Redwood to complete his analysis.

There are two points in Mrs. Cox's evidence which should be noted. Firstly, she quoted Charles as saying to her, "I have taken poison; don't tell Florence"—a form in which other witnesses were to state she had repeated it to them. Dr. Johnson alone records—and on this point he was emphatic—that the phrase she used to him was: "I have taken *some of that poison;* don't tell Florence." Secondly, one should remember her observation: "Most probably he took it medicinally."

3

The funeral having been fixed for Saturday, the 29th, Mrs. Cox was sent to Brighton on Thursday, the 27th, to find a house where Florence could afterwards recuperate. Having taken 38 Brunswick Terrace—in that lovely row of Regency houses overlooking the sea which has so far escaped the attention of vandals both at home and from abroad—she called upon Dr. Dill and, since no mention of the inquest had appeared in the Press, told him the whole story of Charles' fatal illness, including her allegation that the sick man had admitted to her he had taken poison and besought her not to tell his wife.

CHAPTER SEVEN

THE RESUMED INQUEST: FRIDAY, 28TH APRIL

I

WHEN the inquest was resumed Mr. McCalmont was accompanied not only by Mr. Reid—whose notes were once more to supplement the cursory jottings of the Coroner—but also by Mr. Carlyle Willoughby, who was soon to take the initial step in calling the attention of Scotland Yard to the mysterious death of Charles Bravo.

Mary Ann Keeber deposed that she had been in Mrs. Ricardo's employment for two years before her marriage to the deceased; Mr. and Mrs. Bravo had gone to London on the morning of Tuesday, the 18th, and Mrs. Bravo had returned for luncheon. That night, after deceased had gone to his bedroom, witness had heard him calling for his wife. "I heard him call 'Florence'! and say 'Hot water! Hot water!' as loud as he could from his bedroom door. He was in his night-shirt. Mrs. Cox was then in Mrs. Bravo's room." Mr. and Mrs. Bravo usually occupied the same room, but had not done so since her illness nine days previously. "In general they lived together very happily." Witness described how she had been sent for the hot water and how, on returning, she had found deceased seated on the floor. "Mr. Bravo did not speak a word; I obtained some mustard and Mrs. Cox mixed some in hot water in my presence and it was administered to him, but he could only swallow very little. . . . At no time did he speak as to his illness; he did not make use of the word 'poison' in my hearing, nor was it made use of by Mrs. Cox on Tuesday night."

Mr. Reid's notes add the following: "*Mrs. Cox said, 'Give him mustard and hot water'* . . . *Mr. Bravo did not call me, but called 'Florence' twice.*"

Dr. Harrison, recalled, stated: "I was not told that deceased had said he had taken *poison*; Mrs. Cox said she was sure he had taken *chloroform*."

Dr. Joseph Frank Payne stated that he carried out the *post-mortem* in the presence of the four medical men in attendance. "The following is the result of the same—*Body*: perfectly well-nourished, no external wound or bruise; *Head*: brain membranes quite natural; *Chest*: pleura containing blood-stained fluid arising after death; *Heart*: natural, blood unusually fluid; *Mouth, oesophagus and stomach* shewed no marked change, except in the large intestines: these contained blood and were generally congested, especially at the upper part, which was ulcerated, the ulcers being small and shewing signs of haemorrhage; *Liver, spleen and kidneys*: fairly natural. No change in any other part of the body. I took away the contents of the stomach and intestines. That I sealed in the room in the presence of Mr. Royes Bell and Dr. Moore. Also I took away part of the intestines and some portions of the heart in a sealed jar. I took them to Professor Redwood's laboratory together, to make my analysis of the contents of the intestines, also sealed up. I did not find any disease of the body or head as accounting for death. The *post-mortem* was held at the request of the family, who also got the analysis made."

Mr. Reid's notes contain the sentence: "*There was no attempt on the part of the family at anything like secrecy, from what I saw it was quite the contrary.*"

Hutchinson Royes Bell, F.R.C.S., said that the deceased was his cousin. When he arrived at The Priory deceased was insensible. On recovering consciousness "he said in answer to Dr. Johnson that he had taken laudanum for neuralgia. Dr. Johnson said: 'That won't do; it doesn't explain your symptoms.' He then said: 'If it wasn't laudanum, I don't know what it was.' He did not make any further admission of having taken anything. . . . I was present when Sir William Gull asked him if he had taken anything and he repeated the same thing."

Professor Theophilus Redwood: "I am a professor of Chemistry to the Pharmaceutical Society of Great Britain, and have been an analytic chemist for the past 30 years. I received a bottle containing about 20 ounces of semi-solid matter that had been vomited and which consisted of masticated but undigested—principally animal—food. I submitted the whole of these to analysis and I detected antimony in the vomited food. Emetic tartar, a salt of antimony, soluble in water and tasteless—comparatively—may have been taken. Upon analysis and evidence my opinion is that death arose from the taking of antimony into the body in a sufficient quantity to cause death."

Mr. Reid's notes supply the following supplementary information: "*In small quantities antimony has been used as a slow poison in many cases. There is one form alone in which it could have been administered, and that is emetic tartar. . . . I apprehend that that is the only form in which it could have been taken. We have not many well-authenticated cases of poisoning by antimony in large doses, but symptoms are recorded similar. The symptoms might be like chloroform. The effect of antimony is to produce prostration; the first effect is to produce vomiting. I got as much antimony from the vomited food as would make ten grains of tartar emetic.*"[1]

The Coroner's notes here record: "After Professor Redwood had given his evidence it was suggested by Mr. Bravo, sen., whether the antimony might not have been in the food partaken at dinner. Mrs. Cox was recalled, and, in answer to the Court, said it consisted of fish, roast leg of mutton, spinach, and eggs and anchovy toast; that she and Mrs. Bravo partook of this diet, but neither she nor Mrs. Bravo became unwell. Mr. Bravo then said he was satisfied with this explanation."

Mr. Reid's notes: "*The Coroner was here proceeding to sum up the evidence to the jury when it was pointed out to him that there was no evidence before him as to the deceased's state of mind on the day of the seizure, and the next witness, Mr. Frederick Hayes McCalmont, volunteered evidence upon that head.*"

Frederick Hayes McCalmont: "I am a barrister-at-law and reside at Clement's Inn, and occupied, conjointly, Chambers with the deceased gentleman. I did not hear of his death until Friday morning, coming here to inquire as to the state of his health having heard he was dangerously ill. I had seen him on

[1] One ounce of tartar emetic is equivalent to about 150 grains.

the afternoon of the previous Tuesday. I met him in Piccadilly, accidentally, walking with a gentleman. I walked with them as far as the bottom of St. James Street, and thence with him only to Victoria railway station. I was with him half-an-hour. He was in his usual health and spirits, and made an engagement for me to come here on the following morning and spend the day. He had nothing in his hand that I am aware of. I had met him and his wife. He was a person not, in my opinion, likely to commit suicide—a most unlikely person."

As Mr. McCalmont returned to his seat Dr. Johnson rose and, announcing his identity, said he would like to add his evidence to that of the other medical witnesses; but Mr. Carter informed him that the Court already had all the medical evidence it required. He was again beginning to sum up when a juryman asked that the dead man's widow should be called, to which Mr. Carter replied that he thought her feelings ought to be spared.

Neither the Coroner himself nor Mr. Reid seems to have made any notes of the former's summing-up, but at a later date Mr. Reid informed the Authorities that the following was the substance of Mr. Carter's remarks: "*They*" (the jury) "*would have to say whether the poison spoken of by the medical men was taken by Mr. Bravo himself, or administered to him, or taken by accident. If they believed Mrs. Cox, he had taken the poison himself—and the word employed by the deceased was 'taken'. If that were so, it was a case of* felo de se, *unless he was insane, of which there was no evidence.*"

Mr. Carter's notes end abruptly thus:

"*Verdict:* That the deceased died from the effects of a poison—antimony—but we have not sufficient evidence[1] under what circumstances it came into his body."

2

On the evidence before them the jury could have brought in no other verdict, for there was nothing to support, and no one to corroborate, Mrs. Cox's allegation. Had Sir William Gull been called and made the statement which he did at the

[1] The words "to shew" evidently omitted.

second inquest, expressing the conviction that Charles had taken the poison himself, this, combined with the weight of his reputation, would probably have been decisive. But he was not called because neither the Campbells, nor the Coroner himself, imagined for an instant that the verdict could be anything other than *felo de se*. But even if Sir William had failed to convince the jury, and even supposing a verdict of "Wilful Murder against some person or persons" had been returned, it would have remained for the police to find a suspect and bring a charge; in which, as events were to prove, they would have failed, and interest in the case would have died down. It was Mr. Carter's incompetence; it was what the *Daily Telegraph* was to describe as "the secret and unsatisfactory" manner in which he had conducted the inquest, which was to give the case a blaze of publicity. It was the ill-feeling already existing between the Bravos and the Campbells, occasioned originally by Mrs. Bravo absenting herself from the wedding, which worked upon the mind of Joseph Bravo until the suspicion inherent in his dark blood turned venomous.

The first signs occurred immediately after the verdict while he was awaiting his carriage to return to London. Mr. Campbell observed that he had never heard of antimony in his life, to which Mr. Bravo replied that it was commonly used by grooms to "condition" horses and could be found in most stables. William Campbell then said that the coachman had assured him there was none in The Priory stables, which Mr. Bravo evidently took to imply that the fatal dose had come from the stables at Palace Green, for he retorted with sweeping acrimony:

"There are poisons in every room in this house!"[1]

The Campbells gave no further thought to the incident, but Joseph Bravo went home to nurse his anger in company with his grief-demented wife.

---

[1] "He called all homoeopathic medicines 'poisons'."—Mrs. Cox in evidence.

CHAPTER EIGHT

AFTERMATH: SATURDAY, 29TH APRIL—MONDAY, 3RD MAY

I

WHEN the mourners gathered at The Priory on the afternoon of Saturday, 29th April, the Campbell family could scarcely have failed to notice that Mr. Carlyle Willoughby ostentatiously refrained from entering the house, but waited outside the door to join the funeral cortège. He had known Charles for some four years and, as he was to tell the Court, having seen his friend's body lowered into the grave at Lower Norwood cemetery, he made up his mind to report to Scotland Yard first thing on Monday morning "several circumstances which were worrying me in connection with my friend's death."

On that Saturday, too, Joseph Bravo, returning from the obsequies with Mr. Henry Smith, repeated his observation that there were "poisons in every room" at The Priory and shewed his companion those high-spirited letters which Charles had written his mother up to within twenty-four hours of swallowing the fatal dose. He went on to say that Florence's extravagance had been a source of anxiety to Charles, who had been doing his utmost to curb it, and on this account wished to be relieved of the expense of Mrs. Cox who "was costing the establishment £300 a year". He described how he himself had tried to persuade her to return to Jamaica in her own interests—"all in vain". Mr. Henry Smith suggested that, if any suspicions were troubling his mind, he would do well to impart them to Scotland Yard.

So on Monday, 1st May, not only did Mr. Carlyle Willoughby visit the Yard and unburden his mind, but Mr. Bravo, having first called at Ely Place to consult and retain the services of Mr. George Lewis,[1] whose reputation as a criminal

[1] Afterwards Sir George Lewis.

MR. ROYES BELL
DR. MOORE

DR. GEORGE JOHNSON
MR. GEORGE HARRISON

The four medical men summoned on the 'fatal Tuesday'

MRS. ROBERT
CAMPBELL
The wife of the
County Magnate

JOSEPH BRAVO
The City Merchant
of Jamaican origin

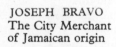

lawyer was largely to be established by this case, also made his way there and, not content with voicing his suspicions, hired—as could be done in those days—the services of Inspector Clarke to pursue all possible lines of investigation and try to trace the sale of antimony to some member of The Priory household.

Meanwhile, in the neighbourhood of Balham the verdict instantly set tongues wagging, and over the same weekend in that popular resort the Bedford Hotel, next the railway station, Mr. Carter was severely criticized for refusing to call the widow and to hear Dr. Johnson's evidence, while his failure to notify the Press of the proceedings served successfully to stimulate the gossip. Over the pint-pots the attachment between "the old doctor" and the former Mrs. Ricardo was recalled; and it was remembered that up to within a few days of the fatal Tuesday he and Mrs. Cox had been seen meeting at the station and travelling up to London together. Someone reminded the company that Griffith, who had been employed for years by Dr. Gully and then by Mrs. Ricardo, had made no secret of the fact that he conditioned his horses with "white antimony" and had been discharged, only a week before the wedding, at the instigation of Mr. Bravo himself; then, with the effect of a match tossed into tinder, somebody else recalled how on the very morning of the wedding and in that very bar—as Mr. Stringer, the landlord, could confirm—Griffith had predicted that "Mr. Bravo would not live four months"!

All this and more besides was available to the ears of Inspector Clarke when, in search of both information and refreshment, he dropped into the Bedford Hotel; and as a whirlwind gathers momentum in one place and passes on to another, so the gossip in Balham was carried to London, there meeting and mingling with the suspicions being voiced by the Bravos and the dead man's friends.

The wider public was to remain in ignorance of the "tragedy at Balham" for another ten days yet.

2

On Monday, 1st May, while the machinery of the law was being set in motion, Mrs. Tom Campbell drove over from

Kingston to spend the day at Balham and comfort her niece
and sister-in-law. She found them in Florence's bedroom,
where packing for the departure to Brighton was going on and
Mrs. Cox was busily trotting in and out with various things to
be included. Presently she appeared with Dr. Gully's bottle of
laurel-water bearing its crimson *Poison* label.

"Shall I include this?" she asked.

"No," said Florence. "You needn't keep it; you can throw
it away—perhaps they'll say that, too, is a poison!"

Mrs. Cox having borne it away, Mrs. Campbell asked what
the bottle contained. Florence explained that when she had
been sleeping badly after her miscarriage, Dr. Gully had sent
it to her through Mrs. Cox; but by then the sitz baths and
compresses which he had recommended through the same
agency had given her so much relief that she had no need of
it. The two ladies asked her if she had known Mrs. Cox was
meeting Dr. Gully: she replied that the first she had heard of it
was when Mrs. Cox had told her about the treatment for her
back. They expressed surprise at, and disapproval of, these
clandestine meetings, and Mrs. Tom Campbell—inspired, no
doubt, by Joseph Bravo's remark—suggested that she took the
bottle away with her. Florence went up to Mrs. Cox's room.

"I have been talking to Mamma and Auntie about Dr.
Gully ordering me the sitz baths and spinal washes, and sending me the little bottle to make me sleep. Auntie will throw it
away."

"She needn't trouble to do that; I'll see to it."

The matter was still on Mrs. Tom Campbell's mind, and as
she was making ready to go home she said to Mrs. Cox:

"Can I take the bottle?"

"Oh no, you needn't trouble; I'll throw it away."

"I did not do so then," said Mrs. Cox in evidence, "but next
day, or the one after, I threw the medicine away. I thought the
bottle a useful little one, so I emptied away the contents,
keeping the bottle for vinegar. . . . The white leather was over
the top as I had received it. The bottle was full at the time I
emptied it."

This episode led Mrs. Campbell to reflect that if Mrs. Cox

was capable of such indiscretion as to meet Dr. Gully and discuss Florence's intimate affairs with him, she might be guilty of worse breaches of confidence nearer home. She believed in the truth of her assertion that Charles had told her he had taken poison, for otherwise she would hardly have dosed him with mustard and water. But why, after first calling for his wife, should he "beseech" Mrs. Cox—in her own words— "not to tell Florence"?

Many of her late son-in-law's actions had gone against the grain with Mrs. Campbell: his persistence in hurrying on the marriage and his insistence on concealing Florence's "attachment" from his mother; the fact that, though he himself had brought only £100 to the marriage, he had harassed her to curtail the expenditure of her own income. She recalled certain things he had said to her at Buscot, certain phrases in his letters, and the more she thought upon the problem the more convinced she became that Mrs. Cox, and Mrs. Cox only, held the key to the mystery of his death.

Next day, with the arrival of William to see his sister off to Brighton and to escort her back to Buscot, Mrs. Campbell's anxiety gave place to dismay: Mr. Bravo, he informed her, "had had the detectives put on". That could only mean one thing: he believed his stepson had been *murdered*.

CHAPTER NINE

BRIGHTON: 3RD–8TH MAY

MRS. CAMPBELL, while she thought it right to pass this information on to Mrs. Cox, particularly asked her not to mention it to Florence, for although the latter's weakness and nausea had greatly diminished, the strain through which she had passed had taken severe toll of her nerves.

Except for Dr. Johnson's chance observation on the night of 18th April it would seem that Mrs. Cox's allegation that Charles had admitted taking poison had never been communicated to Florence. Now, as the train carried the two women through the smiling Sussex landscape Mrs. Cox was to assert—and Florence to deny—that she told her of it, but with a startling addition which was to colour and affect all the subsequent proceedings.

"I told her that when I went to Charlie he said to me: 'I have taken poison *for Gully*; don't tell Florence.' "

Whether those words were spoken in that railway carriage, or two days later as Florence alleged, is of no great moment, but it is of immense significance that Mrs. Cox, as soon as she had been warned that Joseph Bravo "had had the detectives put on", should have added two words to her original statement which supplied what had hitherto been conspicuously lacking—*a motive for suicide*.

When questioned later on as to why she had withheld them from her evidence she replied that she had done so to spare Florence's reputation and to avoid "scandal". This may have been so—and may also have been the reason why she withheld them from the Campbells, who did not realize that Florence's relations with Dr. Gully had been immoral. Her further claim that she included them in the account of Charles' illness which she gave to Dr. Dill on Thursday, the 26th, was never substantiated as he did not appear as a witness.

It was to prove most unfortunate that Mrs. Cox, who had

hitherto remembered her promise not to tell Florence that Mr.
Bravo "had had the detectives put on", should, on 5th May,
have forgotten it. On that day Florence had a letter from
Mr. Brookes informing her—no doubt with the usual professional circumlocution—that Mr. Bravo had, in the presence
of himself and another witness, sealed up all Charles' effects in
his Chambers at the Temple. Florence took this to mean that
Mr. Bravo had improperly interfered with Charles' property
and proceeded to write him the first of two letters which not
only quenched any spark of compassion for her which might
have been lingering in his heart, but when read out in Court
gave the impression of a woman so obsessed with cupidity that,
less than a fortnight after her husband's death, her sole concern was to lay her hands upon even the most paltry of his
possessions.

"38 Brunswick Terrace,
"Brighton,
"May 5th, 1876.

"My dear Father Joseph,

"I am astonished to hear from my solicitor, Mr. Brookes,
that you have had dear Charlie's drawers sealed, as, legally,
nobody but myself has the power to touch one single thing
belonging to him, he having left all he possessed to me, and
I must ask you to see that nothing he possessed is touched
by anyone.

"With regard to what he died possessed of I must leave to
you: he told me he had £200 a year of his own coming
from investments, and of course his books, pictures and
private property at Palace Green are now mine. His
watch he left at your house, and by his wish I give it to Mr.
Royes Bell. Please see that it is delivered to him.

"My father will take care that I have all my dear husband
left me. Poor fellow! How he would have grieved at all this
unkind feeling shewn me.

"Hoping you and Mrs. Bravo are better,
"Believe me,
"Yours sincerely,
"Florence Bravo.

"P.S.—Poor Charlie told me you had promised to allow him £800 a year."

To make matters worse this letter was next day followed up with another one, equally ill-judged. Charles, on his death-bed, had asked her "to do something for the child—Katie", but had said nothing of the £500 he owed his mistress' sister. By the first post on 6th May Florence had a letter from Royes Bell to the effect that Charles' ex-mistress had written to him requesting maintenance for the child and the repayment of her sister's £500.[1] Florence immediately jumped to the conclusion that Charles had been driven to borrowing this money by Joseph Bravo's parsimony and that the woman had been dunning him for it.

"May 6th.

"Dear Father Joseph,

"A letter received this morning from Royes Bell fully confirms my suspicions as to poor Charlie's committing suicide. Hence his motives for reducing our expenditure, as he could not tell me how hard he had been pressed by that dreadful woman. I wish he had, poor fellow, for I should not have been hard upon him: but it is a sad reflection on his memory for me, and I intend to sift this matter. We have Sir W. Gull's evidence, and I shall not allow the living to be under any imputation such as is cast upon them by such a wicked verdict.

"I leave it all in my father's hands and shall abide by his decision.

"Yours sincerely,
"Florence Bravo."

Two days later a full realization of the misunderstanding upon which she had acted with such impetuosity was brought home to her, firstly through a letter from Mr. Brookes explaining that the sealing of Charles' effects at the Temple had been carried out in accordance with legal requirements by Mr. Bravo in the presence of himself and another witness; and secondly

[1] Royes Bell had apparently already shewn this letter to Mr. Bravo.

through what must have been an icy rejoinder from Joseph Bravo. Instantly she responded with what was an appeal as well as an apology: but it was now too late; from now on Joseph Bravo would give her no quarter. The stage was set for a bitter family feud.

"May 8th, 1876.

"My dear Father Joseph,

"The letter I wrote you on Friday was written under the impression that you had forced dear Charlie's drawers at the Temple, and I regret being so impressed, as ever since I knew you I have only experienced kindness and consideration. Please try to think of me as your loving daughter and do not address me as 'Mrs. Florence Bravo'; it pains me more than I can tell you, and it is only in legal documents that I must be so addressed. I hope you are all recovering from this dreadful and sad last fortnight. My life is a complete blank and I feel very ill.

"With love to you and yours,

"Ever your affectionate daughter,

"Florence Bravo."

Dr. Dill had known all the circumstances of her "attachment", and in him she reposed almost as much confidence as in Dr. Gully himself. He was visiting her twice daily and to him she poured out all the details of Charles' death; her own disappointment in twice losing her hopes of motherhood; and the depression and sickness from which she had suffered until recently. As they sat together in the window of her drawing-room overlooking the sea he gave the closest attention to all she had to tell him.

CHAPTER TEN

THE GATHERING STORM

I

AT the trial in Scotland, in 1858, of Madeleine Smith, accused of poisoning her lover, the Lord Advocate, in his charge to the jury, said that if the guilty party "is not immediately detected in some such way as to leave no doubt of actual guilt, suspicions arise, often most unjustly, and obtain great weight, and a great hold over the public mind." The Bravo case is an outstanding instance of this.

On 10th May there appeared in the columns of *The World* a guarded report of the main facts relating to Charles Bravo's death, and, though all names were omitted, it was so worded as to pique curiosity, while the question-mark following the heading—*A TRAGEDY?*—was itself suggestive. But it was not until twenty-four hours later that a startled public learned that what appeared to be a case of murder by poisoning— that foulest of crimes—had taken place in the higher ranks of Society, when the *Daily Telegraph* gave a well-informed account of the fatal illness of Mr. Charles Bravo, Barrister-at-Law, of The Priory, Balham, together with the names of some of the doctors who had been in attendance; and in a trenchant leading article severely criticized the "secret and unsatisfactory manner" in which the inquest had been conducted. There and then this newspaper opened a campaign—which it did not relax until it had achieved its object—that the inquest be quashed and a new inquiry ordered, either in the form of a fresh inquest or through the setting up of a Special Commission.

The account included the menu served at dinner on the fatal Tuesday, and it was pointed out that while no ill-effects had been suffered by the ladies, who partook of it in the dining-room, or by the servants, who did so in the servants'-hall, Charles Bravo alone had drunk Burgundy, as was his custom, while the ladies had drunk sherry, as was theirs.

The Burgundy—so declared the article—had been opened, decanted, and placed on the table by the butler about half an hour before dinner was served, which suggested that anyone familiar with the household routine could have used it as the vehicle for the poison. Suspicion was thus attached to *all* who were under The Priory roof that night, and might even be extended to others who had formerly been connected with the establishment.

In those first days, however, suspicion was hardly directed towards the two ladies at The Priory: people in Mrs. Bravo's sphere of life did not commit murder. It was considered likely to be the vengeful act of a dismissed servant, and this at first pointed to Griffith, who, on Lord Mayor's Day the previous November, when he had been driving Florence in Bond Street, had bumped into a brewer's dray, and Charles, declaring "he was not fit to drive in London", had prevailed upon his fiancée to give him a month's notice forthwith. Turned out of his comfortable quarters at the lower lodge a few days before the wedding, a thoroughly disgruntled Griffith had indulged in defamatory remarks concerning his former mistress in the bar at the Bedford Hotel and uttered his famous prediction that "Mr. Bravo would be dead in four months"—and dead he was, four months and two weeks later, of poison. However, it was soon established that Griffith, having quickly obtained a good situation in Kent, had been nowhere in the neighbourhood of Balham since that time. And into the vacuum created by the collapse of this theory swirled that whirlwind of gossip which had first gathered momentum on the same spot.

Soon it was on every lip that the celebrated Dr. Gully had been the lover of Mrs. Ricardo up to and within a very short time of her second marriage, and had continued to reside at her very gates after it; and since he had recently been seen more than once in the company of her lady companion, it looked as though some sinister plot had been afoot. Rumours arising in London itself underlined those from Balham: the livelihood of the lady companion—"an impecunious and unprepossessing widow" of obscure West Indian origin—had been threatened by the dead man whose wife's extravagance made household

economy essential, while poison, everyone knew, was freely
used in the West Indies as a means of solving tiresome domestic
problems. In fact, all those suspicions were arising which, in the
words of the Lord Advocate, would most "unjustly obtain
great weight with, and a great hold over, the public mind".

On 18th May the *Daily Telegraph* published an article by
Dr. Harrison and Dr. Moore giving an account of their connection with the case. In this article the former stated that on his
arrival at The Priory on the night of 18th April Mrs. Cox had
met him at the door and told him that "she was sure Mr. Bravo
had taken chloroform". Dr. Johnson, who recounted his
experiences in the *Lancet*, declared that Mrs. Cox had distinctly
informed him that the patient had said to her, "I have taken
some of that poison": he had been impressed by the fact that
some particular poison seemed to be indicated and had immediately inferred that the patient had attempted suicide. But
when he had confronted the dying man with Mrs. Cox's
allegation he had replied, "I don't remember speaking of
poison", and would only admit that he had rubbed his gums
with laudanum and "might have swallowed some of it". The
discrepancy in her two statements, made within five hours
of each other to the medical men, hardened the trend of
suspicion against Mrs. Cox.

On 18th May, too, Mr. Serjeant Simon, M.P.,[1] rose in the
House of Commons to ask the Home Secretary[2] "whether his
attention had been drawn to the unsatisfactory character of
the Coroner's inquest on the late Mr. C. Bravo". The Minister
replied that he was "entirely dissatisfied" with the way in which
the proceedings had been conducted, and while he was not in
a position to say what action would be taken, all the relevant
papers were in the hands of the Law Officers of the Crown.

The "Balham Mystery" had now become a *cause célèbre*.
The more it was discussed, the darker grew the portraits of the
suspects and the fairer that of the dead man, until he came to
represent the ideal of English manhood: the dutiful son; the
affectionate husband; hard-working, happy-natured, fond of

[1] Afterwards Sir John Simon (1818–1897).
[2] Richard Assheton Cross, afterwards first Viscount Cross (1823–1914).

outdoor life, a cheerful and agreeable companion: and as thousands of tongues wagged in public places and tattled over teacups, the venomous reached for their pens and a deluge of scurrilous anonymous letters began to rain down upon 38 Brunswick Terrace and Orwell Lodge like white-hot ashes belched from a volcano.

2

The story within the story of this case was meanwhile taking shape at Brighton. Reconstructed from fragments of evidence scattered over the twenty-three days of the second inquest like pieces of a jigsaw puzzle, it is possible to fit the facts together, but impossible to time their occurrence with any exactitude.

There was a constant coming and going of the Campbell family between Buscot, Lowndes Square and Brighton. They were deeply concerned and anxious at Florence's predicament. Their physician at Buscot made a suggestion which sent Mr. Campbell to Brighton to put it to his daughter: that a substantial reward should be offered to anyone who could prove a sale of antimony to any member of The Priory household. Florence at once authorized Mr. Brookes to offer £500, and for the next week the reward was widely advertised in various newspapers. That the offer of so large a sum might be a temptation to manufacture evidence occurred to none of them.

About 8th May Inspector Clarke presented himself in order to obtain Florence's consent to a search being made of The Priory, and having obtained it left without putting any questions to anyone.

Distrust of Mrs. Cox had been seeping into Mrs. Campbell's mind ever since she had learned of her meetings with Dr. Gully. It was significant that not only had no antimony been found in Charles' room, but nothing which could have contained it. Could he have destroyed the container? If not, who had? When he told Mrs. Cox that he had "taken poison", had he told her anything else? "When we were at Brighton," stated Mrs. Campbell, "I discussed the question of suicide with all my family and with Mrs. Cox. We never discussed the question of murder. We never supposed such a thing."

In fact she persistently questioned Mrs. Cox, and while the latter successfully parried the questions she could not have failed to be aware of the suspicion behind them. Dr. Dill, too, seems to have had reason for certain suspicions of his own. But all were careful to keep these things from Florence.

Pressure within the domestic circle, the rising tide of the Press campaign, the first trickle of anonymous letters, all bore down upon Mrs. Cox and under their weight her morale began to weaken. Then on 18th May appeared not only the article by the two doctors in the *Daily Telegraph*, but the Home Secretary's reply to Mr. Serjeant Simon's question in the House. She who had suffered from a lifelong dread of "scandal" was now involved in one more terrible than any she had ever dreamed of—a scandal which was linking her name with *murder*. The following letter gives some indication of her state of mind:

> "38 Brunswick Terrace,
> "Brighton,
> "19th May, 1876.

"My dear Dr. Harrison,

"The reports and comments in the papers make me most unhappy. I do wish you would try to remember what I said to you about the poison. It is so dreadful for it to be said I never mentioned anything about the poison until Mr. R. Bell came. I told you I felt sure he had taken chloroform, for I smelt it when he was sick, but when you afterwards said, 'It couldn't be chloroform' or 'It was not', I said 'I feel sure he took chloroform', and the bottle was empty, and he said he had either taken 'some poison' or 'poison', and I forget which, and I also told you I had given him mustard and water to make him sick, and that I had put his hands and feet in hot mustard and water, and mustard plasters on his feet. All this I did to keep him awake, and you told me afterwards I could not have done better. It is so dreadful to have such things said as they are now saying.

"I know you will, with your usual kindness, forgive my troubling you, and will you kindly reply to this per return post.

"With kind regards, believe me,

                                "Yours truly,
                                        "Jane C. Cox.

"P.S.—I did not tell Dr. Moore because I was expecting you every moment, and I quite thought also that he would recover from the effects of chloroform, and he would be so angry at my having told he had said he had taken poison."

Dr. Harrison replied promptly:

                                "Streatham Hill,
                                        "May 20th, 1876.
"Dear Mrs. Cox,

"I am willing to do my best to relieve your mind. You did not use the word 'poison' to me, nor did you say he had told you he had taken it, but you did tell me he had taken chloroform, and you told me so in such a manner as to imply he was poisoned by it, but Dr. Moore and I hunted for poison all over the room before Bell arrived. As you may remember, we examined the liniment bottle, etc., and directly the vomiting of blood commenced we became certain that it was an irritant poison, so that no difference could have been made in the treatment.

"Believe me, ·

                                "Yours very truly,
                                        "George Harrison."

His letter was quite firm: that it was also kind may or may not have brought some comfort to Mrs. Cox, who had neither friends, family nor money to support her in her tribulation. It would seem that the blow which ultimately broke her was the arrival by post of a crude but vigorous drawing of herself, complete in spectacles, dangling from a gibbet over the mouth of Hell with a bottle labelled *Poison* clutched in one hand.

The next thing we know is that an urgent telegram summoned Mrs. Campbell to Brighton. There she found Florence
in a state of collapse, and Dr. Dill so alarmed at her condition,
which he diagnosed as "brain fever", that he had taken up
residence in the house: Keeber, *not Mrs. Cox*, was in attendance
on the invalid. The latter abruptly quitted the premises and,
pausing only to collect her belongings from The Priory,
retired into London lodgings.

When Inspector Clarke paid a second call at 38 Brunswick
Terrace to inform Florence that her servants would be required
to appear before the Treasury Solicitor, who had been instructed to hold a preliminary inquiry, he was startled to hear
her make "a charge of a very grave nature against her late
husband"; but when he pressed for further details she would
only reply that "if he wanted to learn more he had better see
Dr. Dill".

Such is the summary of events at Brighton between 8th and
22nd May.

CHAPTER ELEVEN

THE STORM BREAKS

I

ON 27th May the *Daily Telegraph* announced that the Treasury Solicitor, Mr. A. K. Stephenson,[1] had closed his inquiry after examining some thirty witnesses. "The concluding sentence of this apparently inspired paragraph," writes Sir John Hall, "is significant: 'For various reasons neither Mrs. Bravo nor Mrs. Cox, though questioned by the police, has been asked to give evidence.' " Indeed, the inference was obvious: Florence Bravo and Jane Cannon Cox were suspected by the higher Authorities of having wilfully murdered Charles Bravo.

A family consultation was held immediately: it was decided that the two suspects must take some action to demonstrate their innocence; but their request to submit themselves for examination met with the reply that any statements they wished to make must be tendered in writing and read over on oath to the Treasury Solicitor and that no questions would be put to them.

Every lawyer knows the danger of voluntary statements. "The excited suspect," as Sir Patrick Hastings has pointed out, "proceeds to pour out a long rigmarole, in the optimistic belief that it is going to be of use to him. . . . When he appears in Court ready to support a most excellent defence carefully prepared by his legal advisers . . . he flounders about in an effort to reconcile the statement with his present evidence, with a result that almost invariably leads to disaster."[2]

When on 1st June Florence, from Brighton, and Mrs. Cox, from her lodgings in Manchester Street, Manchester Square, converged on Mr. Brookes' office and "poured out their long rigmaroles" for him to take down, the result was more than to

---

[1] Later Sir Augustus Keppel Stephenson, K.C.B., K.C. (1827-1904), Queen's Proctor and Director of Public Prosecutions.

[2] *Cases in Court*—Sir Patrick Hastings.

justify Sir Patrick Hastings' observations. Their action, in fact, was most untimely and ill-advised, for on that date not even the Home Office itself knew whether or not a writ to quash the Coroner's inquisition would be issued and an order for a fresh inquiry granted. Indeed, the odds were against it, for the Lord Chief Justice, Sir Alexander Cockburn, Bart.,[1] was known to disfavour such action and in 1861 had refused a similar application in the case of Constance Kent in face of far more serious charges against the Coroner and a far greater weight of public opinion. It was, indeed, Mrs. Cox's statement in which she admitted that she had suppressed evidence at the inquest, and the amendment of her original allegation into the form "I have taken poison *for Gully*", which influenced the Lord Chief Justice to grant the application.

2

Florence had blindly clung to the belief that no more would ever be known of her *liaison* with Dr. Gully than that it had been a romantic attachment on the part of an unhappily married young woman for an elderly and distinguished physician who had earned her gratitude. Only Charles and Mrs. Cox had been told the true nature of that relationship, and Mrs. Cox, if only for the reason that her condonation of it would reflect discredit on herself, could, she thought, be trusted, even now, to keep the knowledge to herself.

The similarity of their written statements, as well as their later evidence in regard to what the Press termed "the inner life at The Priory", have resulted in suggestions of collusion and the suspicion that they invented or exaggerated the accounts they gave of Charles' "ebullitions of temper", stress being laid on the fact that there was no other evidence to support their contentions. But this proves no more than that the façade they had erected had proved efficacious, while corroboration is provided by Florence's two hasty departures to Buscot, and by the tone of Charles' letters while she was there.

---

[1] 1802–1880. Attorney-General 1851; prosecuted Palmer the poisoner, 1856; Lord Chief Justice 1859. Succeeded to baronetcy 1858. Twice declined a peerage.

Neither woman dreamed that the words they were uttering in the privacy of Mr. Brookes' office, and which they read over in private to Mr. Stephenson, would in a few days' time receive the widest publicity in the Press. So Florence, in her statement, emphasized the innocent nature of her attachment to Dr. Gully, and laid equal stress upon Charles' unreasonable jealousy concerning it and on the financial difficulties in which she quite honestly believed him to have been, trusting that this, combined with accounts of his uncertain temperament and violent displays of temper, would suggest a motive for suicide. Both she and Mrs. Cox overlooked the fact that it might also suggest a motive for murder.

After recounting the story of her disastrous first marriage, and the growth of her friendship for Dr. Gully—"During that time," she said, "Dr. Gully had taken a great and increasing interest in me and my welfare and I became attached to him and grateful for his care"—she described how she had met Charles Bravo at Brighton in October 1875. Before becoming engaged to him she had "broken off" completely with Dr. Gully. "A compact was made between us that Dr. Gully's name should not be mentioned, as I had told him, and requested him to tell his family, of the attachment." And now she proceeded to a gratuitously false assertion: "This attachment was quite innocent, and nothing improper ever passed between us"; then continued: "But although I never heard from, or spoke to, Dr. Gully after my marriage, he" (Charles) "was constantly —morning, noon and night—speaking of him, always abusing him and calling him 'that wretch', and upbraiding me for my acquaintance with him."

Except for "casual allowances" from his stepfather, her husband had had no money of his own. He had pressed her to "put down" her garden and the cobs—"my two great hobbies" —and had wished her "to turn away Mrs. Cox by which he hoped to save £400 a year. . . . I used to ask him why there was the necessity for this retrenchment, as I had always been accustomed to live within my income." His mother, too, had shown a "disposition to meddle" in their affairs, and she instanced the quarrel during which Charles had threatened to

cut his throat as an example of what arose out of that interference. The "ebullition of temper" on Good Friday, which
arose out of her wish to rest after luncheon, was then related
and she wound up this part of her statement with the words
that, before this, "we had had a happy three weeks, and I got
quite to like him and forgot his meanness which had previously
disgusted me".

These are strange words on the lips of a woman whose
affection for her husband, living, dying and dead, had impressed itself on all beholders. Did they spring from the bitterness of some recently acquired knowledge which had turned
that affection to wormwood and gall?

The drive to London on the morning of the fatal Tuesday,
the quarrel and reconciliation in the carriage, Charles' return
home in cheerful mood, his ride and its unfortunate outcome,
were all described. "At dinner he got a letter from his stepfather which made him furious. It was about money—the
sale of Caledonian Railway shares. . . . A sale note of this
transaction was enclosed and this was not found after his
death."

The final portion of Florence's statement contains two
passages of importance. The first relates to her husband's fatal
illness: "*He did not tell me he had killed himself, nor did he charge
anyone with having killed him. He made no inquiry as to what caused
his illness.*" The second stands out by reason of its apparent
irrelevance: "*When we first married he thought I took too much
sherry, and I gave it up to please him.*"

3

The first words of Mrs. Cox's statement were an admission
of perjury:

"I was examined as a witness at the inquest on the late
Mr. Bravo, but from confusion and from a mistaken idea of
shielding, as I thought, the character of Mrs. Bravo, I did not
tell the full particulars which I am now anxious to state.
There was no cause whatever or the slightest reason for his
committing suicide for Dr. Gully, and therefore there was no
reason why I should not have stated this before. 'Mrs. Cox,

I have taken poison for Dr. Gully; don't tell Florence' were the words he used, beseechingly, when he first told me he had taken poison. The words 'don't tell Florence' were used emphatically, in a most imploring way. I said: 'How could you do such a thing?' He only screamed out as loud as he could three times for hot water. Before the hot water arrived he was sick out of the window, and detecting the smell of chloroform when he vomited I rushed to look at the chloroform bottle which I found nearly empty. *There was a good fire burning in the grate.*"

These words are stressed because, like those above, their apparent irrelevance provides a clue to the final solution of the mystery. The statement continues:

"I told Dr. Harrison, who was the regular attendant, directly he arrived that he" (Charles) "had taken chloroform. I did not tell Dr. Moore, thinking suicide from such a cause[1] such a scandal. Mr. Bravo's temper was so violent. Had he recovered, as I thought he would if it was only chloroform, he would be so angry. He had no reason to take poison as she, I knew, had not had any communication with Dr. Gully since her marriage, and their acquaintance before marriage was, though very imprudent, I conscientiously believe[2] entirely of an innocent nature."

Having described the various "ebullitions of temper", she passed on to the incident which she alleged had taken place on Wednesday, 19th April, when Royes Bell had gone downstairs to lunch and she and Charles were alone together for the first time since Dr. Johnson had told him she had said he had admitted taking poison.

"He asked me 'Why have you told them? Does Florence know I have poisoned myself? Don't tell her'—imploringly. I said I had not. I said, 'I couldn't let you die'; I asked, 'What have you taken, Charlie?' He turned his head away from me and said, 'I don't know'. . . . He was jealous of Dr. Gully, though he knew everything before marriage."

[1] I.e. jealousy of Dr. Gully.
[2] When again charged with perjury on account of this statement by Mr. George Lewis, she immediately retorted that what she had actually said was "I conscientiously *believed*"—not "*believe*".

She, too, described the scene at dinner on 18th April, and having touched on minor matters concluded with the words:

"I told Mr. Royes Bell that he had told me he had taken poison, and I repeated it to Dr. Johnson. That is all."

It was to be more than enough.

CHAPTER TWELVE

THE COURT OF THE QUEEN'S BENCH:
19TH JUNE

I

THE Attorney-General, Sir John Holker,[1] familiarly known as "Sleepy Jack", had attained eminence and an income estimated at £22,000 from a practice mainly consisting of Patent cases: had he possessed equal experience of criminal law it is unlikely that the proceedings in the Bravo case would have taken the form they did.

On 19th June, 1876, in the Court of the Queen's Bench, sitting in Westminster Hall, the Lord Chief Justice, Mr. Justice Mellor and Mr. Justice Field heard his plea for a writ to quash the Coroner's inquisition and for a rule *nisi* calling upon the Coroner to show cause why a fresh inquisition should not be held before him, or by Commissioners appointed by the Court. After the usual preliminaries Sir John Holker read the Coroner's erratic jottings and compared them with Mr. Reid's notes, and having commented on the fact that Mr. Carter had resisted a request from the jury that the widow should be called, he read her voluntary statement. Commenting next on Mr. Carter's refusal to hear the evidence of Dr. Johnson—the physician under whose care the deceased had been—he read an affidavit made by him. From this, quotations have already been made, and only the following points need now be noted.

Concerning Mrs. Cox's allegation: "I remember her very words—'I have taken some of *that* poison.'"

Concerning the patient: "He certainly thoroughly understood what I was saying. I said, 'That'" (laudanum) "'won't explain your symptoms.' I don't remember if he made any definite

---

[1] 1828–1882. Solicitor-General and knighted in 1874. Attorney-General 1875.

reply to this, but certainly I got no further explanation from
him in answer to my remarks about his symptoms. . . . From
the time he recovered consciousness he never lost it while I
was there. I saw him five or six times in two days . . . but we
learned nothing more."

Concerning Florence's conduct: "While talking in the presence
of Mrs. Bravo I unintentionally referred to Mrs. Cox's
statement that he had taken poison, and Mrs. Bravo, turning
to Mrs. Cox, asked her: 'Did he say he had taken poison?'
Mrs. Cox replied: 'Yes, he did.' . . . I was rather astonished
that Mrs. Bravo did not display more feeling when this was
mentioned. I had never seen Mrs. Bravo before this case and
her usual manner was unknown to me. I saw her evince great
anxiety as to her husband's recovery, and the occasion I
mentioned was the only one which caused me astonishment.
Her conduct at other times was, under the circumstances,
perfectly natural."

Concerning the cause of death: "My decided belief and impression is that he had not knowingly taken antimony or
any other poison than laudanum."

Concerning Mr. Campbell's attitude: "On the morning of the
adjourned inquest Mr. Campbell, senior, called on me, and
told me he had been advised by Sir William Gull to come to
me. He said: 'The question is, what verdict shall we get?' He
said: 'I can get a verdict of suicide in five minutes.' I said:
'How?' He said: 'By repeating Sir W. Gull's opinion.' I said:
'Then Sir W. Gull believes it to be suicide?' He said: 'Yes.'
I said: 'Well, it may be suicide, but so far as I can see there is
no evidence to show it, and the only possible verdict is an
open one—that he died by poison.' I added that I thought of
going to the inquest. He begged that I would not, and said he
would telegraph for me whether I should come or not. I
received no telegram, but I went to Balham and attended the
adjourned inquest. I saw the Coroner was about to sum up
and tendered myself as a witness. I said I had seen the deceased
several times. The Coroner said: 'We don't require any further
evidence; it is quite unnecessary to examine you.' "

This passage in the affidavit, when it became known next

day in newspaper accounts of the proceedings, naturally influenced public opinion unfavourably to the Campbells. The affidavit ended with the declaration:

"I have never in my experience met with a case of suicide by antimony."

Laying this document aside, the Attorney-General then addressed their lordships:

"Now, my lords, here we have witnesses who could certainly have carried the matter further. It is clear that Mr. Bravo stated what practically amounted to a denial of suicide. The evidence on this important point was offered and not received. The Coroner refused to receive important evidence and his doing so amounts to misconduct, which misconduct renders necessary the re-opening of the inquiry.

"I hope to shew your lordships that I make this application in the interests of public justice and from the desire of ascertaining some facts which will enable the Crown to make a charge against someone, but I think that if we had a fresh inquiry, with the opportunity of cross-examining witnesses, some important evidence might be obtained. I think it very much to the interest of Mrs. Bravo and her family that there should be such further inquiry, and perhaps for the family of Mr. Campbell. They have come forward and said they are anxious to make statements and, acting upon the Law Officers' advice, the Treasury Solicitor heard those statements.

"From these statements there was, it appears, some reason for Mr. Bravo committing suicide. There had been quarrels between himself and Mrs. Bravo, and other evidence in favour of this statement which may satisfy a jury that it was a case of suicide. If the Coroner had examined Dr. Johnson, his view as to the suicide might have been shaken. He might have come to the conclusion that it was not a case of suicide, but one of murder, and would have made investigation as to what was partaken of at dinner. There was a bottle of Burgundy of which Mr. Bravo took three or four glasses, and no one else touched it, the ladies taking sherry, and we find that when Mr. Bravo went upstairs a glass of Marsala was taken up to Mrs. Bravo's room. In fact, but for the view of suicide entertained by the Coroner, a great deal of light might have been thrown on the matter.

"It appears most important that the servants living in the house should be examined and cross-examined, in order to elicit all they know of the matter. It appears to me, therefore, that the interests of justice require that a fresh inquiry should be granted which might result in a charge being preferred against an individual. But even if the effect were a verdict that Mr. Bravo did commit suicide, the inquiry would at all events be complete."

"Their lordships," said the Press next day, "shewing some reluctance to comply, notwithstanding that the Attorney-General stated plainly that 'if a new inquiry was granted facts might be elicited which would justify a charge against someone or other', Sir John Holker was reluctantly compelled to read Mrs. Cox's statement from beginning to end."

Holding it aloft he said:

"Then there is the statement of Mrs. Cox to which I am reluctant to refer, but it certainly appears she withheld important information from the Coroner's jury." He read the opening sentences with great deliberation. On reaching Dr. Gully's name he paused and said, "Here comes a name I must not mention," and omitted it throughout. "You see, my lords, from her own statement," he said as he laid it aside, "she deliberately kept information from the jury."

The Lord Chief Justice: "There is no use shutting our eyes to the fact that in your view it is not a case of suicide."

The Attorney-General: "If it turned out to be a murder, as I suspect it was, I hope we will be able to elicit facts which would justify a charge against someone or other."

The Lord Chief Justice: "I think you have shewn sufficient grounds, Mr. Attorney-General, to warrant us giving you a rule *nisi*."

2

The shrill voices of running newsboys pierced the roar of traffic in the sunlit London streets that June evening. Their papers sold as fast as they could pluck them from the bundles under their arms. In residential roads they zigzagged from pavement to pavement at calls from windows, or from magpie-uniformed parlour-maids at doorways. In omnibuses, in trains and hansoms; in public-houses and West End clubs; in drawing-rooms and servants' halls, the account of that day's proceedings was eagerly read and discussed. Clearly the Attorney-General believed that Charles Bravo had been murdered by the placing of antimony in the Burgundy he had drunk at dinner, and, equally clearly, he believed that it would not be necessary to look far to find who had placed it there and why.

From that moment the public did not doubt that Florence Bravo had desecrated the cherished standard of female virtue with a lover, and had she been charged then and there with her husband's death she would have stood small chance at the hands of a Victorian jury. But such prejudice was by no means confined to the nineteenth century: it was her illicit love for Frederick Bywaters rather than proof of complicity in his crime that brought Edith Thompson to the gallows in 1922; while the exclamations of delighted horror which greeted the disclosures wrung from Florence Bravo at the second inquest in 1876 of her relations with Dr. Gully were aroused by precisely the same public passion which in 1935 drove Mrs. Rattenbury to take her life after the Court had acquitted her, and convicted her chauffeur-lover, Stoner, of the murder of her husband. These feelings were epitomized in the following malicious parody of Goldsmith's well-known lines which were sent anonymously to Florence:

> *When lovely woman stoops to folly*
> *And finds her husband in the way,*
> *What charm can soothe her melancholy?*
> *What art can turn him into clay?*

> *The only art her aims to cover,*
> *To save herself from prison locks*
> *And repossess her ancient lover,*
> *Are Burgundy and Mrs. Cox!*

Part III

THE SECOND INQUEST

CHAPTER ONE

THE SECOND INQUEST: 11TH JULY

I

ON 26th June Mr. Serjeant Parry, having presented a medical certificate to the effect that Mr. William Carter was laid up with an attack of erysipelas and unable to appear in person, told their Lordships of the Queen's Bench that his client deeply regretted that the inquest had not ended satisfactorily and was anxious to submit himself to the Court to act in whatever way it might direct. After a lengthy discussion on legal technicalities the Lord Chief Justice and his Associate Judges made absolute the rule *nisi* quashing the inquest and directed the Coroner to hold a fresh inquiry with a fresh jury. The opening date was fixing for 11th July; the place, the Bedford Hotel, Balham; and Mr. R. Burleigh Muir was appointed to sit as legal assessor to the Coroner.

Mrs. Cox was at Handsworth, near Birmingham. Over and above the admitted difference in her statements to Dr. Harrison and Dr. Johnson; over and above her misjudgment in having the vomit thrown away, and her confession that she had withheld evidence from the Coroner, there was another reason for suspicion against her: if Charles Bravo had told her he had taken poison, why had she not let Dr. Harrison know that when she had sent for him, so that he could have arrived equipped to deal with the emergency? This point had struck Florence and the Campbells as well, as is clear from the following letter which Mrs. Cox wrote to Dr. Harrison on 15th June:

". . . Mrs. C. Bravo has told me several times that she thought, had the stomach-pump been used, Mr. C. Bravo's life might have been saved. I told her you told me afterwards it was impossible to use it. . . . Mrs. C. Bravo said Sir William Gull said it might have been used, but I told her Sir William Gull could not know, as you and Dr. Moore did, the state that Mr. Bravo was in. Of course this has grieved me dreadfully, and I should feel so much obliged to you if you would kindly write to me on the subject. . . .',

Dr. Harrison did so, to her satisfaction, and in his evidence repeated his assertion that the use of the stomach-pump would have caused the patient's death.

Meanwhile the vicious anonymous letters had continued to pour through the letter-box at 38 Brunswick Terrace; groups of people gathered on the Promenade to stare up at the windows, and the gaze of every passer-by was instinctively lifted to them. Florence, now an object of evil notoriety, could no longer sit before them; nor could she go out walking or driving. The sense of horror and calamity lay upon her even while she slept, and was heavy upon her when she awoke each morning. There was no moment of relief from it. She paid her servants a month's wages and left for Buscot.

From the moment the Campbells heard that Mr. Joseph Bravo "had had the detectives put on" and had retained the services of the cleverest criminal lawyer in London, they realized that he meant to exact not only his pound of flesh, but to squeeze out with it as much blood as possible. The only link that now remained between Florence and Mrs. Cox was that of mutual danger; and since the cause of one was the cause of the other, and Mrs. Cox had no resources wherewith to pay legal costs, Florence, to protect herself, must pay not only for her own but also for her companion's defence. The affairs of each, therefore, were placed in the hands of the only other two reputable firms of solicitors which then handled criminal cases, and these respectively briefed Sir Henry James, Q.C.,[1] and Mr. John Biron[2] to appear for Florence, and Mr. J. P. Murphy, Q.C., and Mr. R. M. Bray[3] for Mrs. Cox. After the proceedings were over the *World* was to say:

[1] 1828–1911. Afterwards first and last Viscount James of Hereford; Attorney-General 1873; refused Lord Chancellorship, 1886, rather than assist in establishing Irish Home Rule; a wit and *bon viveur*; Byronic in his handsomeness.

[2] Father of the late Sir Chartres Biron, Chief Magistrate, Bow Street.

[3] Afterwards Mr. Justice (Sir Reginald) Bray.

"The inquiry which began on 11th July occupied 23 working days, on each of which Sir Henry James was present. . . . Sir Henry James received a heavy fee with his brief and a hundred guineas a day; Mr. Murphy, who was called on the 17th of July, received in addition to his retainer fifty guineas a day. . . ."

On 22nd June Mrs. Cox returned to London to begin her consultations with her solicitor. About the same date Florence stayed in London for the purpose of consulting her own advisers. and then, with her mother and William, returned to The Priory.

2

The billiards saloon at the Bedford Hotel formed the setting of what was to be described by the *Saturday Review* as "one of the most disgusting public exhibitions which has been witnessed in this generation".

In that exceptionally hot summer, while the sun blazed down upon its walls, the sash-windows had to be kept closed, except for a narrow aperture at the top, against the hubbub of the crowd outside and the thunder of the trains crossing the nearby railway bridge. In consequence, the atmosphere at times grew almost unbearable.

As to the conduct of the proceedings, "public feeling", said *The Times*, "has been revolted by the manner in which the investigation has been conducted". In a Criminal Court a Judge would have suppressed Mr. Lewis' assumption of the rôle of avenging angel, quelled the turbulence of the jury and promptly cleared the Court of an over-excited public. Above all, he would have limited the business of the inquiry to its proper purpose, which was to ascertain how the antimony had entered into Charles Bravo's body. But Mr. Carter, abashed by official displeasure, and over-awed by the presence of the Attorney-General and the other legal luminaries, "sat in blank helplessness and apparently quite incapable of keeping Counsel in order or of confining the examination of witnesses within due limits".[1]

On Monday, 11th July, as soon as the jury, numbering seventeen, had been sworn, they were taken to Lower Norwood cemetery to view the exhumed body of Charles Bravo. The lid of the coffin had been removed and an aperture, large enough to display the head and shoulders of the corpse, had been cut in the lead casing and a pane of glass inserted. As, hat in hand, the seventeen men filed slowly past, their glances froze as they fell upon that dead face: for here was no sign of three months' burial; the flesh was as firm, the eyes as serenely closed, as though life had only just fled, but in gruesome contrast some contraction of the muscles had curled back the upper lip in a snarling grimace exposing completely blackened teeth.[2] So shocking was the sight that one of their number fainted and was carried away to attend the proceedings no more. Pallid and shaken, the remaining sixteen returned to Balham.

It was afternoon before the first witness was called. This was Mr. Joseph Bravo. His "moist, thick-lidded eyes, old-fashioned Dundreary whiskers, and coffee-coloured skin" attracted the notice of the reporters. His evidence, given in a tone matching the funereal garb he wore, lasted until the Court adjourned. Throughout he referred to the dead man as his "son".

"It should be borne in mind," the *World* reminded its readers when the investigation had ended, "that this inquiry into Mr. Bravo's death had about it a good deal of the nature of a family quarrel—and these quarrels are the bitterest of all—fought out in a public Court. It was the

---

[1] *Saturday Review.*

[2] At the trial of George Chapman (1903) Dr. Thomas Stevenson stated: "On December 9th, 1902, I examined the body in a coffin bearing the name-plate of Mary Chapman, who died on 25th December, 1897. The body was altogether remarkable: the face and head were those of a woman who might have been coffined that very day from the appearance." Her death had been caused by 25–30 grains of antimony administered by her husband. Until this exhumation the preservative properties of antimony, when taken during life, had not been established.

'Philosophical Physic'
SIR WILLIAM GULL, BART., M.D.
From a *Vanity Fair* cartoon, 1875
'His sense of the mystery of the universe was deep'

SIR JOHN HOLKER
The Attorney-General

SIR HENRY JAMES
Counsel for Mrs. Bravo

The crowd outside the Bedford Hotel during the Second Inquest

object of Mr. Bravo's friends not only to find out how he died, but to clear his memory from a stain. . . . To vindicate his character it was necessary, if possible, to disprove the veracity of the two chief female witnesses. . . . These considerations go some way towards explaining why questions . . . which can have been little less than torture, were pressed with a relentless pertinacity."

In reply to *Mr. George Lewis*, Mr. Bravo stated that it had been Sir William Gull who had told him that deceased was suffering from an irritant poison but would admit to taking nothing but laudanum. Deceased had told witness nothing to account for his condition, and to his knowledge nothing had been found in writing which would explain it. Deceased had taken a great interest in surgical matters and used to attend operations at one of the hospitals. "I knew him intimately down to his death—he was ever my friend and companion. I brought him up from a child and educated him. It was his own wish that he should assume the name of Bravo, which he did when he came of age. Up to the time of his death he was on terms of great affection with me, and the greatest love existed between him and his mother. . . . Knowing him thus intimately I can say he was not a man likely to commit suicide."

In reply to *the jury*: "There is no truth in the suggestion that deceased was pressed for money. I allowed him whatever he desired to have. Between December and April I had given him £1,100. . . . If he had been pressed for £500, or even £1,000, he could have had it for asking."

Sir Henry James: "From what sources would this have come?"

Witness: "From deceased's own resources. He had £1,100 at his stockbroker's, and he could have had £1,000 more for the asking."

But later on, when *Mr. Murphy* pressed for details of the gift of £1,100 made "between December and April", the scale of the witness' alleged munificence underwent considerable shrinkage, and he was compelled to admit: "£500 was a loan on the joint acknowledgement of his wife and himself; £100 was a gift made in January, and £500 was the proceeds of a security which was realized and the amount placed to deceased's credit in the books of the firm." In fact, only the £100 had been a gift—a circumstance amply confirming Mrs. Campbell's contention to be made on 26th July that Charles Bravo had brought only £100 to the marriage. Continuing, witness said: "Since his death the sum of £1,160 has come into my hands arising from the sale of my son's securities, and out of it the £500 he borrowed has been repaid."

In reply to *Mr. Lewis*: "My wife did not approve the marriage. After it my son discussed with me the expense which Mrs. Cox was to the establishment—a matter, he said, of £300–£400 a year. I agreed with him that it was not a wise thing to have a charge of that kind, and about two months after the marriage I advised Mrs. Cox to return to Jamaica. . . . She said she should not return. . . . The deceased was always a man of high spirits and took an interest in all questions; we debated everything and all things. . . . Mrs. Charles Bravo told me nothing to account for my son's serious illness. Dr. Johnson informed me that Mrs. Cox had told him that deceased had said he had taken poison. I said he never could have taken poison. I disputed with Mrs. Cox that he could ever have done anything like that, and I have disputed it all through."

Mr. Lewis: "Did your son either by speech or manner ever indicate that he had a feeling of jealousy towards anyone?"

Witness: "Never."

Mr. Lewis: "Did your son ever mention to you the name of a doctor—Dr. Gully?"

Witness: "Never. . . . Deceased and his wife were always most affectionate to each other when I saw them. Deceased never seemed unhappy." But next moment his bitter animosity against the widow took charge of him as he answered questions about the illness. "She did not appear much grieved in any way. There were members of her family there, and the dinners at her table were served in the usual way—in several courses."

And now an attempt was made to give point to suspicion. "I recollect my son coming early in the month of March to my house at Palace Green and complaining of sickness. He had never before his marriage complained of nausea or sickness. He had been with me to Jamaica several times and never suffered from sickness even on the voyage. My son died in the most dreadful agony, there can be no doubt of that."

Sir Henry James, cross-examining on behalf of Florence, quickly elicited that his client had sent at once for deceased's cousin, Royes Bell; that she had telegraphed as soon as she could for his mother and the witness; that upon her own initiative she had called in Sir William Gull, and only in response to his mother's special request had she given up her position at deceased's bedside. "I do not think Mrs. Charles Bravo kept away from my son from any other cause than that she knew the wish of my wife to nurse the deceased. I knew that Mrs. Charles Bravo had been ill, and that she had kept to her room before his illness."

Witness agreed that deceased's mother had been alone with him on many occasions between her arrival at The Priory and the death—thus giving him ample opportunity to express any suspicions he might have entertained. "After my son's death I was informed that he had known a person at Maidenhead. I have heard, too, that this woman's sister had left £500 in his hands. I have found out nothing about it, or that he had to pay her £30 a year—I have only heard it. . . . I know he was ill in Jamaica with a reputed sunstroke. . . . He was quick in temper; I have never told anyone that he had 'a horrible temper'; I have said he had a rough edge to his tongue. . . . I communicated with the authorities of Scotland Yard, and I thought it right to take legal advice."

In reply to *Mr. Gorst, Q.C.*,[1] for the Crown, witness amplified his account of deceased's alleged sickness in March. "He said that coming up the lane to Balham station he had vomited so much that he was afraid people would think he had been drunk the night before. . . . He looked very ill. His mother suggested various remedies; he refused them and asked to have a glass of curaçao, and feeling better went to Westminster."

[1] Later Sir John Gorst.

2ND, 3RD AND 4TH DAYS OF THE INQUEST

I

The Second Day: Wednesday, 12th July
Evidence of Dr. Moore and Dr. Harrison

DR. MOORE, having described how he had been called by Rowe and given a detailed account of deceased's symptoms, stated that when he informed Mrs. Bravo that he considered her husband "unlikely to recover" her "grief appeared altogether natural".

On Dr. Harrison's arrival they had together made a search "to see if they could discover anything to account for the symptoms", which they thought suggested poison. They had found nothing but the bottles labelled chloroform, laudanum and liniment. The patient had recovered consciousness about half an hour after the arrival of Mr. Royes Bell and Dr. Johnson. Mr. Bell had asked, " 'What did you take, Charlie?' He did not reply and was asked again. He then replied that he had taken nothing, but afterwards said he had rubbed some laudanum on his gums. He also said he had taken a little laudanum for the pain in his face. When he recovered consciousness he had asked his wife to kiss him, and she had done so. He treated her with affection and there was no trace of temper or bad feeling towards her. He continued to treat her with every sign of affection up to the last. . . . I saw no acting in her conduct. . . . She appeared to reciprocate his affection."

Sir Henry James: "Is it your opinion that if he had entertained suspicion that he had been treated foully he was in a condition to express that opinion?"

Witness: "Certainly."

Continuing his evidence witness stated: "I heard nothing said to him in which the word 'poison' was used. . . . I never saw a case of poisoning by antimony. . . . I never heard of suicide by antimony."

Dr. Harrison described how he had been met at the door by Mrs. Cox on his arrival. She had said to him: "I am sure he has taken chloroform." After seeing the patient witness had told her that he "did not believe he could live an hour. . . . We did all we could for him, and could not have done more had we known he was poisoned." Dr. Johnson had then arrived and taken charge of the case. The patient "was repeatedly asked by the medical men, 'What have you taken?' He never admitted to having taken anything in my presence. He never spoke of poison in my hearing. He twice repeated distinctly in my hearing that he had taken nothing at all, and that all he had done was to rub his gums with laudanum."

Witness had been present when Mrs. Cox made her statement to Dr. Johnson. She had said: "When I first went to Mr. Bravo's room, he said, 'I have taken poison; don't tell Florence.' " Witness continued: "I asked her why she had not told me that before. She said she thought she had told me. I said, 'You certainly did not: you told me you were sure he had taken *chloroform.*' . . . She did not tell me he had taken *poison*, but I understood her to mean that Mr. Bravo had taken chloroform in a poisonous dose."

Witness went on to say that Mrs. Bravo had been a patient of his before her marriage to the deceased, and that he had attended her afterwards—in January. "I saw not the slightest sign of feigning or acting on the part of Mrs. Bravo. She seemed to be natural in her affectionate remarks to her husband."

In reply to *Mr. Gorst*: "The system would become tolerant of antimony after frequent small doses, and to a person accustomed to take it a largish dose could be given without producing immediate poisoning. I never knew of a case of suicide by antimony. I once took a large dose by accident: vomiting did not come on till two hours afterwards."

2

The Third Day: Thursday, 13th July
Evidence of Mr. Royes Bell and Dr. Johnson

Mr. Royes Bell, having stated that he had received a note
written at The Priory by Dr. Harrison on the night of 18th
April, said that he had asked Dr. Johnson to accompany him
to Balham. The patient on regaining consciousness would
admit to taking nothing except laudanum for neuralgia.
Witness could not quote Mrs. Cox's actual words—"She gave
me to understand that my cousin had taken poison. . . . The
name of the poison was not mentioned." Witness had there-
upon protested that she should have informed the doctors of
this before, and had then fetched Dr. Johnson to hear her statement. "She told Dr. Johnson that my cousin had taken poison.
He asked her what he had taken. She made no definite reply.

"Dr. Johnson," continued witness, "told my cousin what
Mrs. Cox had said. He replied, 'I have taken nothing but
laudanum.' That was all he said. Dr. Johnson said, 'That won't
explain your symptoms.' My cousin said he could offer no
other explanation."

In reply to *Mr. Lewis*: "In the early hours of the morning
deceased asked me several times if he would recover. I said,
'I hope so, Charlie, but you are very ill indeed.' Before he made
his Will he asked for prayers. This praying was after he had
denied knowing anything about what had poisoned him. He
was not a man of strong religious feeling. . . . I discovered no
trace of unkind or jealous feeling towards his wife—quite the
contrary. He kissed her and addressed her by her pet name—
Florrie. On Wednesday morning, when he was very ill, he
commissioned me to ask his mother 'to be kind to Florence'. . . .
From first to last deceased denied that he had taken anything
but laudanum. . . . I have known him since 1850. The last
time I saw him was the Sunday before Good Friday when I
spent the afternoon with him. He was then in perfect health
and good spirits, and full of fun. In my judgment he was not
at all a man to commit suicide."

In another passage of his evidence, witness, answering questions about Florence's miscarriage on 6th April, said: "When this miscarriage occurred I went and advised as to the treatment. *I advised them to call in Dr. Harrison if further medical assistance was required.*"

Dr. Johnson, much of whose evidence has already been incorporated in the narrative, repeated his statement that Mrs. Cox had quoted Charles as saying, 'I have taken *some of that poison*'. Referring to Sir William Gull's return to the sick-room at Charles' request he said: "I understood the patient to say he was afraid Sir William Gull did not believe he had told the whole truth, and he assured him that he had. He repeated this in an earnest manner and added 'So help me, God.' We were struck by his earnestness. . . . It was my impression Sir William said, 'Whatever you took, you took it yourself?' and the patient said, 'Yes'. That immediately followed his denial of having taken anything but laudanum, and preceded my statement as to the accusation of someone." [1]

3
The Fourth Day: Friday, 14th July
Evidence of Sir W. Gull and Professor Redwood

Sir William Gull was a commanding figure as he stood before the Court, drawn to his full height and with his gaze fixed unwaveringly upon his questioner. The first part of his evidence turned upon the question as to whether or not he had known the patient was suffering from poison before he saw him. He contended he had not. Florence's letter was read out and witness stated:

"I received that note from Mrs. Cox who brought it to my house. She made no statement to me regarding Mr. Bravo. . . . I found a gentleman in bed, pulseless, but quite mentally coherent. After examining him a minute or two I said, 'This is not disease,' or words to that effect, 'you are poisoned,' or 'dying of poison—pray tell us how you came by it.' To which

---

[1] "Unless you tell us more than we know at present, someone may be accused of causing your death."

he replied, 'I took it myself.' I said, 'What did you take?' He said, 'Laudanum.' I said, 'You have taken more than laudanum,' or 'much more than that'. I then, as solemnly as I could, asked him to tell me what it was, and I went on to say it might help us to find an antidote—but instantly I checked myself and said, 'That would not be quite fair, as I fear no antidote would do you good.' I added, 'It is not for me to press a dying man.' He repeated, 'I took it myself.' I believe Dr. Johnson made some remark. I said, 'Where was he sick?' One of the windows of the room was pointed out to me. . . . I and the others saw the vomited matter lying in the gutter. A servant was directed to get out of the window in our presence, and he collected the vomit into a clean jar with a silver spoon. . . . While Dr. Johnson was sealing it the dying man sent for me. I thought he would probably communicate more to me, but he merely asked if he were dying. I replied that I could not doubt it."

In reply to *Mr. Lewis*: "I had known the family of Mrs. Bravo before, but not herself. I knew Mr. Campbell very well as a patient and an acquaintance. Dr. Johnson communicated to me the symptoms of the case on the way down. All he told me was that the patient had suffered from neuralgia and had been in the habit of using laudanum to the mouth. As far as I can remember, Dr. Johnson did not tell me before we went into the sick-room that Mr. Bravo had taken laudanum. I was then in entire ignorance of the statement made to the other doctor and of the statement made by Mrs. Cox. The three sentences deceased used to me were, 'I took it myself', 'I took it myself' and 'Before God it was only laudanum'. He cried out with pain and distress. Mr. Royes Bell and Dr. Johnson were in the room at the time. . . . I believe the latter said, 'If you die without telling us more, someone may be suspected of poisoning you.' Mr. Bravo, I think, said, 'I am aware of that, but I can tell you nothing more.' . . . I told him he was dying of poison; there was no expression of surprise and that surprised me. *It would be surprising to me if I were to tell a man he was dying of poison and he was not surprised; it would induce me to think he knew it.* He was in full possession of his faculties. The whole time he was talking to me I saw not the slightest indication in his manner that he had suspicion against anyone of having administered poison to him. . . .

"I saw Mrs. Bravo for only a few seconds. She came into the room to embrace her husband, and I went out of the room. I don't think she spoke to me." Indignantly witness repudiated Mr. Lewis' next suggestion: "She did not come to *me* with her arms spread out! She went to *her husband* with her arms spread out!" Continuing, witness said: "I think the Court should know that I told the dying man on my own responsibility, and without consultation, that it was not disease: that he was dying of poison. . . . The absence of surprise may have resulted from one of two causes: either from indifference due to exhaustion, or because the sick man, being conscious of all, could not be surprised by my statement."

As the witness left the Court none could doubt he had expressed his innermost conviction that Charles had admitted a fact when he had twice declared, "I took it myself."

Professor Redwood, who repeated the evidence he had given at the first inquest, made it clear that it was from the matter lying on the leads that he had obtained his results.

"On the analysis of this vomited matter I found neither arsenic nor mercury. I found lead (from the roof) and antimony, and had no difficulty in getting abundant and conclusive evidence of the presence of antimony." From one half of the sample he had obtained "$2\frac{1}{2}$ grains of precipitated sulphide of antimony, which corresponds to 5 grains of tartar emetic. The whole matter, therefore, would have yielded 10 grains. . . . Taking into account that it would only have represented part of what was originally present, that would be sufficient to account for death."

In reply to *Mr. Gorst*: "Antimony has a diaphoretic effect when taken in small quantities, an emetic effect in larger quantities, and a powerful reducing and sedative effect in still larger amounts, such as 2 to 3 grains. A depressing effect will also result from repeated small doses, on account of which it has been used as a slow poison. The suspicion of it being so used at one time led to its being interdicted by the Parliament of Paris: it was not allowed to be used in France, even by medical men, for nearly a century. A dose of $1\frac{1}{2}$ to 2 grains will act as an emetic in half an hour more or less, according to the state of stomach, or whether it is full or empty. Taken in water, twenty minutes to half an hour would be the minimum time. If taken with Burgundy or food I should expect the action to be delayed. The quantity taken by deceased could not have been less than 20 grains and probably ranged between 20 and 40."

Mr. Gorst: "It is on record that Palmer's wife died through the effects of antimony, and there is the case of Dr. Pritchard of Edinburgh."

Witness, in reply to *Sir Henry James*, said he had sometimes put tartar emetic into laboratory spirits which servants were taking in quantities to cause them "inconvenience, but not harm. . . . I have heard, too, that women in the country have come for tartar emetic to put into their husbands' drink, to wean them from their fondness of it."

CHAPTER THREE

5TH, 6TH AND 7TH DAYS OF THE INQUEST

I

The Fifth Day: Monday, 17th July
Evidence of Frederick Rowe, butler

SPRUCE and slender, with neat mutton-chop whiskers, Rowe typified the manservant of the day. He had entered Florence's service a month before her marriage to Charles Bravo. He was to state that The Priory was "a liberally run household", to which the fact that his predecessor had left to open a shop and the suspicious confusion of his own cellar-book both bore ample testimony.

He had gone to the door to meet deceased on his return from London on the afternoon of 18th April, and shortly afterwards deceased had called for his riding-breeches. He did not know that deceased had returned from his ride until, glancing into the morning-room to see if the fire needed attention, he "saw Mr. Bravo there looking ill and wretched". Soon afterwards the morning-room bell had rung and Mrs. Bravo had given the order for the hot bath. Witness had seen no wine-glasses in the room.

At dinner "I poured Mr. Bravo out three glasses of Burgundy. I cannot say how much was left, but some was. It was placed in the cellarette by myself. I was not struck by any peculiar appearance in the wine. . . . I next saw Mr. Bravo in his bedroom at half-past ten or a quarter to eleven that night. I had previously been sent by Mrs. Bravo for a doctor and I brought Dr. Moore. Before this Mrs. Cox had pushed open the pantry door and said, 'Tell Parton to go for Dr. Harrison; Mr. Bravo is ill.' . . . On returning from the lodge Mrs. Bravo, who was crying as she came, called out to me to fetch someone quickly—'Go and fetch someone, Rowe!' I told her Dr. Harrison had been sent for. She said: 'Never mind, get

someone! Get someone from Balham—I don't care who it is!'
She screamed it at me. . . .

"Mr. Bravo was cheerful on the 18th. He was always lively
in company, but I used to think he looked sad sometimes
when he was alone. . . . I think he used to be bothered about
stocks going down. He used to speak of such things. . . . He
was a very kind and considerate gentleman—one of the kindest
gentlemen I ever knew."[1]

And now the cellar-book was produced, and witness, much
to his discomfiture, was questioned about its entries.

"I decanted on the 18th two bottles of sherry and one of
Burgundy. I opened one bottle to fill a flask for Mrs. Cox before
she went to Worthing that morning, but I do not remember
at what time I decanted the other and the Burgundy. . . . My
wine-book was made up once a fortnight. In the fortnight ending March 11th there were 30 bottles of wine drunk; in the fortnight ending March 5th, 44 bottles; from 9th to 18th April, 26
bottles. They were chiefly sherry and Marsala—65 sherry and
14 Marsala. . . . I cannot swear whether I did or did not see the
remains of that bottle of Burgundy after that night. . . . I find
by my wine-book that I opened a bottle of Burgundy on the
19th; I made the entry on that day, but I find that while I
entered the wine of the 20th on that day I did not enter
the Burgundy. I was in a muddle with my book at the
time," witness confessed, "and I was making it up." That
he was in a muddle was obvious, and the Court may be
excused if it suspected him of "making it up" in a different
sense.

Continuing, witness said, "Mrs. Bravo used to drink sherry,
Marsala and champagne, and Mrs. Cox the same." He had no

---

[1] In connection with this statement it must be remembered that all who
had been beneath The Priory roof on the night of 18th April were, to a
greater or less degree, under suspicion. Both Rowe and Keeber would have
had ample *opportunity* to administer the poison, and it was therefore to their
interest to suggest that their feelings towards the dead man were as warm
and cordial as possible in order to banish the idea of *motive*. While Charles
could make himself agreeable towards servants he liked, he made short
shrift of those who displeased him, as is shewn by his treatment of Griffith
and his intentions towards an under-gardener with which he acquaints his
stepfather in a letter of 9th April. See Appendix II.

knowledge that Mrs. Cox was about to leave The Priory, nor
had he ever heard any disputes regarding her.

In reply to *Sir Henry James*, witness said that "from first
to last" he had never heard his master express the slightest
suspicion of anyone. "I have never heard the name of Dr. Gully,
and since I went into this service in November I never knew
of his coming to The Priory, and I never knew of Mrs. Bravo
seeing him."

Sir Henry now read extracts from certain letters of Charles
to his parents "to account for the wine shown to have been
consumed". On 3rd January he had written: "*We are expecting
half-a-dozen people and, with children, shall have 31 guests in
the house*"; on 19th March: "*We entertain company next Wednesday*"; and on 22nd March: "*There has been a great slaughter
of cocks and hens and pigeons for the feast.*" On the same theme
witness stated: "There was at times company staying in the
house, and other people who came from London have stopped
for luncheon. . . . Mr. Bravo chided me once for not keeping
the glasses filled and told me always to do so."

Regarding the fatal Tuesday witness said that at dinner
"Mr. Bravo leaned forward at the table and kept turning his
head round as if he were in pain; he appeared like a man out
of sorts—dissatisfied with everything. He had a good taste
for wine, and could tell the difference between the classes of
wine I brought up. On the night he was dying he sent back a
bottle of Moselle for one of the best champagne, one having
been sent up by mistake for the other. If there had been
anything wrong with the taste of the Burgundy, I think he
would have noticed it."

In reply to *Mr. Murphy* (for Mrs. Cox): "Mrs. Cox was
treated with consideration by Mrs. Ricardo before her marriage, and the same consideration was shewn her by Mr. and
Mrs. Bravo after the marriage. I saw no difference in the
demeanour of deceased towards Mrs. Cox during his illness
from what it had been before."

In reply to *Mr. Gorst:* "On one of the occasions that Mr.
Bravo 'looked sad' he said he felt sick. It was after breakfast
and he asked me for brandy. That was about a month before

he died. I never heard of his vomiting.[1] . . . When he took Burgundy he did not take sherry too. The sherry was taken by Mrs. Cox and Mrs. Bravo—they drank a good deal of sherry. I cannot say if the Burgundy was in the cellarette all the afternoon: if I decanted it for luncheon it was; if for dinner, it was decanted only just before dinner. If Mr. Bravo had a glass of Burgundy after his ride, he helped himself to it. It was quite possible for either him or Mrs. Bravo to have got a glass of wine out of the dining-room without my seeing it. I don't remember noticing that a glass had been used."

2

The Sixth Day: Tuesday, 18th July
Evidence of Mary Ann Keeber, housemaid

Young, neat and pretty Mary Ann Keeber brought a breath of something fresh and wholesome into the stale atmosphere of that tawdry room. The male witnesses had given evidence standing, but she was provided with a chair in which she sat alertly forward, one gloved hand resting lightly on the table. She had, she stated, entered Mrs. Bravo's service two years and three months previously.

The first questions put to her indicated that the water-bottle in deceased's bedroom was now being regarded as a more likely vehicle for the poison than the Burgundy.[2] Witness stated that she saw to the filling of this bottle and refilled it every night. "The water from it was frequently used. I never saw any difference in the character of the water in it."

She next described how deceased had complained to her of toothache the night before his seizure, and continued: "On the 18th Mrs. Cox left after breakfast for Worthing before I settled Mr. Bravo's room. I do not think I had filled up his

[1] A reference to the occasion "early in March" when according to Joseph Bravo deceased had arrived at Palace Green complaining of sickness.

[2] It had already been pointed out in the *Lancet* and elsewhere that if a salt of antimony were added to a liquid containing tannin, such as Burgundy, a precipitate would be formed and the resulting turbidity could hardly escape detection.

water-bottle before she left. . . . I do not remember seeing her go to his bedroom on her return."

Witness then stated that she had taken a can of hot water up to Mrs. Bravo's dressing-room at about nine o'clock. "I found Mrs. Bravo undressed. I set her can of hot water in the basin, and I was about to take another up to Mrs. Cox's room when Mrs. Bravo said: 'Mary Ann, fetch me a little Marsala.'" Witness described how she did so, and all the events that followed up to the time she roused the sleeping wife to come to the side of the stricken husband.

"I went to Mrs. Bravo's room," said witness, "and found she was asleep. I woke her and told her Mr. Bravo was ill. I helped her on with her dressing-gown, and she went with me to Mr. Bravo, saying as she went: 'What's the matter? What's the matter?'"

Witness had heard Mrs. Bravo telling Dr. Moore on his arrival: "My husband has been taken ill. I don't know what is the matter with him. He had his dinner as usual." . . . "I heard her say, 'We had better send for Mr. Royes Bell; Mr. Bravo, senior, would like it'; and she asked if Mr. and Mrs. Bravo should be sent for, saying, 'I know that if anything happens they will never forgive me.'"

In reply to *Mr. Lewis*: "Before Mrs. Ricardo was married to Mr. Bravo she was visited by a Dr. Gully. . . . He was in the habit of coming very frequently—I don't know about his coming 'morning, noon and night'. . . . I don't know if he opened the door himself. I don't know how old he is—sixty or seventy I should think. He never came after Mrs. Ricardo became Mrs. Bravo.

"I used to wait on the newly married couple in their bedroom, and have seen them together constantly. I never heard Dr. Gully's name mentioned by either. I never saw any indication of jealousy in the deceased towards his wife, and I never heard him speak to her except in an affectionate way. She always tried to make him happy, and he did the same towards her. . . .

"I think only ten minutes elapsed between the deceased calling out and my fetching Mrs. Bravo. I did not notice anything peculiar about her. It did not strike me that she had taken too much wine. She came directly I told her that her husband was ill. . . . I did not hear either of the ladies upbraid him or make any suggestion to him that he had taken poison. . . .

"Generally there was a little water in his water-bottle in the morning. I did not notice the bottle the night before he was taken ill, but I remember filling it next morning, the 19th. I filled up the bottle on Tuesday evening, the 18th, after he came down to dinner. He had used about a tumblerful. I do not think he used tooth-powder. It was usual for Mrs. Bravo to have wine in her bedroom at night, both before and after her illness. I knew Mr. Bravo to be cheerful mostly. There was not the slightest reason that I know of why he should have committed suicide.

"The tumbler of Marsala I fetched was a small one, and I about half-filled it. I had no reason to think Mr. Bravo would be displeased at my taking wine to his wife, but when I saw him on the stairs I thought he looked as he had never looked before —so pale and silent. I do not know if his looks were caused by illness or temper."

At this point the Court adjourned to allow the jury to visit The Priory in order to study the arrangement of the rooms— with particular reference as to whether or not Charles' cry could have been heard in Florence's bedroom if both doors were shut.

3

The Seventh Day: Wednesday, 19th July
Evidence of Mary Ann Keeber (continued)

The water-bottle and tumbler from Charles Bravo's bedroom were displayed before the Court as exhibits, and witness, in reply to *Sir Henry James*, stated that she recognized them.

Neither Mrs. Cox nor Mrs. Bravo had risen to take notice of Mr. Bravo's cry. "I don't know if Mrs. Bravo was asleep, but I think if she had not been asleep she would have got up. I think Mrs. Cox preceded me in going to Mr. Bravo's bedroom. . . . While he stood at the window he cried again for hot water, and then turned to me and told me to fetch some. I did so as quickly as I could. . . . I held the basin for him to be sick. . . . Mrs. Cox told me to throw the vomit away and wash the basin out. . . . I did not hear any talk of Mr. Bravo having taken poison. I have talked about this with Mrs. Bravo at Brighton. . . . She told me that the newspapers said he had been poisoned by antimony."

Mr. Gorst: "Where did she say he got it?"

Witness: "She said that if he had taken it he must have got it himself."

Sir Henry James: "The learned Counsel for the Crown ought to give an explanation of the word 'got'—whether by 'got' he meant 'bought' or 'obtained', or how it 'got' into the body."

Mr. Gorst: "I am the best judge of the intelligence of my question. I object to being called to order by Sir Henry James, who has no position in this Court which entitles him to interrupt." To witness: "When you talked with Mrs. Bravo at Brighton, what did she say about him?"

Witness: "She said she did not know how the antimony came into his body and could not account for it."

Mr. Gorst: "When you were examined at the Treasury on this point, did you say, 'Since we have been at Brighton we have seen by the papers that it is said he died through taking antimony, and Mrs. Bravo said to that, if that were so, he must have taken it himself'?"

Witness: "Yes, I think I did say that." (After a pause): "I say now that Mrs. Bravo did say that to me."

Mr. Lewis now put some questions suggesting that Florence's miscarriages had actually been abortions brought about by drugs sent to her by Dr. Gully through Mrs. Cox.

Witness: "Before her miscarriage in April Mrs. Bravo had had a miscarriage in January. I did not notice that Mrs. Bravo had medicines immediately before her last miscarriage. She did take medicine occasionally between the first and last miscarriages. I don't remember anyone except a boy from the chemist's at Balham, or the doctor's messenger, calling with medicines."

In reply to *Sir Henry James*: "So far as I know the medicines

Mrs. Bravo had were made up from prescriptions of Mr. Bell and Dr. Harrison."

The next witness, *Charles Parton*, coachman at The Priory, described how deceased had returned from his ride "shaken and unnerved" and had complained that the cob had bolted with him. He did not use antimony for horses and had found none in The Priory stables. He did not know Dr. Gully by sight and had never heard of him coming to The Priory.

George Younger, groom, corroborated the evidence of the last witness.

CHAPTER FOUR

8TH, 9TH AND 10TH DAYS OF THE INQUEST

I

The Eighth Day: Thursday, 20th July
Evidence of Amelia Bushell and Miss Ann Maria Bell

AMELIA BUSHELL, having repeated the evidence she had given at the first inquest, stated in answer to *Mr. Lewis* that deceased was of a cheerful disposition and his general health while at home had been good. As soon as Sir William Gull had left the sick-room, deceased "had called out loudly, 'Sir William!'" and Sir William had been fetched. He had told deceased that "he was in a dying state, and deceased said he was aware of that, and added, 'before my God' that he had taken nothing but laudanum. Immediately after that he had said, 'With that we will have the Lord's Prayer', he commencing 'Our Father' and asking us all to repeat it after him, which we did.

"Mrs. Bravo, senior, nursed deceased until the conclusion —his death. I have left her at Kensington. She is seriously ill and quite unable to be examined at this inquiry. The deceased was always very pleased during his illness to see his wife."

Witness was not aware of any reason why deceased should not have frankly communicated anything to his cousin, Mr. Royes Bell. "He was a very outspoken man. . . . I can say he would be a most unlikely person to commit suicide."

In reply to *Mr. Murphy*: "When deceased was at home he frequently suffered from neuralgia. He was asked during his illness if a clergyman should be sent for and said 'No.'"

Miss Ann Maria Bell stated that she had accompanied Mr. and Mrs. Bravo to The Priory. Like everyone else, she had left the sick-room on the arrival of Sir William Gull. "When they" (the doctors) "left, I went into the room at once. Deceased called out: 'I want to see Dr. Gull! I want to see Dr. Gull!'" When witness had returned with Sir William, deceased was moving restlessly on his bed. "He said, 'Sir William, I wish to tell you now that I have told you the truth, the whole truth and nothing but the whole truth.' Sir William said, 'You must consider the gravity of your situation and of all that you say and do.' He then implied that deceased's end was near. Deceased said, 'I know that; I know I am going to appear before my Maker. I have told them all so and they will not believe me.'[1] Sir William said, 'Under the circumstances I do not wish to press you. If we could only know what you have taken we might be able to give you an antidote.' Deceased said, 'I have taken laudanum.' Sir William said, 'That does not account for your symptoms. It must be something else.' Deceased said, 'I have taken laudanum. If it is not laudanum, so help me God, I don't know what it is.' "

Deceased then asked Sir William for something to relieve him, and inquired again if there were really no hope for him. Sir William replied: "Looking at your condition it would not be right for me to give you any hope. There is little life left in you: in fact, you are half-dead now."

Witness then described how deceased had asked all present to pray with him. From her intimate knowledge of him he was not a man at all likely to commit suicide. She was not aware that there was any reason for him to keep anything hidden from her brother. Deceased had seemed particularly happy in his marriage.

In reply to *Sir Henry James* witness said that after the marriage she had spent a few days at The Priory. She had heard nothing about Dr. Gully until public attention had been directed to his name.

2

The Ninth Day: Friday, 21st July
Evidence of George Griffith, Charles Robinson and Percy Smith

It soon became clear that *George Griffith*, with his shifty eyes and bitter mouth, bore the dead man a deep-seated grudge for being the cause of his dismissal from an easy and comfortable situation. Until employed by Dr. Gully his career had been a

[1] No other witness mentioned any of these particular phrases.

chequered one, and it was obvious that he hoped his evidence would earn him the proffered reward of £500.

He always used antimony for his horses, he stated: he had used it both at Malvern and The Priory. At the latter place he kept it in large quantities in an unlocked cupboard in the stables. He had never told Mrs. Ricardo he used it, but had included the cost of its purchase under the heading of "Extras" in his expense account. He had bought it from the chemists both at Streatham and Balham. When he had been dismissed in December 1875 he had thrown it all down the stable drain at The Priory. He was now in the service of Lady Prescott, of Strode Park, Kent, and had a supply of antimony in the stables there.[1]

In reply to *Mr. Lewis*: "Mrs. Ricardo gave me notice to leave, and for her reason said it was the wish of Mr. Bravo, he saying I was not careful enough to drive in London. I should have been there now if it hadn't been his wish I should leave. I had driven him and her before they were married, in and out of London."

Mr. Lewis: "How long before you drove him had you driven Dr. Gully with Mrs. Ricardo?"

Witness: "From four to six weeks."

In answer to further questions from *Mr. Lewis*, witness said that the only reason he had heard why Dr. Gully broke up his establishment at Malvern was because he was retiring from practice; that he had seen in the newspapers that Mr. Bravo's death was attributed to tartar emetic; that regarding his claim to have bought antimony in Balham—"I think I did swear that I only bought a quarter-ounce of tartar emetic twice, but I recall that it may have been half an ounce—or," he added grandiloquently, "half a pound."

In reply to *Sir Henry James*: "My mind is a perfect blank as to the date Dr. Gully and Mrs. Ricardo were at Malvern—and the date they left it."

In reply to *Mr. Archibald Smith*[2] (for Dr. Gully), witness stated that he had learned the uses of tartar emetic from *The Pocket Farrier*. His mind was "a perfect blank" as to the date he

---

[1] This statement he subsequently retracted, but it did not save him from dismissal from the situation.   [2] Later Sir Archibald Smith.

had entered Dr. Gully's service; it was also "a perfect blank" as to whether he had ever told Dr. Gully he used antimony for his horses, and it continued to be a "perfect blank" whenever he was confronted with an awkward question.

Mr. Lewis: "You remember hearing talk about Mrs. Ricardo's marriage with Mr. Bravo—did you ever express the opinion that he wouldn't live long?"

Witness: "I don't remember. I can't swear I didn't."

Mr. Lewis: "Now just reflect and tell me if you didn't say, 'Poor fellow!'—in relation to Mr. Bravo's marriage with Mrs. Ricardo—'he won't live long'!"

Witness (uncomfortably): "I might have said so. I said all I could about him when he got me out of my home at The Priory."

Mr. Lewis: "Did you say Mr. Bravo wouldn't live four months after the marriage?"

Witness: "No! I didn't say that."

Mr. Lewis (beckoning forward the manager of the hotel): "Do you know Mr. Stringer? Now will you say that you did not use this expression in relation to the late Mr. Bravo—'Poor fellow! he won't live four months'? Answer that question standing face to face with Mr. Stringer."

Witness (hedging desperately): "I don't know that I said *four* months. I may have said five or six."

Mr. Lewis: "Now tell me what you meant by it."

Witness: "I said it in aggravation—nothing else. I looked upon him as having got me out of my place."

Mr. Lewis: "But why should he die?"

Witness (hopefully): "Well, he was bitten by a dog."

Mr. Lewis: "Did you think he might die of that?"

Witness (grasping at the straw): "Well, yes, perhaps I thought he might die of the bite."

Mr. Lewis: "When you read the account of Mr. Bravo's death you were not surprised to see that he did not live more than four months?"

Witness: "Well, I *was* surprised."

Mr. Lewis: "Did Dr. Gully tell you that he would write them a letter that would make them 'very uncomfortable' after their marriage?"

Witness (emphatically): "No—that I swear positive."

In reply to *Sir Henry James*: "What I said about Mr. Bravo's death was after Mrs. Ricardo gave me notice to leave."

In reply to *Mr. Archibald Smith*: "The dog bit Mr. Bravo about a fortnight before he was married. He was very upset, and Mrs. Ricardo ordered me to kill the dog. Dr. Harrison came and said there was no danger in the bite. I shot the dog."

Charles Robinson, chemist and dentist, Streatham, produced his poison book, of which a leaf for the year 1871 was found to be missing. He knew Griffith to be coachman to Mrs. Ricardo of Leigham Court Road, but had never sold him any antimony.

Percy Smith, chemist, Balham, stated that he had been at Balham for five years. He had known Griffith by sight, but had never sold him any antimony. "Antimony," he said, "is a rare thing to be sold in Balham."

3

The Tenth Day: Monday, 24th July
Evidence of Joseph Frank Payne and John Pritchard

Joseph Frank Payne, F.R.C.P., stated that he had known the deceased slightly, and that he had conducted the *post-mortem* on 2nd April.[1]

In reply to *the jury* witness said that if the poison had been taken in the Burgundy he did not believe it would have been retained for two hours. If taken in water when deceased was going to bed it was possible he would be sick in about a quarter of an hour: a medicinal dose would act in that time; a larger quantity in five or six minutes. Immediate and copious sickness would be likely to prevent fatal consequences. The fact of deceased having been sick and fallen down insensible would be consistent with his having taken a dose of 30 grains about 15 minutes before. The vessels of the stomach were particularly absorbent about two hours after dinner, and absorption into the blood was much quicker then. "The effects produced by antimony are many and varied," said witness, concluding his evidence, "more so than in any other poison."

[1] For further details of the results of the *post-mortem* see the evidence given by Dr. Payne at the first inquest, page 156.

John Pritchard, butler to Dr. Gully for twenty-two years and still in his service, stated in reply to *Mr. Lewis* that his master had given him orders the previous autumn not to admit Mrs. Ricardo or Mrs. Cox to his house. This provoked an outburst of laughter from the public benches, causing Mr. Serjeant Parry (for Dr. Gully) to start to his feet and protest, at the same time rebuking Mr. Gorst for having smiled.

Mr. Gorst: "I plead guilty to having smiled. If evidence is given which is amusing I shall smile, for I shall not attempt to go through a case with a wooden face."

Mr. Serjeant Parry: "This is a case in which two learned gentlemen are representing the Crown, and they are here in reality for the purpose of fixing the guilt upon three individuals. All their questions are directed to that object, and not to ascertaining what is the cause of this unfortunate young man's death."

Mr. Lewis: "I cannot help saying that this is rather an unjust observation on the part of Mr. Serjeant Parry, to charge anything of that kind to Mr. Gorst. Mr. Gorst has acted most impartially on the part of the Crown and has fairly brought out evidence telling on both ways."

Mr. Gorst: "I am instructed to come here to endeavour to lay before the Coroner and jury all the evidence which can throw any light on the death of this unfortunate young man. I do not suppose it will be possible for me to conduct my case in a manner pleasing to my learned friends, but I shall carry it out to the best of my ability in accordance with my instructions. I emphatically say again that these instructions are not to bring any charge against any person."[1]

This legal breeze having died down, the examination of Pritchard continued.

In reply to *Mr. Lewis*, witness stated that Mrs. Cox had called at Orwell Lodge before breakfast on 20th April and requested to see his master. He had admitted her because she had told him that "poor Mr. Bravo was dying" and he imagined she wished Dr. Gully to go and see him. Dr. Gully had consented

[1] This hardly accords with the views expressed by the Attorney-General in his speech to their lordships of the Queen's Bench. See page 184.

to see her. Until that visit witness had not seen Mrs. Cox to speak to since the previous October or November. "I was aware that there was a great attachment between Dr. Gully and Mrs. Ricardo. I should think Mrs. Cox knew about it. Each returned the other's presents."

In reply to *Mr. Serjeant Parry* witness said that on Dr. Gully's order he had returned the key of The Priory gate to Mrs. Cox, and Dr. Gully had not, to witness' knowledge, been to The Priory since.

In reply to *the jury*: "I am not aware of Dr. Gully meeting Mrs. Cox by appointment. He told me he had met her once at the station—or it may have been two or three times. I told him I thought it was very unwise of him to speak to her. . . . What Dr. Gully said about Mr. Bravo's death was that it was 'a bad job' and that the last inquest was not satisfactory. Mrs. Cox has been with Mrs. Bravo for the last four or five years. I had never seen her before, and I shouldn't be sorry if I had never seen her at all."

With this Parthian shot Pritchard's evidence ended.

CHAPTER FIVE

11TH, 12TH AND 13TH DAYS OF THE INQUEST

I

The Eleventh Day: Tuesday, 25th July
Evidence of Dr. Johnson, Charles Bravo's friends and Mrs.
Campbell

A CONSIDERABLE stir was created by the appearance, for
the first time in the proceedings, of the Attorney-General
himself.

Dr. Johnson was recalled and, in reply to *Mr. Lewis*, stated
that as he had driven down to The Priory with Sir William Gull
he had described the patient's symptoms and Sir William had
remarked, "That looks like poison." To this the witness had
answered that there were only two doubtful points: the exact
nature of the poison and how it got into the body. He had also
repeated the conversation he had had with Mrs. Cox, and the
patient's denial of taking anything but laudanum.

"I cannot conceive," declared witness, "how Sir William
can have been under the impression that he was going to see a
case of disease, unless he had forgotten what I said or dis-
believed me. . . . He did not ask the patient a single question
about his symptoms, or as to the length of his illness, and this
was because he had heard the whole history of the case from
me."

In reply to a suggestion of *Sir Henry James*, witness retorted: "I was not 'thrown off the scent' by not finding arsenic
—only off a false scent," and concluded by observing: "If Sir
William Gull thought he was going to see a case of disease,
then he placed more reliance upon a lady's note than upon
what I told him."

And now five of Charles Bravo's friends gave evidence. *Mr.*
McCalmont repeated the evidence he had given at the first
inquest and testified as to the friendly relations that seemed to
prevail between deceased and Mrs. Cox: an opinion confirmed

by *Mr. Edward Stanley Hope*. *Mr. Carlyle Willoughby* recounted the feelings which had led him to lay information at Scotland Yard and refrain from entering the widow's house when he attended the funeral. But it was the evidence of *Mr. Jepson Atkinson* which made the deepest impression. This witness stated that he and deceased had gone up to Oxford in the same term and had had "digs" together from 1866 to 1868. "I noticed that before going to bed he always took a deep draught of water. He used to drink it straight from the water-bottle in his room—or my room, or wherever he happened to be— without using a tumbler. This was an inveterate habit of his. He very often used my water-bottle, that is when we have been together. He was in the habit of coming into my room when I was in bed to read over what he had written during the day, and so I noticed it. I visited his stepfather's house up to about two or three years ago, when they lived at Lancaster Gate, and often slept there. Thus I had opportunities for observing that he still had the same habit, and I also observed it when we went to Paris together two years ago.

"*He was, I can say, the last man in the world to commit suicide, and I should like to say why I think so : he was better acquainted with medical jurisprudence than any barrister I knew; he was a very clear-headed man with a great deal of common sense and very little sentiment, and no feeling for any woman would make him take a painful and uncertain poison with the effects of which he was thoroughly acquainted.*"

Mr. Atkinson's evidence made it plain to all in Court how simple it would be for anyone knowing this nightly habit of the dead man to slip into his bedroom and drop into the water-bottle a deadly dose of tartar emetic. On the night of the fatal Tuesday the dead man's wife and her companion were alone together on that floor of the house for about twenty minutes while he was downstairs in the morning-room and the servants at their supper—there can hardly have been a mind in that motley assembly that did not form a picture of those two women, the companion sitting by the bedside of her accomplice while both listened attentively for that cry of agony which would herald the successful outcome of their plot.

The last of Charles Bravo's friends was *Mr. J. Meredith Brown*, stockbroker, who stated that he had known deceased ever since he had first matriculated and was on intimate terms with him. Deceased had done transactions in stocks through witness' firm since April 1873. "He liked to see if he could make £5 or £10. At the time of his death we had stock he had sold to the sum of £1,176, which we handed to his father after his death in exchange for the securities. I never knew him short of money. He was anxious about his wife's securities. He shewed me a list of her investments, and some I margined as dangerous and advised should be sold. The deceased took a deep interest in financial questions. He was a very careful man, the reverse of a spendthrift, and would be likely to be worried by losses."

The next witness was *Mrs. Campbell*. A chair was placed for her, and at the sight of that plump, matronly figure, the sweetness of her countenance overlaid with sorrow and distress, a wave of sympathy went out to her, and in the proceedings which followed even Mr. Lewis moderated his acerbity. With simple dignity she told the story of that first marriage of her daughter's which had had so promising a beginning and had come to so pitiful an end; she told of the struggle to wean Captain Ricardo of his vice, and how at last it was decided that he should undergo a course of treatment at Malvern. "My daughter and Captain Ricardo placed themselves under Dr. Gully's care. . . . I went in November 1870 to Malvern. I fetched my daughter to Buscot Park. . . . She was afraid to stay in the house with her husband because of his violence. She stayed with me until February 1871. . . .

"My daughter lived at Mr. Brookes' house for nine months to a year. . . . We had become aware of the frequent visits of Dr. Gully. That intimacy met with our entire disapproval. I had remonstrated with her on the subject. In addition I observed that she drank more wine than I approved. . . . She took a house at Streatham, and then moved to The Priory. . . . During this time neither my husband nor myself had seen anything of her."

Such, continued witness, had been the state of things until, in the previous autumn, her daughter had written and promised

to give up Dr. Gully " 'entirely and completely'. We received
her back as affectionately as before. . . . I became aware about
this time that she was about to marry Mr. Charles Bravo. . . . I
thought she was much attached to Mr. Bravo, and I understood
from her that she had told him the 'position of things' in
regard to Dr. Gully. I did not accept her position with Dr.
Gully as being criminal, but I thought she entertained an
extraordinary infatuation for him. . . .

"On my first interview with Mr. Charles Bravo I told him he
ought to inform his mother of all the circumstances. That was
in the presence of Mrs. Tom Campbell, my sister-in-law. . . .
She also urged the necessity, but he entirely and distinctly
refused either to tell his mother himself or to let Mrs. Cox do so.
. . . The marriage was from our house in Lowndes Square.
. . . They spent Christmas at Buscot, remaining there about a
fortnight."

Charles' letters to witness were now read,[1] also those, dated
10th and 16th April, which she had received from Florence.[2]

"When deceased was at Buscot at Christmas," continued
witness, "he spoke to me about my daughter taking too much
wine—that she took a glass of wine before she dressed for dinner.
That was her habit, I said, and he said, 'I'll cure her of it', but
he did not say how. I said,'You may do so by kindness and
firmness.' He made no reply to this. . . .''

2

The Twelfth Day: Wednesday, 26th July
Evidence of Mrs. Campbell (continued)

In reply to *Sir Henry James*, witness described her arrival at
The Priory on Thursday, 20th April. She related how her son-
in-law, having refused her suggestion that he should see a
clergyman, had burst into tears and recited the Lord's Prayer.

After Sir William Gull had told them next day that deceased was dying of poison, Mrs. Cox had told witness that
deceased had informed her he had taken poison. Witness had

[1] See Appendix I.   [2] See pages 98 and 108.

then repeated this to Mr. Royes Bell, who had replied, "He makes no admission."

In reply to *Mr. Lewis*, witness said: "Captain Ricardo settled £40,000 upon my daughter—the interest makes a portion of the £3,000 or £4,000 of her income. She also has £200 or £300 a year from her grandfather's estate. Mr. Bravo, senior, on the second marriage, gave his bond to the trustees of the first marriage settlement to pay the interest on £20,000 to his stepson."

Mr. Lewis' next questions were directed to that aspect of the case which was to become his main theme. "I am under the impression," said witness, "that the infatuation of my daughter for Dr. Gully commenced after the death of her first husband." Witness had no knowledge that the infatuation was a criminal one or that her daughter had conveyed that information to Mr. Charles Bravo. "My daughter is a lady of high education and accomplishments, and he was eager to marry her and proud of her. He was earnestly desirous that his mother should not prevent the marriage." Witness did not know that Mrs. Joseph Bravo was opposed to the marriage, but rather suspected that she did not want her son to marry at all. Deceased was very cheerful and good company. He appeared happy with his wife and she with him. Since his death witness had said that she thought it a great pity Dr. Gully had not left the neighbourhood.

Mrs. Cox had told witness: "Charlie said, 'I have taken poison; don't tell Florence.' The impression Mrs. Cox gave me was that my son-in-law had attempted to take his own life. He was then within a few hours of his death. I said, 'Charlie, what did you take?'—this was after Sir William Gull had gone. I put my hand on his arm as I asked him. He turned away impatiently, saying, 'I don't know.'

"Sir William asked him, 'What have you taken?' Deceased said, 'Laudanum; I took it myself.' Twice he said, 'I took it myself.' . . . He had repeated the Lord's Prayer after denying he had taken anything but laudanum."

In reply to *Mr. Murphy*: "*Deceased seemed to have something on his mind when he was pressed about having taken more than laudanum.*" Witness had heard before deceased's illness that an aunt of Mrs. Cox in Jamaica, who was leaving her some property, was anxious for her to return there; and it was in consequence of this, and not through any wish of deceased, that Mrs. Cox was about to do so, but witness had gathered that deceased did not wish to re-employ her on her return on account of the expense. Deceased had spoken to witness on more than one occasion about Dr. Gully and knew her daughter had asked him to leave the neighbourhood. She had heard deceased say that he wished he could "annihilate" Dr. Gully. "I should say that deceased was a passionate man. I have seen him get livid with passion on slight occasions."

And now the *Attorney-General*, Sir John Holker, rose to question the witness. Mrs. Cox, she said, knew all about her daughter's intimacy with Dr. Gully being broken off. "It struck me as strange that she should be receiving things from Dr. Gully, and that it would have been better if she had not; but it struck me, too, that Dr. Gully had done it out of kindness. . . .

"My daughter gained no financial advantage from the marriage." Her daughter had thought deceased penurious and saving, but had never told witness she was "disgusted with his meanness".[1] "Meanness," said witness, "is according to people's ideas: he had a money-mania."

Her daughter had complained that deceased's mother desired to interfere with their household arrangements—that she did not wish her to have a maid or to keep the cobs. "These things my daughter told me in January. She was angered at the mother, *as no money came from them except the £100 at the marriage*. My daughter did not see why she should not manage her house as she liked. I think she blamed her husband for listening to his mother. . . ."

In reply to *the jury*: "The deceased had a money-mania—he was always speaking of the cost of things. As to his being 'livid with passion', it was on the occasion of my daughter taking wine before dressing for dinner that I saw him so. I also saw him in a passion about the furniture. He was passionate, but it was soon over."

In reply to *Mr. Lewis*, witness said that deceased's feelings

[1] See page 178.

about Dr. Gully had not been given her as a reason why he should commit suicide. Her daughter had taken no steps to find out if deceased were murdered—she did not believe he was. She knew that Mr. Bravo had had the detectives put on, but he had never spoken of murder to her daughter or to any members of her family.

In reply to *Mr. Gorst*, witness said that there had been much discussion as to where this poison had been obtained, and Mr. Joseph Bravo having told witness' husband that he always kept it in his stables, her daughter had suggested that deceased had obtained it from there.

3

The Thirteenth Day: Thursday, 27th July
Evidence of Mr. Joseph Bravo (recalled), William Hemming
and Mrs. Jane Cannon Cox

The rumour that Mrs. Cox was to be called had caused a larger crowd than usual to assemble, including a number of fashionably dressed ladies who tried by every means, not excluding bribery, to get past the police into that erstwhile billiard saloon; but for every one who gained admittance a score were turned disconsolately away.

First of all, however, *Mr. Joseph Bravo* and his coachman were called to rebut Mrs. Campbell's allegation of the previous day that the former had admitted that tartar emetic was kept in his stables. "I never kept tartar emetic," he stated in reply to Mr. Lewis, "and it is not an accurate statement that I ever told anybody I did."

In reply to *Sir Henry James*: "I did not know until the Monday following my son's death that antimony had been found."[1] On the 27th April Mr. Robert Campbell had called at Palace Green and in the course of conversation witness had told him that tartar emetic "was much used by grooms to produce a glossy coat in their horses". Witness had observed

[1] I.e. 24th April; but according to Mrs. Campbell's evidence Florence was not informed until after the inquest on the 28th (see page 164), though, as we are about to see, her father knew of it at least as early as the 27th.

at the same time that he had never heard of antimony being taken to commit suicide, "though it was used by persons to take the lives of others".

In reply to *Mr. Murphy*, witness stated that it was not within his knowledge that Mrs. Cox had received a pressing letter from her aunt asking her to return to Jamaica. He did not know that deceased had had an anonymous letter; none had come to him or to his family that he was aware of. His wife had not objected to deceased marrying, but she had objected to his marrying Mrs. Ricardo.

William Hemming, groom and coachman to the previous witness for the past eleven years, confirmed that he had never used antimony for his horses nor kept it in the stables.

And now the reporters began to sharpen their pencils in eager anticipation. As the *Daily Telegraph's* representative wrote: "There was a great stir in Court when Mr. Burleigh Muir said, 'Call Mrs. Cox,' and orders were given to keep the door clear. Mrs. Cox wore deep black and seemed only a few years senior to Mrs. Bravo, who is thirty-one."

There was scarcely room for the purposeful little figure to move to the chair which had been placed for her, so tightly packed were the spectators. Under the raking stare of those many eyes she held herself erect, her black silk mantle sitting neatly on her narrow shoulders, her bonnet, trimmed with black flowers and egret tips, settled firmly on her smooth, ebony hair. She knew that in all that assembly she had not a single friend; she knew that, though she had not been charged with murder, everyone believed her guilty of it and that her Counsel was at his wits' end how to prevent that charge being preferred: she knew that upon him, and her own wits, depended not only her liberty, but perhaps her very life.

Sir John Hall and Mr. William Roughead both express the opinion that Mrs. Cox made a bad witness, but those who follow her evidence with the attention it deserves can hardly fail to agree with so unimpeachable an authority as the late Sir Douglas Strait, who was present in Court and declared that he "had never seen so intelligent and composed a witness as Mrs. Cox". During four whole days she withstood the exacting, though patient, cross-examination of the Attorney-General, and that of the ruthless and relentless Mr. Lewis, with equal self-possession. Smoothing the table before her with black-gloved fingertips she fenced with them adroitly, fending off accusations of perjury with subtle prevarication, parrying sarcasm with unctuous demureness. She was maddeningly genteel; she never once became shrill—and they never once got the better of her.

In reply to *Mr. Murphy*, she related the story of her life up to the time, in 1871, when, as governess to Mr. Brookes' younger daughter, Mrs. Ricardo had offered her the post of lady companion.

In March 1874 Mrs. Ricardo had moved from Leigham Court Road to The Priory, and that same month witness had had a letter from her aunt, which was read out in Court, asking her to return to Jamaica. In the autumn of that year, Mrs. Ricardo had called for her one day at Palace Green and so met Mr. Charles Bravo. In March 1875 witness had visited the Continent with Mrs. Ricardo and Dr. Gully, and in September witness had gone with Mrs. Ricardo first to Eastbourne and then to Brighton, where they had met Mr. Charles Bravo "in the street" and this had led to his visiting them and ultimately to his proposal of marriage.

At this point *Mr. Lewis* complained that Mr. Murphy was carrying on his examination in "a conversational tone" and witness' replies could not be heard. "A lady who can speak across a dinner-table can surely speak loud enough to be heard," he remarked tartly, and the spectators applauded this sentiment, stamping their feet and thumping their umbrellas on the floor.

Sir Henry James: "This is monstrous!"

Mr. Serjeant Parry: "Applause in a Court of Justice! It is horrible! It is fearful! There is a sort of reign of terror in reference to anybody who is called! I wish to express the utmost indignation at these manifestations."

Mr. Murphy: "It is not surprising the witness cannot be heard if she is subjected to demonstrations like that."

The Coroner: "I shall order the Court to be cleared unless order is kept."

The examination being resumed, witness, speaking "in a somewhat louder tone", described how, before the marriage, she had told Mr Charles Bravo that he ought to inform his mother of Mrs. Ricardo's former acquaintance with Dr. Gully. He refused, and when witness offered to do it for him "would not hear of it". "You know what the consequences of that would be," he had said; "the marriage would be broken off and then I should leave the country and no one would ever see me again."

At the end of November 1875 witness and Mrs. Ricardo had stayed at Palace Green for a week. The wedding had been fixed for 14th December, but at Mr. Charles Bravo's request was put forward to the 7th. He had told witness—as had Mrs. Ricardo and Mrs. Joseph Bravo—that he did not wish her to leave after the marriage.

While staying again at Palace Green after the marriage and just before Christmas Mr. Charles Bravo had received an anonymous letter which "had made him very angry".

CHAPTER SIX

14TH, 15TH, 16TH AND 17TH DAYS OF THE INQUEST

I

The Fourteenth Day: Friday, 28th July
Evidence of Mrs. Jane Cannon Cox (continued)

THE TIMES records that on this day "there was great competition for space in the room, several Members of Parliament being present who stood crowded together in a part of the room where they could see little and hear less".

Mr. Murphy resumed his examination of Mrs. Cox, who stated that the anonymous letter received by deceased had been sent to his Chambers in the Temple. Witness could not remember the exact wording, but it accused him of marrying Mrs. Ricardo for her money.[1] He had been very angry and had asked witness if the handwriting were Dr. Gully's. "I told him I thought not."

Witness next recounted her meetings with Dr. Gully, stating that these had taken place "by accident, certainly not by appointment", and described how Charles had overtaken her on the way to Balham station and compelled her to open the letter in which Dr. Gully had sent her the "treatment" for Jamaica fever.

On 10th April she had found the bottle of laurel-water awaiting her at 150 Lancaster Road. Mrs. Bravo said she did not want it as she was sleeping better. Witness had taken it to her own room. In Jamaica laurel-water "was given to children".

On 11th April witness had had another letter from her aunt which she had read out to Mr. and Mrs. Bravo. Mr. Bravo had said: "It seems that you will be obliged to go; I will take care of the boys while you are away, and I shall be very glad to see you when you return." Witness had decided to go as soon as Mrs. Bravo had recovered from her illness.

[1] Witness omitted the reference to "Dr. Gully's mistress".

"Mr. and Mrs. Bravo seemed to be very happy except when he got into a temper. . . . Although he had a very passionate temper, it was not of long duration and all was made up soon afterwards." He frequently referred to Dr. Gully: witness had heard him say he "wished Dr. Gully were dead; that he would like to shoot him; that he would like to see his funeral crossing Tooting Common".

Deceased's parents were "constantly interfering in the management of the house". A "serious ebullition of temper" had occurred on 7th March: deceased had struck his wife and then rushed out of the house. It was late at night, and witness had followed him and begged him to return. The next serious quarrel was a week before deceased's death—on Good Friday.

On Tuesday, 18th April, witness had gone to Worthing to take the house there. She had returned to The Priory about 7.20 p.m. and had gone up to Mrs. Bravo's room where she found her dressing for dinner. Witness had told her she should have gone to bed "as she was still weak from her illness and had been up to London that day. She replied that she was anxious to sit up for dinner with Charlie, and would go to bed directly afterwards. . . . I went straight up to my room. I went into no other room. I then went down to the morning-room, going into no other room on the way down."

At dinner deceased had been "very much annoyed" by a letter from his stepfather and said "the Governor had no business to open his letters or to write to him in the way he had done". He was greatly put out.

At dinner deceased had had lamb and the savoury; his wife, fish and lamb; witness had had all three courses. He had drunk Burgundy, his wife and witness sherry or Marsala. Soon after they had returned to the morning-room deceased had told his wife "she ought to go to bed". On the way up she had asked witness to get her some wine and water. Witness had half-filled a small tumbler with wine and added water. When Keeber had entered with a can of hot water at about 9 o'clock Mrs. Bravo had handed her the tumbler and asked her to fetch "a little wine". Soon afterwards deceased had entered the room and said in French: " 'You have sent downstairs for more wine; you have drunk nearly a bottle today.' I don't think Mrs. Bravo answered," and Mr. Bravo left the room.

"There had been discussions between deceased and his wife concerning the amount of wine she drank. I have heard him say at dinner, 'You have had quite enough,' and sometimes he would get up from table and drink some of the wine himself out of her glass."

Witness had sat down at Mrs. Bravo's bedside, as had been her habit since her illness, until she fell asleep. "I heard nothing to attract my attention until Keeber came into the room and said: 'Mr. Bravo is ill' or 'very ill'. I do not know if the outer green baize door of Mrs. Bravo's room was open or shut at the time he shouted out. The inner door was shut. Usually both doors were shut when Mrs. Bravo was in bed. I immediately rushed out of the room and into Mr. Bravo's room, and saw him standing at the open window. He said, 'I have taken poison for Dr. Gully; don't tell Florence.' I asked him how he could do such a thing, and he screamed out violently: 'Hot water! Hot water! Hot water!' He was then sick out of the window, and I fancied I smelt chloroform. I rushed to the mantelpiece and looked at the chloroform bottle and found only a few drops left in it. I immediately sent for Dr. Harrison and told Keeber to bring some mustard and water for an emetic. . . . He sank down on the floor as though he had no power." After the mustard and water, deceased had been sick into the basin, and witness told Keeber to empty it and bring it back in case it be needed again.

2

The Fifteenth Day: Monday, 31st July
Evidence of Mrs. Jane Cannon Cox (continued)

After one or two questions to round off the examination of his client at the point where it had been left the previous Friday, Mr. Murphy put into evidence the list of drugs which Dr. Gully had given to provide a remedy for Jamaica fever. To his subsequent questions the witness emphatically denied that she had ever obtained any of them. Presumably the police had already made their investigations and were satisfied as to the veracity of her statement, for the matter attained no further prominence.

Continuing, witness said that she had not told Dr. Moore what deceased had said about taking poison because she was expecting the family physician, Dr. Harrison. "I did not like to tell a gentleman of Balham because I thought it would be such a dreadful scandal, and that Mr. Bravo when he recovered would be very angry with me if I did so. I said to Dr. Harrison, 'I am quite sure he has taken poison—chloroform.' . . . I told Mr. Bell, 'Charlie said he had taken poison and told me not to tell Florence.' Mr. Bell replied, 'You had better tell that to Dr. Johnson: it's no use bringing us here and letting us work in the dark.' I repeated the same to Dr. Johnson. I don't remember what Dr. Johnson said. . . . *The doctors made no further inquiry as to what Mr. Bravo said to me. I was not brought face to face with the deceased to have the matter explained. I wish I had been so brought face to face with him. The doctors never said anything doubting the accuracy of what I said—not for a moment.*"

This further omission on the part of the medical men constituted a strong point in favour of Mrs. Cox.

The next day—Wednesday, 19th April—Mr. Bell asked witness to stay in the sick-room while he went down to lunch. Deceased then said to her: " 'Why did you tell them? Does Florence know I have poisoned myself? Don't tell her'—imploringly. I replied, 'I was obliged to tell them; I couldn't let you die.' I then asked, 'What have you taken, Charlie?' He turned away his head, saying impatiently, 'I don't know.' " Then before witness could ask him anything more his wife had entered the room.

"I asked Sir William Gull what deceased had taken; he replied, 'The symptoms point to arsenic, but he will only acknowledge laudanum.' I said, 'Can't you get him to say what he has really taken?' Sir William said, 'I really cannot press a dying man further.' . . . I told Sir William about deceased being sick out of the window; he said: 'Has that been collected? Let it be collected.' "

On Thursday morning, the 20th, Mrs. Charles Bravo had

asked witness to go to Dr. Gully. She said, "I should never be
happy again if every means were not taken to save him."
Witness had seen Dr. Gully in his library and informed him that
deceased had told her he had taken poison. She had described
his symptoms and said he was so ill that he was not expected to
live. Dr. Gully had said that he thought the condition was
amenable to homoeopathic treatment, and prescribed two
drops of *arsenicum* in a dessertspoonful of water at frequent in-
tervals—witness could not recall exactly how often—compresses on the stomach and a mustard plaster down the spine.

Witness did not know whether deceased had a habit of
drinking water—"There was nothing which would take me
into his room at night so that I should know of this habit," she
observed primly. The mustard she had given deceased had
been mixed with hot water from the can Keeber brought.
Witness had not noticed the state of the carafe on deceased's
washstand.

Having described the laurel-water incident of 1st May and
how Joseph Bravo had declared "there were poisons in every
room in the house", witness concluded:

"Apart from what Mr. Bravo told me I have not the slightest
knowledge of how he came by his death."

And now the *Attorney-General* rose to cross-examine. He
began by asking her what was the oath she had taken at the
first inquest.

Witness: "I was sworn to tell the truth, the whole truth, and
nothing but the truth."

The Attorney-General: "I will read your deposition before the
Coroner which you swore to be the whole truth."

He did so, stressing the sentence, "I have taken poison; don't
tell Florence."

Witness: "That is what I said then."

The Attorney-General: "*Then!* But *now* you say there is a good
deal in it which isn't true?"

Witness' lips quivered, assiduously she stroked the table
before her, her eyes following the rhythmic movements of her
fingers. The Attorney-General repeated his question.

Witness (with careful deliberation): "I will not say that it is not true, but I own I did not use the words that deceased took poison 'for Dr. Gully'."

The Attorney-General: "Then you did not tell the whole truth?"

Witness sat silent. The silence in that thronged Court was weighted with suspicion and hostility against her. It was probably in that frightening moment that she decided that if it became necessary to betray the carefully guarded secret as to the true relationship which had existed between Florence and Dr. Gully in order to divert that hostility from herself, she would do so. But her loyalty held during the next two hours in which the Attorney-General sought to establish the fact that an "engagement" to marry when Mrs. Gully died had existed between Dr. Gully and Florence Ricardo. Secondly he wished to shew that the genteel little widow facing him had been privy to this intention, and by accompanying the "lovers" on their various travels had willingly abetted their flagrant defiance of the rigid conventions of the time. It is in this limited sense only that the term "lover" is used in the ensuing interrogation, for at this stage neither the Attorney-General nor anyone else in Court had proof of the deeper intimacy.

The Attorney-General: "What was the relationship between Mrs. Ricardo and Dr. Gully?"

Witness: "There was great intimacy between them; there was familiarity—gentlemanly familiarity—on the part of Dr. Gully. Mrs. Ricardo had portraits of Dr. Gully and wore one in a locket in her bosom."

The Attorney-General: "Now what do you suppose was the nature of their acquaintance?"

Witness: "I thought he was very much interested in her."

The Attorney-General: "Will you tell us if you looked upon him merely as her friend—or as her lover?"

Witness: "I cannot tell exactly."

The Attorney-General: "I put it to you again: did you know that Dr. Gully was Mrs. Ricardo's lover?"

There was a long pause. The Court sat in tense silence broken only by the droning of flies against the window-panes. Witness' eyes stared fixedly at her busily stroking fingers.

The Attorney-General: "You lived with her for four years, and I ask you—did you not know sooner or later during that time that Dr. Gully was Mrs. Ricardo's lover?"

Witness (reluctantly): "Yes, I think I did."

The Attorney-General: "When did you first know? Was it at Leigham Court Road?"

Witness: "Yes, I concluded so from his coming there so often."

The Attorney-General: "Did you know he was a married man?"

Witness: "Yes, but I was told that he had not seen his wife for thirty years."

The Attorney-General: "You know now that that is not true?"

Witness (sharply): "No, I do not!"

To the Attorney-General's next questions witness replied that she had seen Dr. Gully kiss Mrs. Ricardo. She had never known him stay late at night except once when Mrs. Ricardo was dangerously ill. She knew there was scandal about Mrs. Ricardo, but did not believe it. She knew Mrs. Ricardo used to go away with Dr. Gully from time to time; they did not go alone for Mrs. Ricardo took her maid, and Dr. Gully his man, Pritchard. "I did not think there was anything wrong in Mrs. Ricardo going away with Dr. Gully as a friend."

The Attorney-General: "But surely it is not usual for a lady in her position to do that?"

Witness (amidst titters): "Well, he was an *old* gentleman."

The Attorney-General: "Before they went to Kissingen you knew that Dr. Gully had been visiting Mrs. Ricardo?"

Witness: "I must have known he was coming to see her."

The Attorney-General: "As her lover?"

Witness: "Well, I don't know exactly what you mean by 'lover'. I should like to know what you mean."

The Attorney-General: "You knew they were more than friends?"

Witness: "I knew she was fond of him. He was extremely clever."

The Attorney-General: "You knew she loved him?"

Witness: "I knew she was fond of him."

The Attorney-General: "Will you go no further?"

Witness: "No—well, if Dr. Gully had not been married it might have been a match."

The Attorney-General: "Do you, or do you not, know that she had agreed to marry him when his wife died?"

Witness: "I believe it was so arranged. I don't know how old Mrs. Gully is, but I believe she is over ninety and has been separated from Dr. Gully for thirty years."

In answer to further questions witness replied that from the beginning of 1874 she had accompanied Mrs. Ricardo and Dr. Gully wherever they went, at home or abroad.

The Attorney-General: "Now, what was the demeanour of these people—did they treat each other as lovers?"

Witness: "They kissed each other. They were not often alone; I was there, and never in my presence did they speak of their plans for the future."

The Attorney-General: "Perhaps you left them alone purposely?"

Witness: "Sometimes I had to go to see my children."

The Attorney-General: "But you did not have your children in Italy?"

Witness: "Oh, *there* they were never alone! I occupied the same bedroom with Mrs. Ricardo, always."

The Attorney-General: "Did you tell Mr. Charles Bravo how fond Mrs. Ricardo was of Dr. Gully?"

Witness: "She did so herself. I know he knew everything because he mentioned it."

The Attorney-General: "Do you think—and you know the manner of man Mr. Bravo was—that if he had known as much as you have told us he would have married Mrs. Ricardo?"

Witness (emphatically): "I believe he would have married her."

The Attorney-General: "Did you tell him that Dr. Gully was Mrs. Ricardo's lover? That they had been together for weeks?"

Witness: "I did not tell Mr. Bravo this because Mrs. Ricardo told me she had told him. She told me she had told him everything. I know he knew everything because he mentioned it."

Continuing, witness said that she had known the Joseph

Bravos for many years and was bound to them by ties of gratitude; she had never told anything of Mrs. Ricardo's private affairs to them because Mr. Charles Bravo had desired her not to do so. "Mrs. Charles Bravo never told me she was afraid her husband would find out about her previous conduct with Dr. Gully; she had no reason to fear that as she had told him everything."

Witness was then questioned on the subject of the anonymous letter the deceased had received; on her own meetings with Dr. Gully after the marriage; of the incident of deceased compelling her to open Dr. Gully's letter; and about the bottle of laurel-water. The Attorney-General's questions then passed to the night of the fatal Tuesday.

It might have been ten minutes, said witness, between the time deceased was sick out of the window and the time he was sick into the basin after being given the mustard emetic. "I gave him that emetic in order to get any deleterious matter off his stomach. . . . It did not strike me, as he had told me he had taken poison, that it would be as well for the medical men to see this vomit. There were other receptacles and basins in the room, but I never thought of them. I had no object in throwing the vomit away—what object could I have? I quite thought it was chloroform he had taken; that was why I gave him coffee —to keep him awake. I could not account for his saying 'don't tell Florence' except that he wished to save her pain. I understood that he had taken poison because he was jealous of Dr. Gully—not because he had heard stories about his wife. . . . Dr. Harrison has denied that I used the word 'poison' to him, but that does not alter my impression that I did—it is possible on a night like that he might not remember all that occurred. . . . I did not know deceased was dying; I still hoped the effects would pass off. Dr. Harrison did say that he did not expect the deceased to live long. I did not think about giving him an antidote for poison. *I told the doctors about his vomiting out of the window directly they came.*"

Witness had not told Mrs. Charles Bravo about deceased having said he had taken poison until after Sir William Gull had been on Thursday. "Dr. Johnson did mention it to me in

Mrs. Bravo's presence and she did say 'Has he taken poison?' but she was so exhausted I did not think she understood it fully.

"On April 26th I went to Brighton to take a house. . . . I went to see Dr. Dill; I told him that Mr. Bravo said he had taken poison on account of Dr. Gully; I had not told anyone before that. I told Dr. Dill of this because Mrs. Bravo had been under his care when she broke off with Dr. Gully. Dr. Dill said he thought her reputation would be injured by it being spoken of. I told Mrs. Campbell and Mr. Brookes of it before I made my statement to the Treasury."

3

The Sixteenth Day: Tuesday, 1st August
Evidence of Mrs. Jane Cannon Cox (continued)

In reply to the *Attorney-General*, witness stated that she had known Mrs. Bravo would be seeing Dr. Dill, and in the train down to Brighton she had told her deceased had said: " 'I have taken poison for Dr. Gully; don't tell Florence.' I had not told her before then. When they had all been speculating where deceased could have got the antimony, Mr. Campbell had remarked that Mr. Joseph Bravo had told him antimony was kept in the stables at Palace Green. They had discussed everything which might suggest a motive for suicide. They thought the 'connection' at Maidenhead might have had something to do with it. The question had arisen if antimony were used in The Priory stables: the coachman said he had never used antimony. Mrs. Bravo was very fond of her horses and would go to the stables to give them apples, but I have never heard her speak of 'physicking' them when they were ill."

The Attorney-General: "Was it not said in the presence of Mrs. Charles Bravo that there was no reason for Mr. Bravo committing suicide unless it were on account of Dr. Gully?"

Witness: "It was said this might have been his motive, and it was also said it might have been on account of the connection at Maidenhead."

And now *Mr. Lewis* rose. The Attorney-General had, in the words of Sir John Hall, "put his questions in a somewhat persuasive style", but Mr. Lewis "adopted a sharper tone and more aggressive methods". Indeed, the tension mounted as he set himself deliberately to brow-beat and intimidate the witness, his demand: "Answer my question, Madam!" coming like the crack of a whip at her least hesitation. Under his influence the inquiry lost all resemblance to an inquest bent on discovering how Charles Bravo died, and he was permitted by a cowed Coroner to pursue courses and use methods which would have been sternly forbidden him in a Criminal Court.

But before proceeding to his cross-examination of Mrs. Cox, one must pause a moment and glance at what had been going on behind the scenes. It would appear that the previous day—31st July—Mrs. Cox had had an interview with Mrs. Campbell and her brother, Mr. Orr, at which she told them that the intimacy between Florence and Dr. Gully had been an immoral one. Although there is no evidence that they did so, it may be assumed that Mrs. Campbell and Mr. Orr besought her not to divulge this. But we have Mrs. Harford's evidence that Mrs. Cox told her of it about the same date, and asked her advice as to whether or not she should inform Mr. Murphy of it; and that, after consulting her husband, Mrs. Harford advised her not to do so. When, therefore, Mrs. Cox entered the Court on that morning of Tuesday, 1st August, no one was prepared for what she would presently disclose.

Mr. Lewis came straight to the point: "From the conversations you had with Mr. Bravo before his marriage, and before his engagement, did you believe that he knew that Mrs. Ricardo had had criminal intercourse with Dr. Gully?"

Witness (cautiously): "I knew that she had told him everything before the engagement."

Mr. Lewis: "Will you answer my question, Madam—do you believe he knew she had had intercourse with Dr. Gully?"

Witness: "Knew of it on the 1st November?"[1]

Mr. Lewis: "That is the date I am speaking about."

Witness: "No, not then."[2]

[1] The date the engagement was ratified.
[2] From Mrs. Cox's reply to the next question it would appear she was referring to the semi-confession of 21st October. See page 58.

Mr. Lewis: "Was it your impression from his conversation that he believed her to be a perfectly chaste woman?"

Witness: "I believe before the marriage he knew everything, but not at that time." Then suddenly, without prompting, words that were to strip Florence Bravo of every rag of reputation and bring consternation to Sir Henry James and witness' own Counsel began to pour from her lips. "At that time I had spoken of her to Mr. Bravo in the highest terms—of her disposition, her kindness, and her being able to make him happy. . . . He believed her to be a chaste woman, and I did not create any suspicion that she was different from that. I left her to tell him what she liked. I had spoken to him of Dr. Gully, and he told me that Mrs. Ricardo had told him all about Dr. Gully. I did not keep anything back before the marriage—*well, I did*, but let me understand fully what you mean?"

For no reason that anyone has ever been able to understand, she was ratting. The dead man, the purpose of the inquiry, were forgotten: sexual curiosity held the Court tense and silent.

Mr. Lewis: "You say you kept something back before marriage—what was it?"

Witness: "I kept back from him what Mrs. Ricardo had told me after giving up her acquaintance with Dr. Gully."

Mr. Lewis: "What was it she told you?"

Witness: "Of her intimacy with Dr. Gully."

Mr. Lewis: "What do you mean by intimacy?"

Witness: "You may draw your own conclusions."

Mr. Lewis: "No, I decline to do that—tell me, Madame, was it a *criminal* intimacy with Dr. Gully that she told you of?" Her fingers smoothed the table and Mr. Lewis rapped out: "Answer my question, Madam."

Witness: "Yes, a criminal intimacy." Her words seemed to hang on the air for a long instant before exclamations of shocked excitement broke out. And now she sought to justify herself: "But you will remember that I had no idea of that before she told me. She told me of it the day before leaving Brighton—before the marriage—and I urged her to tell Mr. Bravo. I did not hear her tell him, but he spoke to me on the subject afterwards."

Mr. Lewis: "Did he let you know that he knew his wife's intimacy with Dr. Gully had been of a criminal nature?"

Witness: "Yes; at Palace Green he told me."

Mr. Lewis: "And you have told no mortal subject until this moment that Mr. Charles Bravo knew that his wife had had criminal intimacy with Dr. Gully?"

Witness: "I mentioned it after the marriage to a lady, but I would rather that her name should not be mentioned."

Mr. Lewis requested witness to write down the name and address. She demurred, but he insisted so peremptorily that Mr. Murphy sprang to his feet, and exhibiting the caricature of his client dangling from a gibbet, declared as he tossed it across the table to Counsel for the Crown that Mr. Lewis' methods "were a continuation of this selfsame torture".

Mr. Lewis: "I intend to perform my duty quite regardless of the consequences to anybody. I am surprised that a Q.C. should have spoken to me as he has done after the delicacy I have exhibited in wishing the lady's name not to be made public."

Mr. Murphy (tartly): "I haven't noticed much delicacy displayed by Mr. Lewis!"

Mr. Lewis (to witness): "Did you say at the Treasury: 'He had no reason to take poison, as she, I knew, had not had any communication with Dr. Gully since the marriage, and their acquaintance before the marriage was, though very imprudent, I conscientiously believe entirely of an innocent nature'?"

Witness: "Yes, I stated that."

Mr. Lewis: "How came you to state there, in that deliberate statement, that you 'believe, conscientiously believe', her acquaintance with Dr. Gully before marriage to be 'entirely of an innocent nature' when you knew it to be to the contrary?"

Witness (nimbly extricating herself): "I did not say 'I *believe* it to be of an entirely innocent nature'; I said 'I *believed*' it to be so—and so I did until she told me to the contrary at Brighton." Continuing, witness said: "I kept that back wilfully: I did not think it necessary to bring forward Mrs. Ricardo's name more than there was occasion for. I was not stating the 'full particulars' in regard to that; I was stating the 'full particulars' in regard to the death."

In answer to further questions: "In December, before the marriage, I did have a conversation with Mrs. Joseph Bravo; I won't swear that I did not use the words, referring to Mrs. Ricardo, 'She is everything that is good.' She *was* everything that was good except in this one thing. . . . I did conceal this from Mr. and Mrs. Joseph Bravo," witness freely admitted, adding with unanswerable logic: "It was the son's duty to speak of it to his mother, not mine. I did say Mrs. Ricardo 'would make an excellent wife for Charlie', and she *did* make him an excellent wife; she did all she could to make him happy, and Mr. Bravo told his mother on his death-bed that she had been the sweetest and best of wives. . . . I had a great affection for Mrs. Ricardo, and I had the same when she became Mrs. Bravo. I had the same when she confessed the 'adulterous intercourse'—you cannot change affection."

Mr. Lewis was finding Mrs. Cox a harder nut to crack than he had expected. He now attempted to discredit her evidence of the previous day. Why, he asked, had she not told the Attorney-General that she had known of the "adulterous intercourse"? Again the witness was ready with an answer: the Attorney-General had been questioning her about a time *before* she had known of it; if he had been questioning her, as Mr. Lewis was doing, about a time *after* she had known of it, then she would have answered him as she had answered Mr. Lewis. "I answered according to my knowledge at the time of which he was speaking."

Mr. Lewis: "For how long did Mrs. Ricardo say she had lived upon these terms with Dr. Gully?"

Witness: "She told me upon one occasion only—when they were at Kissingen."

Mr. Lewis: "Why then did you tell the Attorney-General that you did not know they passed as man and wife?"

Witness: "I don't know what you mean by 'passing as man and wife'. If the Attorney-General had asked me what you have asked me, I should have told him what I have told you."

Witness now related how the "attachment" to Dr. Gully

had been broken off and how she herself had met his train at Croydon. After the engagement he had written Mrs. Ricardo a "very angry" letter, then another, saying "he was so grieved at the time he had written it that he had expressed himself hastily". On the eve of the marriage deceased had said to witness: "I think a woman who has gone wrong is more likely to go straight in future than one who has never strayed."

Again witness was questioned in detail about the events of Tuesday, 18th April. As for Mrs. Bravo having taken "more wine than was good for her health" that night, she had had what witness and Keeber had taken upstairs: as to that being too much—"well, perhaps it was". Deceased had screamed out loudly for hot water to Keeber, "but he did not say very loudly what he said to me about the poison. . . . As to when I heard that Mr. Bravo had denied telling me anything about poisoning himself, I heard early on the morning of the 19th that he would not *admit* anything; Mr. Bell told me Mr. Bravo had said he did not *remember* telling me anything. . . . I still feel great affection for Mrs. Bravo. I do not consider I swore falsely because I did not mention certain words: I did not do so because they would have injured Mrs. Bravo's reputation."

Mr. Lewis: "Would you have considered it very wicked to have sworn falsely?"

Witness (with emotion): "I never thought of myself; I thought only of Mrs. Bravo."

Mr. Lewis: "You have eminent Counsel: let me ask you—is that at your own expense?"

Witness (sharply): "That has nothing to do with this inquiry."

Twice Mr. Lewis demanded an answer, and at last witness admitted reluctantly: "It is not at my expense."

Sir Henry James now rose. His face was grave. Suddenly and deliberately, for no reason he could imagine, Mrs. Cox had betrayed Florence Bravo to her deadliest enemy and rendered her position perilous. Only she could have done so, for no evidence existed that criminal intimacy had ever taken place. There was scarcely an hour left before the Court would adjourn. He must devote that time to rehabilitating his client's reputation as well as he could—shew how greatly she had suffered during her first marriage, how compelling had been the influence which Dr. Gully had exerted over her, and how greatly the witness was indebted to her. Before the proceedings re-opened next morning he must make the critical decision whether to pursue or abandon his carefully prepared case.

In answer to his questions witness stated that Mrs. Bravo had "suffered wretchedly with her first husband". Dr. Gully had had great influence over her; "he was a very fascinating man, and one who would be likely to interest women very much". Witness herself had felt his fascination. "I told him all about myself—he knew all about my affairs." Mrs. Bravo had always been very kind to witness and her children. It had been out of gratitude to Mrs. Bravo that she had omitted Dr. Gully's name from her evidence at the first inquest. If Mr. Bravo had made inquiries at Balham, he could have learned the local gossip about Mrs. Ricardo's association with Dr. Gully. Witness had advised Mrs. Ricardo to delay her marriage with Mr. Bravo until the spring when she would have known him better, but he had pressed for it to take place early in December against the wishes of her family.

At this point the Court adjourned, and as Sir Henry James left he was on the horns of a dilemma. Scarcely an eyebrow had been raised over the fact that Charles Bravo had had a mistress, but shivers of excited horror had passed over the Court when Mrs. Cox divulged the fact that Florence Ricardo had likewise been guilty of the sin of fornication. The Church might draw a distinction between fornication and adultery, but to the jury they were one and the same, and in their eyes a woman who was capable of breaking the Seventh Commandment would be equally capable of breaking the Sixth.

It had not yet been stated in Court that Charles Bravo had had an illegitimate child, though that, too, was unlikely to cause excitement: but if Mrs. Cox elected to reveal tomorrow that his client had submitted to an abortion at the hands of Dr. Gully the effect upon the jury might well be catastrophic. Sir Henry James therefore decided—which no doubt was wise—to fore-stall that possibility by eliciting the worst that could be known about his client in such a way as to rob it of its sensational quality. But the decision he made simultaneously to abandon the case he had so carefully prepared to prove Florence Bravo's innocence of her husband's death was to have deplorable results and to prevent the story within the story—though the Crown itself knew its nature—from being heard in Court.

Sir Edward Clarke, K.C., whose own painstaking labour on behalf of Adelaide Bartlett alone saved her from conviction for the murder of her husband, writes thus of Sir Henry James: "As an advocate he was skilful but not very courageous, and for fear of losing a case he often settled it when with a little more energy and persistence he might have won."[1] Never was this criticism truer than in the Bravo case.

4

*The Seventeenth Day: Wednesday, 2nd August
Evidence of Mrs. Jane Cannon Cox (continued)*

Sir Henry James opened the day's proceedings by reading Florence's letter from Kissingen to Mrs. Cox, which shewed her as a woman who in spite of her wealth took a practical interest in the affairs of her household. "Mrs. Ricardo," stated witness in answer to Sir Henry's questions, "took a great interest in domestic affairs. . . . I was on terms more friendly with Mrs. Ricardo than is usual with a companion."

Next Sir Henry elicited how, in spite of his client's estrangement from her family, her brother and his wife, and her aunt, continued to visit her and shew their affection for her; how she had often expressed regret at not being able to see her mother, and how anxious she had been when, in the spring of 1875, she had learned of her mother's illness. He went on to elicit that, as soon as Dr. Gully had left for the Continent and his influence had been removed, "Mrs. Ricardo had grown strong in her desire to be reunited with her family", and that, although Dr. Gully "had been much displeased when Mrs. Ricardo wished to break off the attachment, and had been much displeased

[1] *The Years of My Life*—Sir Edward Clarke, K.C.

at the acquaintanceship with Mr. Bravo, Mrs. Ricardo maintained it notwithstanding that displeasure".

Having shewn the Court that as a result of Captain Ricardo's dipsomania his client had fallen victim to a man whose powers of fascination had been felt even by the witness—a man who had not hesitated to gratify a selfish passion regardless of the consequences to herself—having depicted her to the Court as a warm-hearted, sensitive woman, struggling to break free from the spell of that fascination and be reunited with her family, Sir Henry approached the delicate subject before him with all the skill he could command. His voice was almost casual as he reminded witness of her statement of the previous day that she had not known about the improper intimacy until Mrs. Ricardo had told her of it at Brighton in October 1875, then inquired: had anything taken place after Mrs. Ricardo's return from Kissingen in September 1872?

Witness: "After her return from Kissingen Mrs. Ricardo had an illness and Dr. Gully attended her."

Sir Henry James: "That illness was a miscarriage?"

Witness: "Dr. Gully said the illness arose from a kind of tumour which he removed. No one was in attendance except Dr. Gully. Mrs. Ricardo appeared to suffer a great deal."

Had witness not known the true nature of that illness? asked Sir Henry in tones which expressed his incredulity that the mother of four children could hardly have been in attendance upon such a case without knowing its real cause.

Witness: "At the time I gave credence to the statements made me."

Satisfied that he had elicited this damaging information with the minimum of sensation, Sir Henry now proceeded to emphasize the fact that Charles Bravo had married his wife in full knowledge of it and had hurried on the marriage date against both her own and her parents' wishes.

His next questions produced the replies that witness had never heard Mrs. Charles Bravo say an unkind thing about her husband, either to his face or behind his back. "Mr. Bravo was at times anxious about money matters in relation to household expenditure. Mrs. Bravo's tendency was to be free and open in her expenditure—causing differences. There was also cause for difference in the interference of Mrs. Joseph Bravo in their household affairs. He was very quick and hasty in temper, but apart from these circumstances Mr. and Mrs. Bravo appeared to live on terms of sincere affection. . . . I never heard Mrs. Bravo express the slightest wish to hold any communication with Dr. Gully. . . . Mr. Bravo spoke of Dr. Gully with anger and hatred. These expressions increased in intensity because he knew that Dr. Gully continued to reside in the immediate neighbourhood of The Priory."

Every event of the fatal Tuesday was once again reviewed, and to Counsel's next questions witness replied that Mr. Joseph Bravo had remained at The Priory for some days after the death, and that at Brighton in all matters of business—the offering of the £500 reward "and such like"—"Mrs. Charles Bravo had acted under the advice of others." She was very sensitive on the subject of "her error of conduct with Dr. Gully" and very anxious that "it should not be publicly known". She had been extremely ill at Brighton and the doctor had had to sleep in the house. Since witness had left Brighton she had only seen Mrs. Bravo in the presence of her uncle, Mr. Orr. "I have not had the slightest communication with her on the subject of this inquiry or the evidence I was about to give. Since I have given up my position I have no resources. It was thought fitting that Mrs. Bravo's solicitors should have no communication with me, and Mr. Humphreys[1] was requested by the family to act as my solicitor at this inquiry."

Sir Henry James: "Now, Mrs. Cox, had you any antimony in your possession, or did you know of any being in use at The Priory while you were there?"

Witness: "I never saw any in my life."

Sir Henry James: "From all you heard and saw had you any reason to suppose that Mrs. Charles Bravo had any antimony in her possession, or that she ever used it in any way?"

Witness: "I never did."

Mr. Lewis now suddenly produced a small bottle labelled

[1] Father of Sir Travers Humphreys.

Antimony Tart. and demanded of witness: "Have you ever seen any bottle like that?"

Witness (coolly): "I have seen many bottles like that."

Mr. Lewis: "With that label on it?"

Witness: "I don't know that I have."

It transpired that the bottle was one of the innumerable homoeopathic prescriptions found in witness' medicine cupboard, but so weak a solution as to be entirely harmless.

The Foreman of the Jury: "It has been given in evidence that deceased first called out for his wife—'Florence! Florence! Hot water! Hot water!' Do you not think it strange that when you came instead of his wife he should tell you he had taken poison and say, 'Don't tell Florence'?"

Witness: "*I* did not hear him call 'Florence'. He only called 'Hot water! Hot water! Hot water!' when I was there."

Mrs. Cox's long ordeal was over, but whether freedom or a charge of murder lay in front of her was a matter still in doubt.

CHAPTER SEVEN

18TH AND 19TH DAYS OF THE INQUEST

I

The Eighteenth Day: Thursday, 3rd August
Evidence of Mrs. Florence Bravo

WHAT the crowd in Court expected to see in the person of
Florence Bravo it alone could tell: what it saw was a woman
dressed elegantly but simply in black, her bright hair brushed
up and away from her face under a widow's cap; a woman
with a sweet and gentle face, and eyes laden with sorrow.

"Mrs. Florence Bravo," scribbled the reporters, "was
escorted into Court by her brother, Mr. William Campbell.
She attracted the deepest attention of everyone present.
She is a handsome lady of about thirty years of age, with
large expressive blue eyes, chestnut hair tinged with gold,
and having a graceful figure. She was pale, her voice gently
modulated and her enunciation distinct. She gave her
answers calmly and promptly without any reserve, having a
strange, fixed look, as though her large, beautiful eyes were
searching the past.

"Her attire was in deep mourning, her dress being made
with a becoming black scarf[1] arranged about the shoulders.
She wore little jewelry, except a very valuable emerald ring
upon a finger. Her hand trembled perceptibly as she took the
Book, but she kissed it on being sworn in a decided manner.
She then threw up the crêpe veil which hid her features, and
taking the seat provided for her, soon became composed,
although a deep sigh escaped her lips as she answered the
first question of Sir Henry James. Beside her had been
placed a glass of *sal volatile* and water, which she sipped
now and again. Twice only she faltered, but recovered

[1] A male reporter's attempt to describe a *fichu*.

herself on each occasion immediately. In giving her evidence she did not merely give answers to questions put to her, but added to them and altered them according to circumstances, only breaking down when learned Counsel put point-blank to her a crucial question as to her intimacy with Dr. Gully at Kissingen. Then, after answering the question in the affirmative, she burst into tears and was led from the room by her brother for a few moments. It was evident that she had by a great effort nerved herself for the ordeal."

Sir Henry James took her through the whole story of her ill-starred first marriage and the commencement of her "attachment" to Dr. Gully. From March 1872 she and Dr. Gully were constantly in each other's company. In 1875 Dr. Gully had gone abroad with friends, and witness and Mrs. Cox had gone to Eastbourne, and then to Brighton. There she had encountered Mr. Charles Bravo whom she had met once before at his mother's house. He had paid her considerable attention and they had become engaged.

Throughout this time she had been estranged from, and had had no communication with, her father and mother. Now her mother had fallen ill and witness had determined to seek a reconciliation. She had written to Dr. Gully and told him their acquaintance must end and, about 10th October, he had come twice to Brighton to see her. On the second occasion she had told him that Mr. Bravo was paying her attentions and they had had a painful interview, but Dr. Gully had finally agreed that "whatever was for my happiness he wished me to do". Here witness' voice trembled with emotion.

Witness had told Mr. Charles Bravo the whole story of her attachment to Dr. Gully. He himself had told witness that for the past four years he "had had a connection" at Maidenhead and had promised to give it up.

Sir Henry James: "Now, Mrs. Bravo, I must ask you to state without reserve what you said about your attachment to deceased."

Witness (speaking very deliberately): "I told him that from the time I went to Leigham Court Road I had been constantly in Dr. Gully's company. I told him that we had travelled abroad together and in England—that I had been to Kissingen with him. . . . I told him all. I have to state that there was at one time improper intimacy between Dr. Gully and myself." Here witness broke down in tears and was led from the Court by her brother, but returned in two or three minutes and resumed her painful story. "The first occasion of that intimacy was in 1872 on the visit to Kissingen; there were intimacies on the occasion of that visit—more than one. In November of that year I suffered from an illness, and I was attended by Dr. Gully."

Sir Henry James: "That illness was a miscarriage?"

Witness: "It was, and I did my best to conceal the fact from everyone about me. So far as I know Mrs. Cox did not know what the illness was, and I did all I could to prevent her knowing. I owe my life to her attendance upon me. I had acute physical suffering. . . . That terminated my improper intimacy with Dr. Gully. I did state at the Treasury that it was an innocent intimacy. . . .

"Dr. Gully was a man of great intellectual attainments and in my isolated state, estranged from my family and friends, I found refuge in his society. He was in the habit of coming to The Priory and I was in the habit of going to his house, but I never slept at his house nor he at mine. I never passed as his wife abroad nor had any letters addressed to me in any name but my own. We always had separate rooms at Kissingen and elsewhere when we travelled. . . .

"When I informed Mr. Bravo of the intimacy he made me take my solemn oath before God that I would not divulge to any other human being what I had told him. Previous to this I had told Mrs. Cox of it at Brighton. . . . The anonymous letter referred to my connection with Dr. Gully being an improper one, and Mr. Bravo and Mrs. Cox spoke of the contents of that letter. I did not know that there had been conversations between them on the subject of this intimacy before then. . . .

"On 27th November I received a communication relative to the proposed Marriage Settlement. I never saw the Settlement, but understood from Mr. Brookes that Mr. Bravo wanted the furniture, carriages, horses and everything about the house settled on him. I was angry at this, since it seemed to me that he was going to marry me for my money and not for myself. I sought the advice of Dr. Gully and asked him to meet me at the lower lodge. . . ."

2

The Nineteenth Day: Friday, 4th August
Evidence of Mrs. Florence Bravo (continued)

Sir Henry James: "In begging you now to tell the whole truth I will only ask you to answer 'yes' or 'no' to the question whether you were not improperly acquainted with Dr. Gully before that visit to Kissingen?"

Witness (bursting into tears): "Yes."

Sir Henry James: "Have you any correction to make as to your evidence regarding the period after Kissingen—that there was no improper intimacy?"

Witness: "I have no correction to make as to that. Upon my oath there was no improper intimacy after that. I informed Mr. Bravo of the intimacy during the Kissingen visit only. I was anxious not to appear to him as having been Dr. Gully's mistress for any length of time. . . . I had no such intimacy with Dr. Gully during the lifetime of my first husband."

Counsel's questions moved on to less delicate matters. Deceased, said witness, had paid none of the household expenses at The Priory except the stable bill. She had made over to him the half-yearly interest from her father "as I did not wish him to have to come to me for money, or be bothered by his mother". Witness had given up her maid to please his mother; the carriage-horses had been sold and a pair jobbed to please his stepfather, but she had refused to give up her cobs and deceased "did not insist".

Sir Henry James: "There were occasions when he was harsh to you?"

Witness (in tears): "I do not wish to say anything against him. He did strike me once. . . . I was occasionally annoyed by the expression of his views on money matters—these were all due to his mother." While his mother and stepfather had been away at St. Leonards she and deceased had been very happy. For the last three weeks of his life he had been at home all the time and very kind to her—reading aloud to her, and taking a great interest in domestic matters. His good qualities had been appreciated by her family and by all who knew him. She had always received his friends at The Priory and made them welcome. "This portion of my marriage with Mr. Bravo formed the happiest part of my married life with him."

But although they had solemnly agreed before marriage that the name of Dr. Gully should never be mentioned, deceased was constantly doing so—complaining of his presence in Balham and at having to pass his house every day. At Brighton witness had asked Dr. Gully to leave Balham to spare her embarrassment, and had offered to "pay his rent", but he had "indignantly refused". She herself had tried to surrender the lease of The Priory, but the landlord would not agree.

Details of the fatal Tuesday were now recounted. "Deceased had recently been looking the picture of health from living in the open air, for he often said the bad air of the Courts injured him, and that he went in a strong man and came out a weak one." But at dinner that night, after the receipt of Mr. Bravo's letter, "he looked very ill and very angry—altogether unnerved".

On going up to bed witness had asked Mrs. Cox to get her a glass of Marsala and water, and when Keeber entered her dressing-room she had sent her for more. "I have no recollection at all of my husband upbraiding me in French for drinking too much wine that day. . . . He had remonstrated at previous times about my taking more wine than he thought good for me. . . . That habit had originated at the time of my first husband's death."

Witness had been thoroughly tired that night, and was asleep in a few minutes. "I had seen Mrs. Cox close the double doors of the bedroom when she came in with me. . . . If I had heard Keeber come in and say my husband was ill I should have got up at once. . . . I knew nothing of what had happened until

Keeber awoke me by touching me and told me my husband was very ill. I got up immediately." Witness described the events that followed and said: "Mrs. Cox could not have done more for my husband if she had been his mother. . . . I had not the strength she had, but I helped her as much as I could."

Witness had suggested sending for Royes Bell "who knew my husband's constitution and in whom he had great confidence. . . . Mrs. Bravo made the request to me that she should take charge of her son. I reluctantly gave my consent; I did not refuse because I knew it would have produced a scene and distressed him. . . . I did not understand from Dr. Johnson's remark" (to Mrs. Cox) "that my husband had taken poison to kill himself, but that he had taken an overdose of laudanum, which I knew he was in the habit of using. . . . I did not understand that he had taken it intentionally.

"During the whole time he was conscious he shewed me signs of affection. . . . He shewed not the slightest signs of distrust or dislike towards me, nor did he shew any signs of distrust towards Mrs. Cox." As soon as he had regained consciousness he had asked witness to kiss him. "After I had kissed him I asked him, 'What have you taken, Charlie, to make you so ill?' He cried out, 'Oh Lord, have mercy upon me! Oh Christ, have mercy upon me!' . . ."

Witness had called in Sir William Gull because he was "the first opinion in London". She had not heard her husband say "before God" after he had said "I took it myself". It was only then she realized that he was suffering from poisoning. "I had been searching around in my mind for the cause of his illness; I told Miss Bell I thought it was due to something he had eaten at the St. James Hall restaurant."

When there seemed to be no hope of recovery witness had sent Mrs. Cox to Dr. Gully, who had saved Sir William Heathcote's life when the "regular practitioners" had given him up. She believed him to be "the cleverest medical man in the whole world".

Deceased had requested her to be kind to the child Katie, daughter of the woman at Maidenhead. She had no knowledge that Griffith had ever given antimony to her horses; the drug had never been entered in his expense book. It was not in witness' knowledge that Mrs. Cox had been seeing Dr. Gully until after witness' miscarriage in April. Mrs. Cox had told her then that she had met him by accident at Balham station and that he had recommended sitz baths and compresses for the pain in her back. This had given her relief and she had not required the laurel-water which Mrs. Cox had brought on 10th April. In regard to the letter written to the Coroner, it was Mr. Joseph Bravo who said, "it would be more pleasant to have the inquest at The Priory". After witness had been at Brighton a few days her attention had been drawn to statements in the Press—she had "understood what those statements meant". She had been taken ill and everything had been placed in her father's hands. On 2nd June she had made a statement to the Treasury.

Sir Henry James: "I shall have to ask you some questions on that statement." He read the statement, and in answer to the ensuing questions witness said that Mr. Royes Bell had recommended her to go to Worthing for a change after her miscarriage. Deceased's mother had objected to her going on the score of expense, and witness had been angry. Deceased had ambitions to enter Parliament and wished to save money to meet expenses.

Mr. Lewis now rose to begin his cross-examination and the manner in which he did so provoked the severest censure of the Press. The following quotations will serve as examples.

Saturday Review:

"The question to be determined by the jury was simply how Mr. Bravo came by his death. . . . It was not the business of the Court to pass judgment on the moral character of Mrs. Bravo. . . ."

The Times:

"When the fact of the previous existence of a criminal connection between Dr. Gully and Mrs. Bravo had been established the main object of the exposure had been gained, and it was a cruel, and even barbarous, act to subject a most unhappy woman to hours of cross-examination for the mere purpose of eliciting details of this connection, and even, in one instance, of endeavouring to extort the circumstances under which, nearly six years ago, this fatal passion arose. ... That a cross-examination, even in a Coroner's Court, of a crushed and humiliated woman should have been pushed to the lengths it was at Balham, was a disgrace to the Court which allowed it, and to the manliness of everyone who was in the least degree responsible for it."

Mr. Lewis first asked witness if she had any letters written by her husband. She immediately volunteered to send for them.

Mr. Lewis: "I will thank you for them."

A messenger was despatched.

In answer to his next questions witness said that she had never heard her husband speak of antimony—or of poison, except to order the gardener to get rat poison. Until his death she had never expressed the opinion that he would commit suicide. It had never occurred to her during his illness that he had attempted to take his own life; neither the quarrels they had had nor anything else had ever put that thought into her mind. He was fond of his profession; he was very ambitious and full of spirits; he was fond of his home, always pleased to bring his friends to it, and very much attached to herself. He was a man who made friends everywhere, and witness was very fond of him. "I saw no trace of ill-feeling or jealousy in him at the time of his death. ... He appeared thoroughly unconscious as to what had caused his fatal illness; he never asked a question about that, and this fact astonished me very much. ... He was not a man of strong religious principles. I should say he was not a particularly truthful man. He prayed most earnestly on the Wednesday morning. I understood from the doctors that down to the time of his death he denied administering anything to himself except laudanum. ... There had been no actual dispute about Dr. Gully between us. Taking our married life as a whole we lived most affectionately, and had it not been for this inquiry no one would ever have known there were any disputes between us. Mrs. Cox was the only person who would have known of it."

The letters which Mr. Lewis had asked for were now put into his hand. He picked out that of 22nd October [1] and read it to the Court.

Her candid replies and general demeanour had created a favourable impression, and that impression Mr. Lewis was determined to dispel. He now therefore attempted to establish that witness had acted with deliberate deceit towards the dead man by accepting his offer of marriage *before* acquainting him with the fact that criminal intimacy had taken place between Dr. Gully and herself. Witness admitted that, before that date (22nd October), she had told deceased of her "attachment" to Dr. Gully, but "not the whole story", and that deceased "had laughed and asked how old Dr. Gully was".

Mr. Lewis: "Did he not say that he did not wish to make any further inquiries: that he was perfectly satisfied?"

Witness: "That was on the occasion of the second communication I made to him."

Mr. Lewis: "But I am speaking of the first. Did he propose to marry you on the first occasion of which you are speaking?"

Witness: "Yes . . . but he told me his mother was opposed to his marrying anyone, and of course I thought that included myself. Although the engagement was not made until later, I had then accepted him and there was an understanding that we were to be married—before the letter of 22nd October was written—this understanding depending upon the ratification of his parents."

[1] See page 60.

CHAPTER EIGHT

20TH, 21ST AND 22ND DAYS OF THE
INQUEST

I

The Twentieth Day: Monday, 7th August
Evidence of Mr. Henry Smith, F.R.C.S., Mr. George Brookes
and Sundry Others

BEING August Bank Holiday, and because of the crowds that
would collect, it was decided to discontinue the evidence of
Florence Bravo and to call various other witnesses instead.
The first of these, *Mr. Henry Smith, F.R.C.S.*, was called at
the instance of Mr. Murphy and the evidence he gave, the full
significance of which will appear later, is of the utmost importance.

"My wife," stated this witness in reply to *Mr. Murphy*, "was
a sister of Mrs. Joseph Bravo. I knew the late Mr. Charles
Bravo from a boy. I was asked by Dr. Johnson to come down
to Balham during the fatal illness and I drove him down. We
arrived at The Priory about two o'clock in the afternoon of
Thursday, April 20th. Dr. Johnson's opinion was that Mr.
Bravo was suffering from an irritant poison, but what poison
he did not know. He led me to believe that at the time he
thought it was a case of suicide, and it was with that impression that I entered the sick man's room. I did not ask him
any questions because I knew others had done so before me.
Mr. Bravo had some knowledge of medicine; certainly he had
of surgery.

"It is a common thing for people to put tartar emetic—
not a poisonous dose—into the wine of a person whom it is
desired to cure of drinking habits. I have done so myself. A
person who wanted to procure tartar emetic, like Mr. Bravo
—a sharp fellow, as most barristers are—might write a prescription and get it thus.

"Mr. Bravo was a rather excitable man at times: supposing he had taken laudanum in a fit of passion, and had then taken tartar emetic—which he might have had for any purpose, such as to cure his wife of her drinking habits—to get rid of the laudanum, vomiting might have been brought on in ten minutes, though the action of the antimony would probably be deferred if laudanum had been taken in any considerable quantity. Assuming the vomiting to occur, a great portion of the tartar emetic would come away with the bulk of the vomited matter, but, dinner having been taken just before, the digestive organs would be fully at work and absorption would be rapid. Though a large portion would be thrown off, a portion would be absorbed. Absorption into the system, too, would be going on all the time he was insensible. The *post-mortem* shews that a large portion was easily ejected, but I cannot say that the small quantity of antimony found in the large intestine shews that only a small quantity was absorbed. The fact that Mr. Bravo called for hot water himself shews to my mind that he had taken something which he was anxious to be rid of. There is nothing in the *post-mortem* inconsistent with the theory that he took laudanum himself, and then tartar emetic to get rid of that narcotic poison."

In reply to *Mr. Lewis*: "There is nothing in the *post-mortem* which points to Mr. Bravo having taken laudanum and then tartar emetic. I have been 28 years in the profession and during that time I have never 'known, heard or read' of a man taking laudanum and then taking a poisonous dose of tartar emetic to make himself sick. If a man had swallowed, or thought he had swallowed, laudanum, hot water would be the proper thing to call for to make him sick—it is a very common emetic. There is nothing about the evidence inconsistent with the idea that he received poison ten or fifteen minutes before he called for hot water, by means of a poisoned water-bottle. I knew Mr. Bravo very well. I saw him about a fortnight before his death in good health and spirits. I never knew him in possession of poison. In my opinion he was not a man likely to commit suicide. Death by antimony is a most dreadful death so far as suffering is concerned.

"I think that anyone who wrote a prescription would be served with tartar emetic. I never heard of Mr. Bravo writing a prescription. I never heard of him putting tartar emetic into wine for any purpose. He had never spoken to me about such a thing, nor I to him. I suspected a servant once of taking my spirits, and I put in some antimony—it had an admirable effect. Dr. Johnson's first impressions that it was suicide changed after the *post-mortem*. I was the first person to suggest that the detective police should be employed. Mr. Bravo used to come to the hospital to see operations. He had no opportunity on his visits of obtaining poisons; the drugs are kept in a part of the hospital altogether apart from the operating theatre. It is my impression that Mr. Charles Bravo was a truthful man."

In reply to *Sir Henry James*: "Deceased never mentioned to me that his wife took too much wine and that he wanted to cure her. He never mentioned to me that he had told her mother he would try to cure her.

"I do not know anything of Mr. Charles Bravo's father; the late Mr. Bravo never mentioned him—he died when Mr. Bravo was quite a baby. His mother never mentioned his father to me. One sister of Mr. Bravo's is deaf and dumb, and the other is feeble in mind and body—she is in a convent. As a rule Mr. Bravo was cheerful in temper, but there were times when he shewed excitement. I have seen him excited in argument, but I have never seen him 'almost in a frenzy'. I cannot describe him as a man who would be 'likely to commit suicide', but I have known both cheerful and melancholy men do that."

In reply to *Mr. Gorst*: "To 'doctor' a bottle of wine in order to cure a drunkard I should not put in more than 2 or 3 grains of tartar emetic. A pull at that would make him feel very uncomfortable and would not hurt. I cannot say how many grains of tartar emetic a man might get possession of by writing a prescription.

"A man who took a large dose on a full stomach might begin to feel sick in 5 or 6 minutes, but I cannot say exactly how long it would take to make him sick. Hot water is a common domestic remedy for nausea, and the fact of deceased calling for hot water would lead me to no conclusion of any kind."

A Juror: "Do you think if Mr. Bravo had taken antimony with the intention of committing suicide he would be likely to have called for hot water?"

Witness: "Well, that would depend: if a man is suffering a good deal of pain, even if he had committed suicide, or wished to commit suicide—it is like the case of a drowning man: when he gets under water he would like someone to pull him out. If a man has taken antimony and begins to feel the excruciating agony of an irritant poison, his courage and determination might fail him and he might wish to get out of the mess he had got into. It is possible, and I think with some natures probable."

So ended the evidence of Mr. Henry Smith—a family connection of the Bravos and one who had been intimate with the dead man since childhood. It was clear from his testimony that his underlying conviction was the same as Sir William Gull's: that *"whatever Mr. Bravo had taken, he had taken it himself"*, *and that he had known, moreover, what the substance was.*

Mr. George Brookes gave evidence concerning the marriage settlements. Deceased, he said, had been very angry at the suggestion that the effects at The Priory should all be included in his wife's settlement. "He said in the presence of Mrs. Ricardo's father that it would put him in a most humiliating position. Mr. Campbell gave way on the point. Mr. Bravo made not the least difficulty about the settlement of Mrs. Ricardo's fortune upon herself, and he did not in the least encumber the furniture or the lease, and they passed again to his wife." In the event of her own death "every shilling she possessed" would have passed to Mr. Bravo.

In reply to *Sir Henry James*: "Mr. Bravo brought nothing to the marriage, and would not have done so until the death of his mother and stepfather. He had insisted upon the furniture being left as it was, and if he had not recovered consciousness and made a Will that day, its value would have been subject to distribution.

"When he called upon me on November 15th I rose from my chair to shake hands with him and to offer my congratulations upon his being about to marry an old friend of mine. He said:

'Damn your congratulations! I've come about the money!' I was annoyed at his manner and referred him to my partner when he called again."

Dr. Harrison (recalled) stated in answer to *Sir Henry James*: "I saw an ordinary water-bottle on the table in the sick-room about three-parts full. After midnight I poured myself out about half or two-thirds of a tumbler and drank it. There was only one water-bottle in the room that I saw."

Dr. Moore (recalled) corroborated Dr. Harrison's statement and added: "Not to my knowledge was that bottle of water interfered with by anyone between the time I came into the room and the time Dr. Harrison drank of it." It had not occurred to him that deceased might have been poisoned through the medium of the water in the water-bottle.

Mrs. Harford, in reply to *Mr. Murphy*, stated that she had known Mrs. Cox for twenty years and remembered her calling at her house the previous March to ask advice about going to Jamaica. Witness had helped her to write a letter to her aunt. She remembered Mrs. Cox telling her how deceased had insisted upon her opening and shewing him a letter from Dr. Gully which, she had said, had contained a prescription for Jamaica fever. Witness had remarked how odd it was of Mr. Bravo—"I told her *I* should not have shewn it to him."

"Last Sunday fortnight" (23rd July) Mrs. Cox had made a statement to witness about Mrs. Bravo's previous connection with Dr. Gully. "She asked my advice about telling her Counsel. I consulted my husband and told her it was not necessary to tell her Counsel that."

In reply to *Sir Henry James*, witness stated that the gist of her advice to Mrs. Cox regarding the letter from her aunt was that if the aunt provided the necessary funds Mrs. Cox "should book a return passage and go at once to Jamaica, but not undertake to stop there".

Charles Maddox, assistant to Mr. Smith, chemist, Balham, stated in reply to *Mr. Serjeant Parry* that on 8th April he had supplied Dr. Gully with a half-ounce bottle of laurel-water made up from the prescription in the Pharmacopoeia. Laurel-water could be taken as a sedative in a dose of 5 to 30 drops.

Witness had written the dosage on the label, and had affixed a *Poison* label in accordance with the law.

2

The Twenty-first Day: Tuesday, 8th August
Evidence of Mrs. Florence Bravo (resumed)

The *Saturday Review*, expressing its opinion of this day's proceedings, said:

"The gloating zest with which the audience in Court, including even so-called ladies, gave themselves up to enjoy the spectacle of a woman, to whom reputation was dear, having wrung from her by questions as cruel as the rack an open confession of dishonour, not only a general admission, but in precise detail . . . the wrangling and vulgar levity . . . and the prevailing looseness and dishonour of the whole proceedings, make up a picture of the most unpleasant kind. Not only the ordinary amenities, but the rules of evidence and procedure of a judicial inquiry, were continually broken through, the Coroner sitting in blank helplessness and apparently quite incapable of keeping Counsel in order. . . ."

"Witness," writes Mr. F. J. P. Veale, "was compelled to answer numberless questions concerning her past life on matters utterly irrelevant to the purpose of the inquiry which was for long forgotten by everyone and, in particular, by Mr. George Lewis, who thoroughly enjoyed himself and at the same time earned his fee of a thousand guineas from vindictive old Mrs. Bravo." He adds: "The only fact clearly demonstrated by the cross-examination of Florence Bravo was that our Victorian ancestors were not so far removed from contemporary savages as they imagined. Among the tribes of Darkest Africa . . . a woman caught breaking a sexual taboo would have been subjected to a fate more spectacular and gruesome, but similar in spirit to that to which Mrs. Florence Bravo of Balham was subjected." [1]

In reply to *Mr. Lewis*, witness stated that she did not know

[1] *Verdict in Doubt—the Bravo Case*—F. J. P. Veale.

her husband was in the habit of drinking water from the water-bottle in his bedroom.

Mr. Lewis now read out those letters from Charles Bravo to witness[1] which she had placed in his hands the previous Friday. Having stressed such phrases as "I only want your love, and without your love riches and honours would be as nothing" and dwelt upon such sentiments as his desire to do everything to make her happy, Mr. Lewis adjusted his monocle and, after referring to her statement to the Treasury Solicitor, demanded:

"Now, after hearing those letters read, do you mean to say, and to tell the jury, that your late husband was always— 'morning, noon and night'—speaking in disparaging terms of Dr. Gully?"

Witness: "I do. I told my mother at Buscot in January that he was always talking thus of Dr. Gully. I told my brother who is here in Court, and my other brother who is gone to New Zealand."

Mr. Lewis responded by reading another letter—from witness to Mrs. Joseph Bravo—in which she had written: "Charlie and I are as happy as can be, and never have an unkind word."

In answer to further questions witness said that since her husband's death his jealousy of Dr. Gully had been discussed by her and her family as a reason for his committing suicide, although at that time her family did not know that criminal intimacy had taken place between Dr. Gully and herself. "I have pledged my oath that no criminal intimacy occurred with Dr. Gully during the lifetime of my first husband. At Malvern nothing occurred between Dr. Gully and myself which I wished to keep secret or was ashamed of my servants speaking of."

Mr. Lewis: "Did you ever employ a maid named Laundon?"
Witness: "Yes."

Mr. Lewis (holding up a letter): "Is this your handwriting?"

Witness: "It is."

Mr. Lewis: "It is dated November 16th, with no year, but it

[1] See pages 82, 83, 85 and 86.

will be obvious that it was written in 1870—in the lifetime of
the late Captain Ricardo."

He proceeded to read the letter.

> "Buscot Park,
> "Lechlade, Glos.,
> "Nov. 16th.

"Dear Laundon,

"I am quite satisfied with your apology and, as I
told you before, that had it not been for Field—who is
not worthy of you—you would never have been rude to
me.

"Nobody regrets more than I do that circumstances
compelled my parting with you, for I like you personally,
and you suit me in every way. I will do all I can to procure
you a good situation, and hope you may soon succeed in
getting one. I hope you will never allude in *any way* to *anyone*
of what passed at Malvern. Let it all be buried in the past,
and if *anybody* questions you please refuse to answer *any
inquiries*. I shall remain here till January and then think of
having a house at Clifton.

"With kind remembrances to yourself,

> "Yours truly,
> "Florence Ricardo.

"Burn this."

Mr. Lewis: "What was it, Mrs. Bravo, that was never to be
alluded to to anyone, and was to be buried in the past and no
inquiries answered?"

Witness (with much emotion): "It was to my attachment to
Dr. Gully, but not a criminal attachment then."

"It was at this point," said *The Times*, "that Mrs. Bravo,
with a perfectly just indignation, turned upon her torturers
and refused to answer any more questions respecting Dr.
Gully. Speaking part with tragic force and part tearfully she
said: 'That attachment to Dr. Gully has nothing to do with
this case—the death of Mr. Bravo. I have been subjected to
sufficient pain and humiliation already, and I appeal to the
Coroner and the jury, as men and Britons, to protect me.
I think it is great shame that I should be thus questioned,

and I will refuse to answer any further questions with regard to Dr. Gully.' "

She had the sympathy of the Court. "The audience," wrote the *Saturday Review*, "moved their feet as if applauding", and there were those present who commented on the fact that her own Counsel had let the dead man's own "criminal intimacy" with a prostitute at Maidenhead remain in decent obscurity. But the Coroner allowed Mr. Lewis to pursue his relentless persecution unchecked.

Mr. Lewis: "You see the words wherein you express the hope that she will not allude to 'what passed at Malvern'. Now, Mrs. Bravo, what passed at Malvern?"

Witness: "She knew of my attachment to Dr. Gully—and," she added with rising scorn, "it seems to me that you, and such as you, think it impossible for a woman to love a man without what is wrong occurring. According to you that must occur."

Mr. Lewis (with frigid insistence): "You use the term 'not to say anything of what passed at Malvern'. What passed?"

Witness: "I have explained it."

Mr. Lewis: "Do you mean your attachment to Dr. Gully by those words?"

Witness: "So I have already told you."

To further questions witness replied: "In October 1875 I wrote to break off with Dr. Gully. I cannot say if it was after Mr. Bravo began to pay me attention. I do not know what you call 'attention'." With a wistful smile, as though she had a momentary vision of herself and Charles mingling in that gay cavalcade along the front at Brighton, she added: "He used to walk with me on the Parade," then continued: "I wrote to Dr. Gully about ten days, I suppose, after I had seen Mr. Bravo. . . . It was in October that I offered to pay Dr. Gully's rent if he would go away from Balham. I don't know that he gave any reason for persisting in staying beyond that he liked the place."

Mr. Lewis now read the first of witness' letters to Joseph Bravo written from Brighton after her husband's death,[1] and

[1] See pages 165, 166 and 167.

in answer to his questions witness said: "I did not hear about deceased owing a certain person money until after his death, and I thought it was one of the causes of his death; that he was being pressed for money by this woman. . . . I thought his jealousy of Dr. Gully was another. I think that still even after hearing his letters read today. He was always harping upon wishing he had had 'my first love'."

Mr. Lewis (quoting from witness' letter of 16th April to her mother)[1]: 'Charlie is walking about with a book under his arm as happy as a king'—now Mrs. Bravo, is this not strange in view of the suggestion that two days later he committed suicide?"

Witness: "I do say that it is my impression that two days before his seizure he was 'as happy as a king'. I do say he was thoroughly happy and much attached to me."

Mr. Lewis now turned to the events of the night of 18th April, and witness stated in the course of her replies: "During the illness Mrs. Cox and I discussed the cause of it; we could not make out what had made him so ill. Mrs. Cox never hinted that he had attempted his life because of jealousy of Dr. Gully. I think it was at Brighton, after his death, that she told me he had taken poison 'for Dr. Gully'.

"In April when I had sitz baths and spinal washes I had not suggested to Mrs. Cox that she should seek the advice of Dr. Gully. . . . At the time she was having these interviews the fact that they were occurring was utterly unknown to me. I never asked Mrs. Cox to get the laurel-water—I had never heard of it before—neither did I get any remedy myself from Dr. Gully."

It was now the turn of *Mr. Gorst.* In answer to his questions, witness said that the full confession of her past had been made to deceased at The Priory. "It was after his mother had given her consent." Witness had first seen Dr. Gully when she was twelve years old, and she and her sisters had accompanied their mother to Malvern. "He was very kind to my sisters and myself. He took notice of us by asking us to tea. Between then and going there with Captain Ricardo I did not see him at all. He

[1] See pages 108 and 109.

was only a very kind friend to me in Captain Ricardo's lifetime. Captain Ricardo was jealous of anyone who looked at me, and he was perfectly *au fait* with my acquaintance with Dr. Gully and asked him to take me out. As to there being a time when I was 'willing to give up friends and relations—father and mother—for Dr. Gully', this was after Captain Ricardo's death. There was a legal separation before his death, at my instigation. ... Dr. Gully had discussed marriage with me, but his wife was alive. He went abroad last year without me. He had several times gone abroad without me since our friendship commenced. We had not had the slightest difference before he went. I had not in the slightest degree grown tired of his society. . . . My affection for him was undiminished. I had made up my mind to break off with him long before I met Mr. Bravo. . . . I can say 'carefully and solemnly' that my only motive for this course was to see my mother again and make her happy. . . . In my own mind I had given up Dr. Gully long before the engagement with Mr. Bravo, but I had not told him so. . . . I had written to him on friendly and affectionate terms without intimating that I was going to break off the attachment. . . . I had not the strength of mind to give him up: I was not going to spoil his holiday." Witness now gave an account of the final interview she had with Dr. Gully at Brighton. "It was very painful because I was attached to him, and the parting was a very painful one. . . ."

Mr. Gorst: "The confession of your improper conduct was made to Mr. Bravo at The Priory after your engagement had been ratified by his mother's consent. On that occasion he made you take a solemn oath that you would never mention it to anyone?"

Witness: "Yes."

Mr. Gorst: "Then were you not very much surprised to find — on the occasion of the anonymous letter—that he had talked of it with Mrs. Cox?"

Witness: "No; *I* never extracted a promise from *him* not to talk of it. I looked upon him as a gentleman and therefore did not expect him to talk about it. I suppose he thought Mrs. Cox knew about it and therefore there was no harm in speaking of it to her."

Mr. Gorst: "Did you reproach him for talking of your shame to Mrs. Cox?"

Witness: "I never reproached him with anything, nor Mrs. Cox for talking about it with him. I think it would have been better if they had not. . . . Mrs. Cox made me no promise not to mention it. I never thought she would, though I have seen by her evidence that she did mention it to someone else besides Mr. Bravo."

Witness now described her meeting with Dr. Gully at the lower lodge and Mr. Gorst then asked:

"Did Dr. Gully say anything about the time Mr. Charles Bravo would be likely to live after marrying you?"

Witness: "No. He shewed no trace of anger. . . . He was kindly to me and in his expressions he was the same to Mr. Bravo. He reconciled me to Mr. Bravo's action over the Settlement; he reconciled me to surrender all my goods and chattels into Mr. Bravo's hands. I acted upon his advice and withdrew my objections to Mr. Charles Bravo's view."

Mr. Gorst (ironically): "So, in fact, it was Dr. Gully who made the match at last!"

In answer to the next questions, witness said: "I could not have told Mrs. Cox that I had acquired the habit of drinking more wine than was good for my health during the lifetime of my first husband, for it would not have been true." And now every detail of events on the fatal Tuesday—the quarrel on the way to London, the ride, the arrival of Joseph Bravo's letter was again gone through: then Counsel referred to witness' statement to the Treasury Solicitor, to which she replied: "I should not have made that statement if I had known it would have been published as it has been." Suddenly Mr. Gorst asked:

"Did you make a grave charge against your husband to Inspector Clarke at Brighton?"

Witness: "I do not know whether, just after my husband's death—soon after I went to Brighton—I made a statement making a grave charge against my late husband."

Mr. Gorst: "Did you tell Inspector Clarke that if he wished to know more regarding that charge he could apply to Dr. Dill?"

Witness: "I do not know whether I made a statement to Dr.

Dill making a grave charge against my late husband. When people spoke to me about my late husband having been poisoned with antimony I said he must have taken it himself."

Mr. Gorst: "I do not mean that: *but did you make a statement to Inspector Clarke which involves a grave charge against your late husband?*"

Witness: "I have answered you and can say no more. I saw Inspector Clarke of Scotland Yard at Brighton and knew he was making inquiries about my late husband's death. I told him he might go to Dr. Dill."

Mr. Gorst: "*Did you refer Inspector Clarke to Dr. Dill for the doctor to tell him particulars about the late Mr. Bravo which you could not, but which you had told the doctor?*"

Again witness evaded the question, but on further pressure admitted: "*I sent the Inspector to Dr. Dill to inquire about my health.*" Counsel continued to press the question and witness declared defiantly: "I shan't answer on the subject you mention: I shan't—there!"

Mr. Gorst: "*Did you know that Inspector Clarke would hear a most serious charge against your husband from Dr. Dill—a charge made by you?*"

Witness: "No, I didn't—*I did tell him if he wanted to learn something he could go to Dr. Dill.*"

Mr. Gorst resumed his seat, and in reply to *Mr. Murphy* witness said that both she and deceased had treated Mrs. Cox with the same kindness after their marriage as before it. Mrs. Cox had not wished to leave them to go to Jamaica, but was quite content to go.

Mr. Murphy: "And now, Mrs. Bravo, do you feel towards Mrs. Cox the same kindly regard as you have always felt?"

"I think," answered witness with quiet dignity, "she might have spared me many of these painful inquiries to which I have been subjected."

Two final questions were put by *Sir Henry James*, and witness' reply to the second deserves particular attention:

"Deceased never told me who his father was. He told me before the marriage that he would tell me afterwards—but I forgot, and it doesn't matter.

"I made a Will after I was married and left all I had to Mr. Bravo, even my jewels. I trusted him absolutely."

3

The Twenty-second Day: Wednesday, 9th August
Evidence of Mrs. Griffith and Dr. Gully

The proceedings opened with the reading of the two letters from Mrs. Margaret Cox of Jamaica to her niece, Mrs. Jane Cannon Cox, at The Priory, the first urging her to "come soon", the second, in answer to that composed with Mrs. Harford's aid, to tell her that the money for both outward and homeward passages would be deposited with Mr. Bravo's firm. More conclusive evidence of Mrs. Cox's intention to visit Jamaica could hardly have been produced.

Mrs. Griffith, wife of George Griffith, coachman, said that her husband had at one time kept antimony in the drawer of a table at the lower lodge; she had been afraid of her children getting hold of it and had thrown it in the fire. She corroborated the evidence already given concerning the meeting between Dr. Gully and Florence Bravo at the lower lodge.

And now a wave of excitement passed over the Court as Mr. Burleigh Muir said: "Call Dr. Gully." The shock, the notoriety, the virulent anonymous letters that had descended upon him, had seriously affected his health and he who had borne his years so lightly now looked "the ancient lover" in very truth. But neither this nor the fact that he had come forward voluntarily as a witness restrained the jury from an ugly display of prejudice and rancour when his Counsel asked that he should be allowed to give his evidence seated. For once, however, the Coroner rebuked the outbreak and ordered a chair to be brought.

Mr. Serjeant Parry: "We have heard of your unfortunate intimacy with Mrs. Ricardo—now Mrs. Bravo."

Witness: "Too true, sir; too true. . . . I have read Mrs. Bravo's statement as to that intimacy. I am sorry to say that statement is true and correct, and in having to come here and say so I feel my position most bitterly. I have received many insulting and threatening letters, and I have heard the rumours and suspicions which have been aroused, and upon my solemn oath I declare that I had nothing to do, either directly or indirectly, with Mr. Charles Bravo's death."

Since the interview at the lower lodge in November witness had neither seen nor sought Mrs. Bravo. To his knowledge he had never seen Mr. Charles Bravo. In homoeopathy tartar emetic was sometimes prescribed in infinitesimal doses, "but since I went to Malvern in 1842 I have not had a single grain of tartar emetic in my possession. . . . I did not know of its purchase by Griffith; I forbade him to doctor my horses, for I treated them hydropathically with marvellous results."

Witness had never written an anonymous letter to Mr. Bravo or to anyone else in his life. The advice he had given Mrs. Ricardo at the lodge was "not to squabble about the furniture with Mr. Bravo; she should not desire her husband to come into the house and feel he was not master of it". Witness had been absent from Balham from the time of the marriage until March. Between then and 20th April he had seen Mrs. Cox five times— "the first four of these meetings were entirely accidental: three of them were at the station". He had advised the sitz baths and spinal washes because Mrs. Cox had told him Mrs. Bravo was suffering from pains in the back and sleeplessness. "Knowing Mrs. Bravo was driven frantic by ordinary opiates, I bethought me of laurel-water." On Sunday, 9th April, he had left the bottle at Mrs. Cox's house as she had told him she would be going there next day. "I left the bottle in precisely the same state as I received it from the chemist. I had no tartar emetic to place in the bottle, and any suggestion that I did so, from whatever quarter it may come, is a wicked and infamous falsehood."

In reply to *Mr. Lewis*: "In spite of the orders that I had given that she was not to be admitted to my house I met Mrs. Cox cordially. I was not aware at the time I prescribed the sitz baths for Mrs. Bravo that she was suffering from a miscarriage —Mrs. Cox told me that afterwards. I did not send the laurel-water to The Priory because I regarded all communication with the place as forbidden me."

Witness had first heard of the engagement on 11th November
—"Mrs. Cox sent me a short note telling me." On his second
visit to Brighton—19th October—Mrs. Ricardo had told him
that Mr. Bravo was "approaching her. . . . I asked her if she
were engaged to him. She said no; for he could fix nothing
without his mother's consent. I advised her not to be in a hurry
but to be acquainted with him—and especially his family—for
three or four months before she fixed her fate. She said she
would."

After Mrs. Ricardo had "dismissed him on the grounds that
she wanted to be reconciled with her family", witness had
written her a kind letter "telling her she was quite right to be
reconciled with her family. I told her I should go to Jamaica,
my native place, but I told her on my second visit that I had
said that in momentary irritation. *I* did not say I should not
see her again—it was the other way round: *she* said she
would not see me again. I was at that time much attached to
her and was under the impression she was much attached to
me."

Mr. Lewis, resuming his apocalyptic rôle, now sought to
elicit an admission that witness' intimacy with Mrs. Ricardo
had begun while she was his patient. Although this would have
injured still further an infirm old gentleman's already
damaged reputation, it is inconceivable that it would have
shed much light on how Charles Bravo died.

"Was it during the period that she was a patient of yours
that the attachment between you commenced?" he demanded.

Witness: "After a fashion: it was a friendly understanding;
she was alone a great deal and used to have tea with me at my
house."

Mr. Lewis: "That is no answer to my question. Did the
attachment commence then?"

Witness: "If you like to call it so—yes."

Mr. Lewis: "Do you know what 'passed at Malvern' at this
time that Mrs. Ricardo should desire her servant 'never to
allude to' and 'to answer no questions to anyone about'?"

Witness: "I cannot conceive what that was. There was
nothing between us that need not be known."

Mr. Lewis: "Did you know that she discarded her family for you?"

Witness: "I knew she had discarded her family for me in the spring of 1871."

Mr. Lewis: "You knew that she had given you her entire affections: given up for you her home, family—all—even her good name?"

Witness: "I knew she had been given the choice of giving me up and had refused."

Mr. Lewis: "You knew she had given up her name for you— her good name—her honour?"

Witness: "Well, she had given up her home—but what do you mean by her honour?"

Mr. Serjeant Parry (interposing): "This inquiry is in regard to the death of Mr. Charles Bravo, and the questions which are being put, while inflicting moral torture upon the witness, are irrelevant to that inquiry. I ask the Coroner to stop this class of examination."

But the Coroner took no action and Mr. Lewis pressed his question.

Witness: "There came a time when she sacrificed her honour for me."

Mr. Lewis: "And there came a time when she asked you to sacrifice your house at Balham for her, and you refused?"

Witness: "There did not come a time when she asked me to sacrifice my little home at Balham for her and I refused. She never proposed to pay the rent of my house for me, nor did I refuse it with indignation. I don't see the relevance of these questions."

The Coroner: "Dr. Gully is a witness, and not a judge of the relevance of questions."

Mr. Lewis: "The relevance of these questions lies in the fact that Dr. Gully, after his previous connection with Mrs. Ricardo, chose to stop within five minutes' walk of the house where Mrs. Ricardo's second husband met his death."

In reply to the next questions witness stated that "it did not occur to him" to leave the neighbourhood. He had just furnished his house from "top to bottom". He thought Mrs.

Bravo had confused Orwell Lodge with the house he had had at
Streatham: it was in regard to that house that Mrs. Bravo had
offered to reimburse him, as he had had to forgo a portion of
the lease and had lost money on it. He had refused the offer,
"but not indignantly that I am aware of". . . . Mr. Bravo had
come between himself and Mrs. Ricardo, but he bore him no
grudge for that—he "did not think of him at all". . . . As to his
being in communication with Mrs. Bravo's confidential companion and sending Mrs. Bravo through her a bottle of laurel-
water, "Mrs. Cox might introduce the bottle or not, as she
liked."

In reply to *Sir Henry James*, witness stated that criminal
intimacy had not occurred until long after Captain Ricardo's
death. "No intimacy between myself and Mrs. Ricardo at
Malvern in the lifetime of Captain Ricardo required to be
concealed."

And as the last witness left the Court the Coroner announced
an adjournment until Friday, 11th August, to enable him,
with the assistance of the Assessor, to prepare his address to
the jury.

CHAPTER NINE

THE 23RD DAY OF THE INQUEST: FRIDAY, 11TH AUGUST. THE VERDICT

I

OWING to the peculiar nature of these extra-judicial proceedings the jury was deprived of those benefits which accrue to juries in a Court of Law, namely the closing speeches of Counsel marshalling the evidence in favour of their respective clients, and the impartial summing-up of a Judge putting that evidence in its proper perspective. The extent and complexity of the evidence given in the Bravo case would have presented even a Judge with a formidable task, and that task, complicated still further by a welter of irrelevance, was quite beyond the capacity of the Coroner and his Legal Assessor. Neither they nor the jury managed to perceive any of the gossamer links in the chain which indicated the story within the story, and the final questions which Mr. Gorst had put to Florence concerning the grave charge she was alleged to have made against the dead man suggested to their minds nothing more subtle than venereal disease. Their inquiries on this point receiving a negative reply, they were content to speculate no further. Moreover, Mr. Carter was guilty of certain errors both of judgment and of fact: for instance, in his summary of what took place in the sick-room he repeated almost *verbatim* the evidence of Ann Bell, much of which was uncorroborated from other sources, and who, as a relative of the deceased, might be regarded as a prejudiced witness; and he stated that Griffith threw away the antimony before leaving The Priory in *January 1876*, whereas he had left before the wedding on *7th December, 1875*. Nevertheless, he summarized the alternatives confronting the jury with commendable lucidity.

"You will weigh the evidence," he said at the conclusion of his charge, "as to Mr. Bravo's character and mental condition, and if you are satisfied that he deliberately and knowingly

took antimony with the intention of putting an end to his
existence, you will find accordingly, and you will also find
whether or not he was then of sound mind. . . . If you should be
of the opinion that he took the antimony medicinally, knowing
it to be antimony, but took an overdose of it, or that he took the
antimony in mistake for some other drug or substance, you will
find accordingly. In considering whether antimony was administered by any other person or persons I am unable to point
you to any direct evidence bearing upon the subject, and you
will consider whether or not it is a fact that the only evidence
that antimony was administered by himself or by another is
that antimony was found in the body of Mr. Bravo and in the
vomit found upon the leads. You will consider also whether
there is any evidence of the purchase of antimony by Mr.
Bravo or any person having means of access to him. Griffith
certainly said in evidence that he purchased tartar emetic at
the shops both of Mr. Smith at Balham and Mr. Robinson at
Streatham, but both those gentlemen denied the truth of his
statement. . . .

"Before you can bring in a verdict of murder against any
person or persons, you must be satisfied that that person or
those persons wilfully administered poison to Mr. Bravo, or
laid poison for him and that he took it and was killed by it; for
if the poison were laid the law will presume that the adminis-
tration was malicious, although no particular enmity was proved.
. . . I would, however, state that you must be satisfied by the
evidence that murder has been committed before you find
your verdict. . . . Lastly, if you should be satisfied that there is
no evidence before you as to how the antimony came into the
body of the deceased, you will find accordingly. . . ."

In pointing out that "no particular enmity was proved," the
Coroner acknowledged that no *motive* had been proved; he had
shewn that the only *decisive* evidence was that Charles Bravo
had been killed by antimony, and he clearly indicated that he
expected an open verdict. None was more astonished than he
at the verdict which was returned.

After an absence of three and a half hours the jury filed into
Court and he put the formal question:

"Have you agreed upon your verdict, gentlemen?"

"We have, and have it in writing," replied the Foreman.

The crowded Court, waiting with bated breath, saw him start as he read the words on the paper handed to him and heard the incredulity in his voice as he asked sharply:

"Are you unanimous in delivering this verdict? Have you twelve jurors agreeing with it?"

"We have more than twelve." In fact, three of the sixteen jurors had not agreed with it.

"Then," said the Coroner, "I will take the verdict of the majority."

Amid tense silence he read out the words which imputed a charge of murder against the three suspects: a charge they could never have the means of disproving.

> "*We find that Mr. Charles Delaunay Turner Bravo did not commit suicide; that he did not meet his death by misadventure; that he was wilfully murdered by the administration of tartar emetic; but there is not sufficient evidence to fix the guilt upon any person or persons.*"

Thus ended the Trial by Inquest.

2

Without extracts from the leading articles of the principal organs of the Press after the proceedings had ended with the delivery of that astonishing verdict, this chronicle of the case would be incomplete. All are critical of the inquiry itself and sceptical of its outcome.

Daily News:

". . . It is extremely difficult even for a moment to rest on the theory that either accident or murder or suicide had ended Mr. Bravo's life. Motives and means which would account for either murder or accident or suicide were alike hard to find. In this case there ought to have been some trace of the mode in which tartar emetic, not a substance which is generally believed to be scattered broadcast in families, had been obtained or taken by chance, or administered. The curious demeanour of the dying man, who seemed not indifferent to life, but utterly indifferent to the cause of death, unsuspecting, unwitting, and nearly careless, was so strange as almost to baffle even conjecture. In these circumstances when the story became generally spoken of, and the inadequacy, as it was thought, of the first inquest seemed plain, it may be said that there were good grounds for the general wish that a new inquiry should be held. Unfortunately, the new inquiry has been so conducted as to awaken and satisfy a very different sort of curiosity from that which we have described. The private life of many people was laid bare, and it exhibited, as private life often does when so unveiled, a number of unsuspected wounds and maladies. . . .

"The young man, who might have been envied by his friends: the happy husband, the good fellow, and master of sudden wealth, so mirthful and gay that no one could think of him and things melancholy together, had really, as it seems, a gnawing passion of the sort which possibly not even time can heal. He is displayed as irritable, sensitive, morbid even, and accused of tendencies in his household economy which it is not pleasant to have to mention in connection with one who cannot defend himself against charges which are not made in public against living men. Then the wife who brought him her wealth had her wretched secret, which no one helped her to bear, and, in short, the inner life of the household was one of affection possibly, and even of hope, but assuredly full of all the petty tortures, and some of the greater torments, with which men and women lacerate each other's hearts. . . . But with all these real or alleged motives of unhappiness, there was surely little sign of a tragedy like that of April 18th. There may be a form of suicide which answers to manslaughter as distinguished from murder. A passionate person may hurry himself out of the world almost before he knows what he is about and with no adequate cause for his extreme discontent. . . ."

The World:

"Rightly or wrongly, the general opinion was that the unfortunate young barrister did not commit suicide; and that opinion is confirmed not only by the verdict itself, but by the evidence elicited in the course of the late investigation. On the other hand, there are many features in the mode in which the inquiry was conducted that offend the public sense of propriety and justice, while beyond this there is the conviction that possibly innocent persons lie under the imputation of a horrible charge, the means of substantiating, or effectively disproving, which can never be forthcoming. . . .

"It may be that Mr. Bravo did accidentally administer to himself the drug which produced his death. . . . Mrs. Cox's narrative went definitely to show that he deliberately poisoned himself; but to this narrative the jury, by their finding, shewed that they attached no credit. What may seem morally conclusive to most people against the hypothesis of suicide is not that young Mr. Bravo was, according to the impression of his relatives and friends, an unlikely sort of person to make away with himself—as if an intending suicide would take either friends or relations into his confidence on the subject—but that, knowing the property of drugs, he died by the agency of the most agonizing poison known to the Pharmacopoeia. Again, it is incredible that, had he voluntarily elected the most horrible of deaths that poison could inflict, he should have recalled Sir William Gull to his bedside, and when almost *in articulo mortis* should have uttered in this solemn moment a deliberate lie, in the shape of the reiterated protestation that he had only taken laudanum.

"As regards Mr. Bravo himself, the accounts of his character by different witnesses are strangely conflicting and contradictory. It may even be said that the accounts given by the same individuals are not always consistent. Thus it seems curious that a young husband, whose letters to his wife breathe a spirit of generous and disinterested affection, should inform a professional friend that he does not want congratulations, but the money, and should, according to his wife's shewing, be as happy as a king, and fondness and happiness itself, and yet at the same time be perpetually taunting her with a subject to which he had pledged his word that he would never advert, and carry what would appear to have been a groundless jealousy to mean and violent extremes. He is said to have possessed a remarkable fund of animal spirits and the letters written by him and read in Court certainly have about them much coarse boisterousness, and do not impress one favourably as to his taste or refinement. . . .

"The 'scenes' which took place in Court were the reverse of pleasant or creditable. Both Coroner and jury no doubt gave every attention to the proceedings. But the latter certainly failed to display upon all occasions the taste and temper which the subject and the place demanded, and the former was impotent to check either the rude outbursts of the jurors or the 'licence of Counsel' of which we have heard so much. . . ."

The Spectator:

"The antimony has not been found in the cesspool for all the stirring . . . and on Friday the jury returned a verdict of wilful murder 'but there was not sufficient evidence to fix it upon any person or persons'. That verdict corresponds, probably, with the belief of the majority of the public, though much more evidence had been produced for the theory of suicide than was expected. There is no evidence whatever that Mr. Charles Bravo had taken antimony or had ever possessed any; but there was evidence that he had married under discreditable circumstances, that he lived unhappily at times with his wife, and that he was a man of violently impulsive temperament. Whoever is guilty or innocent there can be no doubt that the inquiry, with all its vast expense, has broken down. . . . There has been, as it were, no judge; and witnesses have been allowed to contradict themselves flatly within half an hour. . . . A more unsatisfactory inquiry never terminated in a more unsatisfactory verdict."

Saturday Review:

". . . Opinions may differ as to the necessity or propriety of so extended an investigation, but there can at least be no doubt that the manner in which it has been conducted throughout has given just offence to all rational and decent people. . . .

"The question to be determined by the jury was simply how Mr. Bravo came by his death; but this was almost lost sight of in the mass of gossip and conjecture as to matters only indirectly and remotely connected with the case. It was not the business of the Court to pass judgment on the moral character of Mrs. Bravo or Dr. Gully, but to form an opinion, as far as the evidence enabled it to do so, as to the manner in which the deceased was poisoned, and the hand which administered the fatal drug. As a matter of fact the only direct evidence which was elicited was that Mr. Bravo was killed by antimony, of which the remains were found in his stomach. The medical evidence was decisive on this point; but there was a difficulty in getting beyond it, and shewing either that antimony was within Mr. Bravo's reach, or that someone else gave it to him. In fact, at this stage the inquiry passed away from the only established basis on which it could rest, and wandered off into a maze of speculation and conjecture.

"The relations between Mrs. Bravo and Dr. Gully had no bearing whatever on the question of poisoning, except in so far as they suggested reasons for supposing that either of these persons might have had a motive for desiring to get rid of Mr. Bravo; but, if even such a motive existed, no one had the right to assume that it would be actually carried out. People may be weak and wicked in many ways, and yet not always ready to commit murder on the spur of the moment. The same remark applies to Mrs. Cox. She probably disliked the notion of leaving a comfortable home, and may have had a grudge against the deceased as the cause of her proposed removal; but even if this were proved, all that it comes to is only a guess as to what she might have done had she chosen. It is unnecessary to place implicit faith in all the statements of the three persons who were practically incriminated by the direction which was given to the inquiry; but in the absence of any facts against them, nothing could be more unjustifiable than trying to set up a mere theory of possible motives and conduct. . . ."

Vanity Fair:

"The task which had to be performed was to discover how it was that Mr. Bravo came by his death . . . whether he knowingly took the antimony himself, or whether it was administered to him by some other person. The point to which anybody who holds the latter theory must address himself is to shew that some other person did administer the antimony, or at least that some person who had access to him was in possession of antimony and might have administered it. This being done, the question of motive might become of very grave importance; but until this is done, it must seem to the unprejudiced observer that the question of motive is one of the very remotest and most inconclusive kind. . . . Yet the whole exertions of those who were engaged in the inquiry into the cause of Mr. Bravo's death appear to have been concentrated upon the effort to prove the existence of motives. . . . But however strong they may have been, they cannot of themselves alone prove anything . . . and the existence of a motive to commit a crime is no proof whatever that such a crime has been committed. . . .

"But though the inquiry has lasted five weeks, we are as far off as ever from any light on the one point at issue— who killed Mr. Bravo?"

Daily Telegraph:

". . . Down to the last moment public opinion was strangely divided, and in every quarter conflicting conjectures were hazarded. Some people anticipated that the jury would return a verdict of suicide; others that they would give an open verdict; while a third class expected they would find that Mr. Bravo had been murdered by some person or persons unknown.

"The precise words which the jury handed in in writing to the Coroner nobody foresaw. They have put upon express record that he did not take this deadly poison by misadventure, and that he 'did not commit suicide', but that as a matter of fact he was 'wilfully murdered', while instead of saying the usual form, that he was murdered by some person or persons unknown, they significantly declare that 'there is not sufficient evidence to fix the guilt on any person or persons'."

The Lancet:

"It is remarkable that, previous to the arrival of the medical man who first appeared on the scene, the patient was treated for poisoning. A mustard emetic had been administered! Supposing a person to be suddenly attacked with vomiting and faintness, that is by no means a remedy likely to be instantly applied, least of all in a family of homoeopathic proclivities. It is necessary, therefore, to assume—indeed, the inference is forced upon us—that either the patient did make a statement as alleged, to the effect that he had taken poison, or it was known or suspected by the person directing the use of the mustard emetic that he had taken something which would require to be removed from the stomach by a powerful stimulating appliance to produce vomiting.

"The hypothesis that the patient himself knew or believed that he had taken poison is further supported by the circumstance testified by one witness, that he called loudly for warm water, although the statement alleging that the words used were 'Florence, Florence, hot water!' is hardly consistent with the evidence given by another witness, to the effect that the patient said, 'Mrs. Cox, I have taken poison for Dr. Gully, don't tell Florence.'

"This, unfortunately, is not the only point overlooked. It is impossible to disguise that a grave omission was made in not at once applying the proper chemical tests to the matter vomited and that passed from the intestines. Had anyone been in a position to say pointedly to this poor man who was conscious after his recovery from the first collapse up to within a very short period of his death, 'You have taken antimony', the truth might have been ascertained.

"In any case the need of at once impounding all bottles and glasses, searching the rooms, the clothes, the belongings and surroundings of the person dying of poison, at the time of his illness instead of a month or two after his death, should certainly have been perceived and acted upon. As it was the opportunity was lost. There is no room for doubt as to the immediate cause of death. Whether antimony was taken alone—that is to say, without some other drug—may be questioned. There are features in the attack which seem to point to the presence of another poison."

Part IV

THE SOLUTION

CHAPTER ONE

NUDA VERITAS

I

ALTHOUGH the twenty-three days of costly proceedings had yielded no evidence whatever to justify any but an open verdict, the jury had returned one of Wilful Murder, and by substituting the words "but there is not sufficient evidence to fix the guilt upon any person or persons" for the usual formula had practically incriminated Mrs. Cox and Florence Bravo.

This unwarranted and unexpected result must have placed the Law Officers of the Crown in something of a quandary, and presumably they reconsidered the whole case very carefully indeed; and it may be accepted as a measure of their respect for the verdict that, except for the rather hollow offer of a reward of £250 for information which would lead to a conviction, they closed the case down and withdrew police supervision from the suspects.

The junior Crown Counsel had been Mr. Harry Poland[1] who was to earn a reputation as "the greatest criminal lawyer of all time".[2] In 1923, after his retirement from the Bar, having read the manuscript of Sir John Hall's account of the case, he expressed the view that "Mrs. Bravo's conduct was generally consistent with innocence", that he "considered there was scarcely sufficient motive to induce Mrs. Cox to commit such a crime", and that Dr. Gully was in no way implicated. In that same year he also informed Mr. Rowlands that he had an explanation for what had happened, "but it was not for publication".[3]

In the light of the opinion he expressed to Sir John Hall, this explanation could not entail murder at the hands of the

[1] Later Sir Harry Poland, K.C.
[2] *Criminal Days*—Sir Travers Humphreys.
[3] *Seventy-two Years at the Bar*—Ernest Rowlands. Sir Harry, having arrived at his explanation as the result of his official duties, no doubt felt himself precluded from publishing it.

suspects, and as the evidence failed to establish any proof of suicide, Bravo's death could only have arisen from some other cause. The inference remaining to be drawn, therefore, is that that cause lay in the "charge of a very grave nature" concerning which Mr. Gorst had tried to extract further information from Florence Bravo in the closing stages of her cross-examination.

A few days *before* Mr. Gorst put these questions, Mr. Murphy had confided the anxiety and bewilderment the case was causing him to his friend, Mr. Arthur Channell; and it made so great an impression upon the latter's mind that forty-seven years afterwards—on the morning Sir John Hall's book was published—he felt himself impelled to write to the author a full account of what had then occurred.

> "The Athenaeum, Pall Mall,
> "S.W.1,
> "Dec. 1st, 1923.

"Dear Sir,

"I read yesterday in *The Times* a review of a book by Sir John Hall (to whom I am intending to address this letter, not seeing in Kelly's Directory any other Sir John Hall, Bart.) entitled *The Bravo Mystery*, and this morning I have procured a copy from the publishers.

"I knew Bravo well, was, under the circumstances I am about to tell you, very well acquainted with all the facts proved at the inquest, and I formed then, and still hold, a clear opinion that there was no crime at all and that Bravo's death was due to a misadventure.

"I have not had time yet to read your book, but I gather both from the review and also from glancing through the book that this view of the case is not dealt with. I have generally found that most people to whom I have mentioned the matter have come to the conclusion that my solution of the mystery is the correct one, and I should like to know what you think of it, and if, as I hope may be the case, your book should reach a second edition you may be able to add something on the point.[1]

[1] The book did not reach a second edition.

"I had been called to the Bar 12 or 13 years when Bravo
died, and I was getting fairly busy. Bravo had occasionally
helped me with my work, and I remember on one occasion
no great while before his death his speaking to me about his
wife, and I am sure that he was devoted to her. Prior to that
time, and before I had much work of my own, I had 'dev-
illed' a good deal for Mr. Murphy, and I believe he had come
to value my opinion and often talked over his cases with
me. The inquest, which he attended on behalf of Mrs. Cox,
as stated in your book, did not sit continually every day,
and one day when the case had gone on for several days but
was not sitting, I walked with Murphy from Westminster,
where the Courts then sat, to the Temple, and on the way
Murphy told me that he never had been so puzzled in any
case as in the Bravo case, and he told me all the facts which
had come out, and all his difficulties, and asked me to think
it over and tell him what I thought the truth was. He told
me particularly of the sickness from which Mrs. Bravo had
suffered and of his difficulty in seeing how best to deal with
that part of the case. We both agreed that there seemed no
motive for murder by anyone under suspicion, and no motive
for suicide, and he particularly pointed out the difficulty
arising from Bravo's denial to the doctors that he had taken
anything but laudanum, and that accidentally. At the time
I did not see any solution, but thinking it over during the
day the view occurred to me which I believe solves the
mystery.

"I believe that Bravo had bought the tartar emetic for
the purpose of putting it in the sherry and curing his wife
of the habit she had unfortunately acquired of drinking too
much, and that her sickness was caused by his having used it
for that purpose. I distrusted the evidence of his having
known very much about drugs and doubted whether he
knew that tartar emetic was a dangerous poison. But if he
did, he also knew the amount that might be safely given,
and he never put enough in the sherry to kill his wife. As I
have said, I knew Bravo well. He was fond of dodges. He
was, I think, just the man likely to adopt such a plan for

curing the unfortunate habit which I am sure distressed him. Then I believe the event happened which he truly told the doctors of, that in rubbing his gums with laudanum to ease the pain of toothache he accidentally swallowed some laudanum. That frightened him, and to get rid of the laudanum he went to the drawer where he kept the tartar emetic, and took what he had left of it as an emetic. I don't think he knew that it was anything but an emetic, but of course he would not be anxious to tell what he had the emetic for and how he had been using it.

"I believe that he quite honestly told the doctors he had taken no poison but laudanum, and possibly never thought of telling them of what he supposed to be the innocent remedy which he had used.

"This view I believe accounts for the whole case, the only difficulty at all in it being his statement to the doctors, and that I think is got over by what I have suggested. Even if I thought that he did know that tartar emetic was a dangerous poison if given in excess of a quite moderate dose, I should still think my explanation of how that poison came to be taken by him was far more probable than any other hypothesis, and that his silence was accounted for by reluctance to tell what he had been doing to cure his wife.

"When this view occurred to me I at once went over to Murphy's chambers to tell him. I found him in consultation on the case with Mr. R. M. Bray, his junior, who died only a few months ago, and the solicitors instructing him and several of the parties. Mrs. Cox was no doubt there, and I am not sure that it was not a joint consultation at which some of the other parties were present. I sent a message in to Murphy and he came out and spoke to me. I told him shortly what had occurred to me, and he said I had better come in and tell it to those present.

"This I did. Almost everyone agreed that it was a probable solution. The next day the inquest was continued. Mr. Murphy put the point to a medical witness[1] as to the effect of taking the tartar emetic as an emetic to get rid of

[1] Henry Smith, F.R.C.S.

the laudanum, and got an answer that it was consistent with
all the symptoms that were known. Mr. Murphy put my
view to the jury as a possible explanation of the mystery,
but he was a very judicious advocate, and avoided resting
his case upon it. He saw his way to getting, and did get, a
verdict which did not, directly at any rate, inculpate his
client, Mrs. Cox, and every advocate who knows his business
knows very well that if you set up an affirmative case, and
the jury do not think it proved, they will be very apt to find
against you generally. The suggestion came too late in the
inquiry to make it safe to rest the case upon it, but Mr.
Murphy and Mr. Justice Bray, as he became, always told
me that they believed I had found the real solution of the
mystery.

"I have not yet read enough of your book to know what
materials you had before you, but I am sure that if you had
anything like a full report of the proceedings at the inquest
you will see that Mr. Murphy did put my point to one of the
medical witnesses called in the case and that he got an
answer supporting the view so far as medical symptoms
were concerned.

"As there are not many now alive who recollect the case,
I am glad of this opportunity of stating my view, and hope
that, whether it commends itself to you as a satisfactory
solution or not, you will be able somehow to put it on record
as a suggested solution of the mystery. At any rate I think
you will be interested in it, if it has never before been
suggested to you.   "Yours faithfully,
                                   "Arthur M. Channell,
            "*Retired Judge of the High Court*
            "*Member of Judicial Committee, Privy Council.*"

2

The words which must claim our first attention in this
letter are: "*We both agreed that there seemed no motive for murder
by anyone under suspicion, and no motive for suicide.*" In fact
they reached the same conclusion as Sir William Gull—that
"whatever Mr. Bravo had taken, he had taken it himself"—

a conclusion with which the thoughtful reader can hardly fail to concur. The questions which Mr. Gorst put to certain of the medical witnesses—notably Professor Redwood and Mr. Henry Smith—concerning the effects of tartar emetic when taken in small quantities, indicate the attention he was paying to this aspect of the case and link up with those final questions which he put to Florence concerning the "grave charge" she brought against her late husband. When carried to their logical conclusion, these suggest the answer to certain flaws in Sir Arthur Channell's argument which we must now consider.

In the first place, Charles Bravo's reputation for "being better acquainted with medical jurisprudence than any barrister they knew" was firmly established among his colleagues, and it is therefore inconceivable that he should have been ignorant of the fact that tartar emetic was a salt of antimony—a substance which had been used for the purpose of criminal poisoning throughout the ages and which, in his own generation, had figured in two classic cases: those of William Palmer, in England, in 1856, and Dr. Pritchard, in Scotland, in 1865.

In the second place, admitting for the sake of argument that Charles Bravo was ignorant of the lethal properties of the drug, was in possession of it for the sole purpose of curing his wife of a propensity for drinking—a purpose for which it was quite commonly used, as the evidence shewed—and had taken it in the circumstances suggested by Sir Arthur, it is equally inconceivable that when the doctors impressed upon him that "laudanum would not have caused his symptoms" he should have "shewn no surprise and asked no questions"; and that, when they further admonished him that "if he died without making an admission someone might be suspected of causing his death", he should continue to withhold his secret even from Royes Bell "with whom he had been brought up like a brother". Nor is his state of mental anguish, of which there is abundant evidence, consistent with Sir Arthur's hypothesis.

We must now consider whether it be not the truth that Charles Bravo had the antimony in his possession, not to cure his wife of drinking, *but to bring about her death*.

CHAPTER TWO

HOW CHARLES BRAVO DIED

I

THE "grave charge" which Charles Bravo's widow brought against him to Inspector Clarke at Brighton was that he had been administering to her small and frequent doses of tartar emetic, adding that "if he wanted to know more he could go to Dr. Dill". And now we must sift the charge for evidence of the deeper implication which appears to be included.

The conduct of the poisoner, as Professor Glaister points out, "when carefully reviewed, is shewn usually to have been activated by a number of concatenating facts relating to the make-up of the criminal and the nature of his surroundings".[1] In other words, should the make-up of an individual include some deep-rooted desire, such as a money mania or a passion for the acquisition of property, which he finds himself in a position to gratify by bringing about someone's death, his desire may develop into an obsession so powerful that he dedicates himself to its fulfilment and becomes wholly indifferent to any suffering he may cause.

Charles Bravo's obsession with money needs no further emphasis. He had, Mrs. Campbell observed, "a money mania". Mr. Meredith Brown expressed a similar opinion more diplomatically—"Deceased took a deep interest in money matters. He was a very careful man, the reverse of a spendthrift." Mr. Jepson Atkinson said that Charles had "very little sentiment".

It is not necessary to prove motive in order to prove guilt, but if motive can be shewn to exist it is an important factor. In reply to the last question put to her by Sir Henry James, Florence said: "*I made a Will after I was married and left all I had to Mr. Charles Bravo, I trusted him absolutely.*" Mr. Brookes corroborated this, adding that in the event of her death "every

[1] *The Power of Poison*—John Glaister.

shilling she possessed" would pass to her husband. Charles, therefore, would have immediately inherited the Ricardo Settlement of £40,000 and made himself heir to the £20,000 Settlement made by Robert Campbell who, until his death, would have had to pay him £1,000 a year interest upon it. And in 1876 there were no Death Duties and Income Tax was 2d. in the pound.

In his *Principles of Circumstantial Evidence* William Wills says:

> "Of the various heads of evidence in charges of poisoning, that of moral conduct . . . represents the natural and unmistakable manifestation of the secret workings of the mind, not only throwing light upon and bringing into relief the character of the act itself, but tending also to discriminate the individual action. . . ." (The poisoner's) "necessities, his antipathies, his falsehoods, subterfuges and evasions—these and many other circumstances constitute most explanatory parts of the story and afford relevant and frequently conclusive evidence from which his guilt may be inferred."

For example, there was absolutely no proof that Seddon (1912) had ever bought, been in possession of, or even handled the arsenic which was fatally administered to Miss Barrow: what was proved against him was his money mania—although *before* Miss Barrow became a lodger in his house it had been inconspicuous. In fact, only when he found himself in a position to gratify it by bringing about her death did he develop into a poisoner. It was the subterfuges he had used to gain control of her capital, and, having persuaded her to make a Will in his favour, the falsehoods and evasions he practised to conceal the cause of her death, which brought him to the scaffold.

From the date Charles Bravo borrowed £500 from the woman at Maidenhead in order to speculate with it, through the coercion he displayed to obtain possession of his fiancée's personal effects and "the falsehoods, subterfuges and evasions" he employed to raise money by playing off his parents against his wife and *vice versa*, there is evidence of a money mania—

evidence confirmed by the fact that, after pretending to all parties that he possessed nothing but £200 a year, his Will was proved at £14,000. Gambler he might be, but fool he was not, and it leaps to the mind that he would never have taken such risks as this double dealing entailed if he were looking forward to a long married life. As we have seen, he twice had to resort to swift action to prevent his wife "having it out" with his mother.

His soaring good spirits proclaimed his relief when Florence's increasing ill-health, and finally her miscarriage, incapacitated her from such action, and his people were safely ensconced at St. Leonards.

When administered in small, frequent doses over a period of time antimony not only has the effect of simulating a state of general debility and natural ill-health, but of aggravating any disorder which may happen to be present: thus, Florence having suffered one miscarriage in January, its debilitating effects might well induce another in April. In any case its action would probably be so masked as to deceive the most experienced medical practitioner.[1] None the less, the poisoner usually prefers to run no risks and tries to avoid calling in his victim's regular medical attendant who knows his constitution. As the evidence shews, Dr. Harrison, who for the past six years had attended Florence and had been sent for when she miscarried in January, was not called in when she miscarried in April: Charles insisted on sending for Royes Bell, a surgeon, and ignored his advice that Harrison should be consulted. He must clearly have gained great influence over his wife to dissuade her from calling in her own doctor, especially when her pain and sickness persisted for so long.

---

[1] As late as 1903 one of George Chapman's three victims whom he murdered in this way was actually treated in hospital without the real cause of her illness being suspected. Dr. James Stoker, who visited her practically every day during the fortnight between her return home and her death, had no suspicions either. He held three separate consultations with three different doctors over the patient: the first, Dr. Sutherland, attributed the illness to inflammation of the uterus; the second, Dr. Thorpe, to a severe form of hysteria; the third, Dr. Cotter, to cancer of the stomach; while finally Dr. Stoke certified death to be due to "intestinal obstruction, vomiting and exhaustion".

Charles to scoop some of the white crystals from the jar marked *Antimony Tart.* into an envelope and slip it into his pocket.

(ii) *How, knowing its true nature, did Charles Bravo come to swallow a fatal dose of it?* The evidence shewed that at luncheon he had eaten a beefsteak, of Victorian proportions, and drunk half a bottle of Burgundy; that Cremorne had bolted with him over a distance of five miles, while no fewer than three witnesses besides his wife and Mrs. Cox—the coachman, the groom and Rowe—testified to the shaking he had received. Florence said he was so stiff that she had to help him out of his chair in the morning-room; Rowe, that when Charles was going upstairs "he put his hands to his sides and cried out in pain". He had been suffering from rheumatism, and the *post-mortem* shewed that his liver, spleen and kidneys were only "fairly natural". The jolting action of the cob had, in fact, both shaken up his liver and brought on the rheumatic pains in his loins, and when he reached his bedroom, where today he might have taken 10 or 15 grains of aspirin, he probably took an equivalent dose of laudanum which, followed by the hot bath, quickly eased him.

Joseph Bravo's letter and dinner arrived simultaneously. The first made him "excessively angry" and with his digestive juices thus upset he ate another heavy meal and drank "three or four glasses of Burgundy"—a rich and heavy wine. "His face worked all through dinner, and he was such a strange yellow colour," said Florence. "He looked very pale, paler than usual, and seemed in pain," said Rowe, adding a touch indicative of nervous exasperation: "He kept twisting his head round." The picture evoked is that of a man both nervously and physically disordered.

When he emerged from the morning-room after brooding in solitude for three-quarters of an hour over "the Governor's shirty letter" and the state of his liver, his appearance shocked Keeber leaving the dining-room with the Marsala for her mistress. Whether or not he "upbraided" his wife for sending for more wine is of little importance, but the fact that he marched past Keeber without a word—"a thing he had never done before"—is a symptom of his state of mind. As soon as he entered his bedroom he probably took more laudanum to calm his nerves and induce sleep, and then decided to take some of the Epsom salts which Royes Bell had prescribed him, and the box containing which the doctors found on his mantelpiece. Perhaps he kept the tartar emetic in a similar box—both substances consist of fine white crystals—and with his mind preoccupied with his troubles and dulled by laudanum, he shook some of the contents from the *wrong box* into a glass, added water and tossed it off.[1] Its lack of taste would immediately inform him of his mistake, and in his first moment of panic he instinctively called to *his wife* for the hot water which, acting as an emetic, would rid his stomach of the poison. When his eyes met the startled gaze of Keeber on the stairs, with the pressure of his guilt upon him he hastily withdrew and made for the window to induce vomiting by putting his finger down his throat. A moment later Mrs. Cox reached his side, and by then he had realized that he must at all costs preserve his guilty secret and get rid of all chances of the poison he had taken being discovered.

(iii) *What part did Mrs. Cox play in the tragedy?* The poisoner works in secret and confides in no one, so it is most improbable that Charles would have made a confidante of Mrs. Cox. On the other hand, she had no idea that he was fatally stricken, and her desire to stand high in his favour so as to ensure re-employment on her return from Jamaica would make her a subservient, even if ignorant, accessory after the fact.

It is through her own evidence that we may briefly reconstruct the part she played that fatal Tuesday night and afterwards. According to Mr. Reid's notes she stated at the first inquest: "Most probably he took it medicinally." In her statement to the Treasury she deposed: "He said to me, 'Mrs. Cox, I have taken poison for Dr. Gully; don't tell Florence.' The words 'don't tell Florence' were used emphatically, in a

---

[1] On 10th August, 1876, a letter appeared in *The Times* over the signature "De Facto" relating how the writer had once gone to his mother's medicine cupboard and taken tartar emetic in mistake for seidlitz powder, owing his life to the fact that he took so strong a dose that he immediately vomited. Dr. Harrison stated in the course of his evidence that he had once done the same thing.

most imploring way. I said, 'How could you do such a thing?'
He only screamed three times for hot water. Before the hot
water arrived he was sick out of the window, and detecting the
smell of chloroform I rushed to look at the chloroform bottle,
which I found nearly empty. There was a good fire burning in
the grate."

To Dr. Johnson she said: "He told me, 'I have taken *some
of that poison*; don't tell Florence.' " Earlier she had said to
Dr. Harrison: "I am sure he has taken chloroform."

In fact she juggled with the truth, adding or subtracting to
suit the occasion. This is what probably happened:

Charles' ghastly appearance when she reached his side at
the window would provoke some inquiry—"Charlie, what's
the matter?" His answer was to turn to Keeber in the doorway
and "scream three times for hot water", then, leaning from the
window, to be violently sick. But as Keeber sped to do his
bidding, pointing to the package of antimony on the mantelpiece he gasped as his legs collapsed under him: 'I have taken
some of that poison; don't tell Florence; *throw it in the fire*."
Instantly she obeyed, asking at the same time: "How could
you do such a thing?" "I took it medicinally." As she
crouched by his side he made her vow to tell *no one*—neither
Florence nor anyone else—what had happened. He would
know that William Palmer had twice dosed John Parsons
Cook with tartar emetic, and each time immediate vomiting
had saved his life and left him little the worse next day.[1]
He would tell Mrs. Cox that so long as he vomited copiously
he would be all right, and to give him a mustard emetic and
stimulate his circulation. He reckoned without the rapid
absorption into the system that would naturally occur soon
after a meal.

But when he lost consciousness and she felt his pulse grow
weak, she became frightened and sent for Dr. Harrison. When

[1] Charles Bravo can hardly have failed to have studied this case, described
by Sir James Stephen, Bart. (author of *The History of Criminal Law*), as one
of the greatest in legal history. The Attorney-General, whose speech for
the prosecution was an outstanding *tour-de-force*, was that same Sir Alexander
Cockburn who had been Lord Chief Justice ever since Charles had been
called to the Bar.

he arrived she felt she must say something to account for Charles' condition, and not daring to tell the truth, blurted out chloroform as the cause, having noticed the bottle was nearly empty. But when Dr. Harrison, after examining the patient, told her that he could not survive, she suddenly perceived her ghastly error in throwing the poison into the fire, *for she had destroyed the only clue as to what it was and the only positive proof that Charles had had it in his possession*. Her dilemma increased when, on regaining consciousness, Charles "made no admission". The only means she had of trying to force one from him was to tell the doctors a portion of the truth, but when she saw the effect of the phrase *"some of that poison"* on Dr. Johnson and understood its implication she subtracted the words *"some of that"*. Similarly, when later on she learned that Joseph Bravo "had had the detectives put on" and realized that a motive for suicide had become imperative, she added *"for Dr. Gully"*.

(iv) *How can the peculiarities of Charles Bravo's behaviour on his death-bed be explained?* The case of William Palmer has already been cited. Sir James Stephen, who knew Palmer and was present at his trial, observed that thirty-four years' subsequent experience only "strengthened and confirmed" the deep impression it made on him. Palmer's career, he says, "supplied one of the proofs of a fact which kind-hearted people seem to doubt, namely the fact that such a thing as atrocious wickedness is consistent with good education, perfect sanity, and everything, in a word, which deprives men of all excuse for crime. . . . He was a model of physical health and strength, and was courageous, determined and energetic . . . yet was cruel, treacherous, and as greedy of money . . . as it is possible even to imagine."

Palmer insured his wife's life for £13,000 and then killed her with antimony. Like Charles Bravo, he possessed an "extraordinary and persuasive *bonhomie*" and his manner "put everyone at their ease". The one practised medicine, the other law. Each had married women of wealth with a stigma attached to them, the one of illegitimacy, the other of unchastity; each, in the eyes of the world, displayed great affection towards his wife;

each wrote her letters protesting extreme devotion. But Palmer seduced the housemaid and consorted with other women, while Charles Bravo systematically deceived Florence over money; each lived in comfort upon his wife's income and each complained in the same terms that his profession gave him endless labour and no reward. Palmer's widowed mother was a wealthy woman; Charles Bravo would inherit a substantial sum on his parents' deaths: but neither had private means and both were governed by a money mania.

But although the background and personalities of these two men—and even their family history—has so many points in common, most striking of all is the conduct of the one at his trial and the other upon his death-bed.

Palmer was arrested on the charge of murdering his friend, John Parsons Cook—to whom he owed a few hundred pounds —while investigations were being made into the death of his wife. The indictment against him was that he had murdered Cook with strychnine—then a new and little known drug— which he was proved to have purchased and with which the fatal symptoms were consistent. The *post-mortem*, however, revealed no strychnine—only a small quantity of antimony which there was strong evidence to shew Palmer had administered to his victim a few days before his death—and had it not been that while the case was pending Dr. Dove of Leeds was accused of murdering his wife with strychnine the charge against Palmer would probably have failed.

Palmer never *denied* that he had murdered his friend, but solemnly declared: "*I am innocent of poisoning Cook with strychnine*"—the poison named on the indictment; and it was the opinion of Sir James Stephen that he had used *brucine*, or some other alkaloid allied to strychnine, which left no traces discoverable by the analytical tests then available. Compare this quibble with Charles Bravo's protestations to Sir William Gull:

"It was laudanum; I took it myself."

"Pray say what other poison was mixed with the laudanum."

"Before God it was only laudanum."

Like Palmer he was stating the literal truth: the tartar

emetic had not been *mixed* with laudanum, but swallowed *separately*. And the words had scarcely left his lips before he was praying for forgiveness. And although Charles Bravo never *admitted* taking any other poison than laudanum, he never *denied* that he had done so.

Sir Arthur Channell found it hard to believe that the colleague he had known and liked could have practised deliberate deception under the very shadow of death; yet the fact remains that murderers, whose guilt admits of no doubt, avow their innocence even at the gallows' foot. But, as Charles Dickens has pointed out, what can the ordinary individual "know of the criminal intellect, which its own professed students perpetually misread, because they persist in trying to reconcile it with the average intellect of the average man, instead of identifying it as a horrible wonder apart"?

The act of murder by violence provides the outlet for the passion which aroused it, and, under the anti-climax which succeeds it, is replaced by guilt and fear which so frequently prompts the murderer to flee the scene of his crime. Slow poisoning is a matter of calculated premeditation over a period of time, and during its application the poisoner develops a species of amnesia whereby he may, in effect, lose the consciousness of guilt and lead an apparently normal life. When Charles Bravo regained consciousness, that amnesia rapidly evaporated and was replaced by a sense of guilt and a desire to repent and make reparation, under the influence of which he prayed and wept, bade his wife marry again, made a Will leaving her every penny he possessed, and implored his mother to be kind to her. But the hope of recovery, the conviction that reprieve from death must somehow come, combined with the egotism and vanity which is part of the criminal make-up, would not permit him to confess.

Charles Bravo was indeed "the last man on earth to commit suicide": he was also the last man on earth to remain mute if he thought he were dying by another's hand.

CHAPTER THREE

THE END OF THE STORY

I

WHAT truth was there in the allegation that Florence Bravo was "addicted to wine"?

It is noteworthy that, though it would reflect no credit upon her, it originated with herself, and first finds utterance in her statement to the Treasury Solicitor, "When we were first married he" (Charles) "thought I took too much sherry." Under cross-examination she said, "He thought I took more wine than was good for my health," and contradicts Mrs. Cox's assertion that she had learned to indulge in the habit during her first marriage with the words "it is not true".

It is equally noteworthy that no faintest hint of any such thing came from the Bravo faction, which used every means at its disposal to blacken her reputation. In fact, in every instance it derives from those connected with Florence and from herself.

Rowe's only definite statement on the subject was, "Mrs. Bravo and Mrs. Cox drank a good deal of sherry", while Keeber merely said that both before and after her illness in April her mistress had a glass of wine and water in her room at bedtime.[1] Mrs. Campbell, in answer to Sir Henry James, after expressing the disapproval with which she had viewed Dr. Gully's increasing influence over her daughter in the spring of 1871, said: "In addition, I observed that she drank more wine than I approved of." She also stated: "When deceased was at Buscot at Christmas he spoke to me about my daughter taking too much wine

[1] It was widely drunk last thing at night to induce sleep. Marsala in the morning and last thing at night was prescribed for the Empress Eugénie during her pregnancy and after the birth of the Prince Imperial. Sherry and seltzer was the popular pick-me-up of the day: Charles Dickens always drank it throughout dinner; Thackeray took it to steady his nerves before leaving home at 3 a.m. with Monckton-Milnes to witness the public execution of Courvoisier, the valet who murdered his master, Lord William Russell.

—that she took a glass of wine before dressing for dinner. That was her habit, I said, and he said, 'I will cure her of it', but he did not say how. I said, 'You may do so by kindness and firmness.' He made no reply to this."

The truth of the allegation emerges from one of Mrs. Cox's statements: "Mrs. Bravo took wine when she was feeling tired and exhausted." Precisely: she drank wine, as everyone did, with their meals; she had learned the Continental habit of the *apéritif*, and she resorted to wine as a stimulant when under the pressure of strain or anxiety, as, for instance, in the spring of 1871 when torn between her family and Dr. Gully, and probably during her domestic conflicts with Charles. Had she had an habitual addiction to it, one can rest assured that Mr. Lewis would have made the most of it: and in view of the source whence the allegation sprang, one can only suppose that it was deliberately introduced in order to lead up to that "grave charge" against her husband upon which Sir Henry James was building his case in order to prove his client's innocence of that husband's death; and it may safely be assumed that he would never have built his case upon such a foundation unless the evidence which supported it was firm and reliable.

2

Florence Ricardo had resolved to dismiss the man she loved in order to be reconciled with her mother. Caught on the rebound by an evil man's superficial charm, and, against the advice of those about her and her own better judgment, she had married him before she had had an opportunity to know him as he really was. The slow death he had planned for her had in a split second and by an ironic twist of fate recoiled upon himself. She faced with admirable dignity the public torture and humiliation inflicted upon her by Mr. Lewis at the instigation of Joseph Bravo, but it, and the treachery that had caused it, broke her heart. The wrong done to Florence Bravo cannot be undone; the agony she suffered cannot be wiped out; all that can be done is to remove the stigma of suspicion which has lain so long upon her memory. The following letter, addressed to the late George R. Sims, contributes largely towards this end:

"3 Coleherne Terrace,
"South Kensington,
"Oct. 20th, 1919.

"Dear Dagonet,

". . . Upon several occasions you have referred in your writings in 'Mustard and Cress', and spoken of, the Bravo case—and again in this week's issue of the *Referee*. . . .

"Well, for twenty years I was the private and confidential secretary of the late Mr. Robert Campbell of Buscot Park, Berks, the father of Mrs. Bravo, and a friend of the family for more than forty years. . . .

"When Mr. Bravo was lying upon his death-bed . . . he was implored more than once by Mrs. Bravo and others (Sir William Gull among them) to admit or deny that he had administered poison to himself, upon the grounds of the awful stigma, if nothing worse, it would cast upon those surrounding him, but although quite conscious at the time he made no response whatever to these appeals and remained as silent as the grave to them.

"Some little time after the trial" (*sic*) "had terminated Mrs. Bravo said to me, 'Mr. Kemp, I shall not long survive this cruel blow.' Nor did she. Whatever the world may have said or thought, at the time or since, Mrs. Bravo was never a party to the crime. If it comes under the category of murder, then Mr. Bravo was his own murderer and he alone, and as sure as there is God in Heaven it will be manifested to all on the Last Day.

". . . I possess no brief, except the one of truth and justice, to defend the memory of a really good, devoted and much wronged woman from the utterly groundless charge which hastened her journey to the grave. . . .

"I am, dear Dagonet,
"Very faithfully yours,
"S. Fortescue Kemp."

3

The roots of Florence Bravo's being had gone down deeply into the soil of The Priory. For a brief spell it had given her a more tranquil happiness than any she had known since she had driven away from Buscot as a bride of nineteen. With her whole life in ruins about her, she clung for another eighteen months to that handful of nostalgic memories, as women cling to the little garments of a dead child. Her former governess became her companion; occasionally she went to Buscot, or to stay with William and Augusta, or Mrs. Tom Campbell—more often they came to see her. But day by day her anguish and shame for the anguish and shame she had caused them all bore down upon her more unbearably. There was no way of proclaiming the truth: now and for all time she must remain notorious as a woman devoid of chastity and suspected of the worst of crimes. In the total despair born of that knowledge, she saw death as her only means of release.

On 20th February, 1877, she made a carefully thought-out Will: each member of her family was invited to choose from among her "jewelry, furs and laces, a remembrance": to her god-daughter, Florence Gully, she bequeathed £1,000; to each nephew and niece a large legacy, and to Augusta all her pictures, silver and glass. Jane Cannon Cox was only mentioned as the mother of her three boys, to each of whom she left £100. The residue of her estate, amounting to some £60,000, went to her brother William in trust for his descendants.

This done, she sought oblivion, becoming now, in very truth, addicted to drink. One year and seven months later, on 21st September, 1878, at Coombe Lodge, Southsea, and at the age of thirty-three, death released her. With other members of her family she lies in Buscot churchyard. Charles Bravo was as morally responsible for her tragic end as he was for that of his mother just one year earlier.

4

Although there was no tittle of evidence to connect Dr. Gully with Charles Bravo's death, nor any that immorality had occurred between himself and Florence Ricardo until after he had retired from practice, Dr. Gully had to submit to having his name removed from all those medical societies of which he had been so distinguished a member, and henceforward he figured in the popular imagination as "the wicked old doctor". His guilt lay, as *The Times* pointed out, in his "violation of the heavy responsibilities of his profession, and with no excuse from the passions of youth, or even middle age, he abandoned himself to a selfish intrigue". His wife survived his mistress by thirteen months, dying at Brighton on 21st October, 1879, aged eighty-seven. He himself lived on until 1882.

5

Jane Cannon Cox was equally innocent of the death of Charles Bravo, in the contrivance of which she has been for so long, and so unjustly, suspected. But being of tougher fibre than Florence Bravo, she withstood far better the "slings and arrows of outrageous fortune". The legend exists that she lived to a ripe old age, winning a reputation as a kind and obliging little woman, "a very present help in trouble".

APPENDIX I

Letters of Charles Bravo to Mrs. Campbell:

I

The Priory, Balham,
Jan. 9th, 1876.

Dear Mrs. Campbell,

Had I not the excuse that I wish you to know how Florence is getting on I should be loath to trouble you with a letter merely for the purpose of thanking you for your kindness to me when I was at Buscot. That were indeed to return evil for good. But as I have the satisfactory news for you that Florence is in excellent health and, though surrounded by bills, in excellent spirits, I will just venture to tell you that I shall for ever count myself a debtor to you and all your family for your great kindness to me.

The reception which my mother gave Florence, and the loving way in which she talked of her, gave me strength to bear up under the affliction of leaving Buscot which I had otherwise been without.

Here I am so thoroughly at home that it almost seems as if I had never lived anywhere else; at times indeed my mind reverts (with regrets that I am not there) to Buscot, where I enjoyed such ease and dignity, together with a liberty of staying at home on Sunday, which I do not enjoy here; but when the thought becomes depressing I go to the stables, over which I am appointed superintendent, or else I seek solace in sleep, which I enjoy like a very Campbell. I am looking forward to the advent of August. Florence sends her love to you all, as does,

Yours affectionately,
Charles Bravo.

P.S.—Florence, who is looking over my shoulder, says she sends, not "her love", but "her very best love". I, therefore, unwilling to be behind her in anything, beg to send my "very, very best love".

Postscript by Florence Bravo:

I do hope Augusta is better; my love to her. Charlie as usual writes tersely as all barristers do; but you must imagine twice the amount of affection, as I had to do when he wrote me love letters, which, by the bye, nobody would have recognized as such, as they were as cold and undemonstrative as possible.

Your loving child,

F. B.

2

The Priory, Balham,
Jan. 23rd, 1876.

My dear Mrs. Campbell,

I have spent the greater part of this blessed Sabbath Day in writing letters, and I find a real pleasure now they are done to write one to you of condolence and hope—of condolence with your past suffering and hope that you may henceforth enjoy the best of health.

Florence is going on finely, and I bless the day I married her. With her usual good nature she has not only had my deaf sister here today, but also a deaf friend of my sister.

We look for a visit from you and Mr. Campbell. When you do come we will show you that the lesson in hospitality which we had at Buscot was not lost.

Trade has been dull with me and I see no signs of revival. This, with a pack of ravenous lawyers feasting on my goods, is distressing to me. However, I suppose it will not make much difference to me at the Great Judgment. It will to the lawyers, though, which is a great consolation to

Yours affectionately,
Charles Bravo.

P.S.—Florence must think you are a born idiot. She imagines that unless I tell you so you will not know that she holds you in her most affectionate love. Know by these presents that she does.

Postscript by Florence Bravo:

Is not Charlie a goose—so dreadfully terse and laconic? I told him to send my very best love to you.

APPENDIX II

Letter from Charles Bravo to Joseph Bravo:

The Priory, Balham,
9th April, 1876.

My dear old Governor,

... Our financial position is steadily improving. ... You may depend upon our not touching capital. I told Brown to buy five Australian Agriculturals at 90. ... He has not sent me a bought note ... so I will tell him to go for something cheaper. I went to your office twice to consult you about the investment, but was not lucky enough to find you.

Poor Florence is still very weak. Royes orders her to remain in bed, which she is very unwilling to do in this beautiful weather. She goes to the seaside as soon as she is well enough. Mrs. Cox is very kind and useful.

I drove yesterday to Norwood to see Mrs. Harford, whose husband I think you know. He has been kind enough to get [me] some oats at a wholesale place where they are not only cheaper but better than they are here. Our fields are to be bush-harrowed and rolled to-morrow, with a view to our getting a good crop of hay from them. Our second gardener has gone to Knole Park, Sevenoaks, to better himself; our third is too good for us and cannot touch his hat or carry a parcel to the station, so I am going to give *him* a chance of bettering himself. ...

Letter from Charles Bravo to Mrs. Joseph Bravo:

14th April, 1876.
(Good Friday.)

My dear old Grannie,

... My fowls lay as if they were Turks and their eggs the money due on coupons, and my spirits are nothing like they would be if the sun was visible. Florence is better but very cross. I went to the library and brought her six volumes of books: three she had read and three contain the uninspired preachings of an idiot. She has finished a pair of slippers for me in a rage, and is slanging me for not being able to tell a good book, as you tell good music, by the look. ...

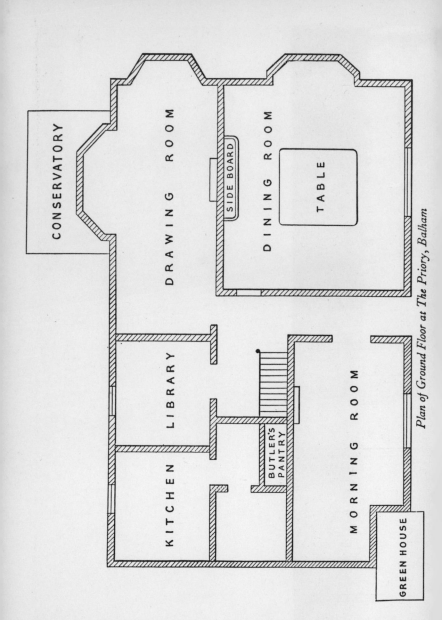

Plan of Ground Floor at The Priory, Balham